COMMUNICATION
and SPORT

COMMUNICATION

and SPORT

Surveying the Field

Andrew C. Billings
Clemson University

Michael L. Butterworth
Bowling Green State University

Paul D. Turman
South Dakota Board of Regents

Los Angeles | London | New Delhi
Singapore | Washington DC

Los Angeles | London | New Delhi
Singapore | Washington DC

FOR INFORMATION:

SAGE Publications, Inc.
2455 Teller Road
Thousand Oaks, California 91320
E-mail: order@sagepub.com

SAGE Publications Ltd.
1 Oliver's Yard
55 City Road
London EC1Y 1SP
United Kingdom

SAGE Publications India Pvt. Ltd.
B 1/I 1 Mohan Cooperative Industrial Area
Mathura Road, New Delhi 110 044
India

SAGE Publications Asia-Pacific Pte. Ltd.
33 Pekin Street #02-01
Far East Square
Singapore 048763

Executive Editor: Diane McDaniel
Acquisitions Editor: Matthew Byrnie
Editorial Assistant: Nathan Davidson
Production Editor: Eric Garner
Copy Editor: Kim Husband
Typesetter: C&M Digitals (P) Ltd.
Proofreader: Sally Jaskold
Indexer: Judy Hunt
Cover Designer: Bryan Fishman
Marketing Manager: Helen Salmon

Printed in the United States of America

Library of Congress Cataloging-in-Publication Data

Billings, Andrew C.

Communication and sport: surveying the field/Andrew C. Billings, Michael L. Butterworth, Paul D. Turman.

p. cm.
Includes bibliographical references and index.

ISBN 978-1-4129-7293-2 (pbk.)

1. Communication in sports. 2. Mass media and sports. I. Butterworth, Michael L. II. Turman, Paul D. III. Title.

GV567.5.B55 2012 070.4′49796—dc22 2010046288

This book is printed on acid-free paper.

11 12 13 14 15 10 9 8 7 6 5 4 3 2 1

Brief Contents

Detailed Contents

Preface

Sports metaphors are abundant in our lives. They are used in our organizational lingo, political discourse, and interpersonal relationships. One common metaphor in sports (and in many other parts of life) involves the search for "the sweet spot," that ideal zone of contact or execution that leads to success. Hitters in baseball know the key to power is finding the sweet spot; tennis players know that hitting the ball purely can make the difference between a routine backhand and a dominating passing shot.

We mention this because our desire to write this book was largely based on our belief that there were many good scholarly books in the marketplace that related to the study of sport, but none that fit the "sweet spot" for communication studies in the broadest and most inclusive sense. Some books deal specifically with sports media, while others deal with the communication of sport through sociological or management-related channels. Some are written specifically about scholarly contributions within communication and sport but are targeted more to graduate students or other scholars within academia who wish to synthesize work that has been done than to the newly initiated undergraduate who wants to learn about the universe of communication and sport. In sum, there were great books within the subject of sport and the field of communication and yet none that we thought was foundational for a communication studies undergraduate survey course on sport. Our hope is that this textbook fills that void. In terms of an undergraduate guide to the universe, we're hoping we've found the "sweet spot."

THE BOOK

Communication and Sport: Surveying the Field is designed to bridge traditional divides between notions of speech communication (a tradition that includes interpersonal, organizational, and rhetorical approaches) and mass communication (a tradition that includes media studies, journalism, and cultural studies), and all of the potential divides and schisms inherently within. The aim was the creation of a book with enough breadth that it would be difficult to have one scholar who could truly claim expertise in all of the terrain. Thus, the combination of the three of us results in a media scholar, a rhetorician, and an applied interpersonal/organizational expert who jointly canvassed what amounts to an amazing amount of work in the field that is now outlined, structured, and synthesized for an undergraduate to grasp the scope and importance of studying communication and sport.

Features of the Book

The comprehensive focus on *communication* scholarship is one of the major features of this textbook. In particular, we orient readers to the enactment, production, consumption, and organization of sport. This entails a wide range of communicative processes, including mass communication productions, interpersonal interactions, family and relational development, public speeches, individual expressions of identity through sport performances, collective expressions of community through sport rituals, and much, much, more. The chapters within this textbook also feature communication scholarship that directs our attention to the ways that sport produces, maintains, or resists cultural attitudes about race, gender, sexuality, class, and politics.

The broad range of topical material is complemented by a pluralistic approach to communication and sport research. We survey scholarship that can be found in each of the major academic research paradigms: social scientific, humanistic, and critical/cultural. Each of these paradigms values different dimensions of intellectual inquiry. Social scientists, for example, are commonly interested in conducting research that allows scholars to explain how communication has worked in the past in order to offer some prediction of how it may happen in the future. Humanists, by contrast, tend to spotlight more particular instances of communication (rather than universal patterns) so that they may reveal deeper levels of understanding of human experiences. Meanwhile, critical/cultural scholars are committed to identifying relationships of power with the goal of sparking productive social change through academic inquiry. Although most researchers tend to identify with one of these paradigms over the others, they are not mutually exclusive, and, in the best cases, the insights from one approach may complement or supplement another. Communication and sport scholars also approach their research using different methodological tools, including content analysis, statistical modeling, ethnography, interviewing, experiments, survey collection, and textual criticism. Throughout this textbook we have included examples of all three research paradigms and various methods of study. It is our hope, then, that we have truly represented the diversity of scholarship conducted in communication and sport.

Another feature of this textbook is the inclusion in each chapter of interviews, case studies, and ethical debates. The interviews feature a range of experts in communication and sport, including renowned media figures such as Christine Brennan and Bob Costas, as well as prominent scholars such as Marie Hardin and Lawrence Wenner. These interviews help to contextualize and extend the ideas that are developed in each chapter. The case studies pick up on a specific dimension from each chapter in order to facilitate discussion about the communicative nature of sport. Along with the ethical debates, which invite a consideration of various cultural, political, and social consequences of sport, readers can expect these inclusions to clarify, extend, and challenge their understandings of communication and sport.

Finally, as those already familiar with sport are well aware, the relationship between communication and sport is one that is rapidly changing. New technologies, changing organizational structures, a pervasive sports media, and the explosion of fantasy sports are just some of the ways that sport has been dramatically altered in recent years. The final chapters of this textbook, then, offer some insights into these developments and provide some cautious glimpses into the future. Although we cannot be certain what the future holds, we are certain that communication scholarship will remain an essential lens through which we can view, understand, and modify the universe of sport.

Acknowledgments

This textbook has been a project that has spanned several years and, while we enjoyed a great deal of synergy among the three of us, we also recognize how fortunate we have been throughout this process. First, we must thank SAGE Publications, particularly Todd Armstrong, for believing in this project from beginning to end. It is nice to have a publisher that is willing to be an advocate for the burgeoning field that is the combination of communication and sport.

Second, the reviewers for this text helped the final version of the book become substantially more interesting than the initial prospectus and the first draft. Their comments and suggestions we incorporated and their insight was terrific: James R. Angelini (University of Delaware, Department of Communication); Kim Bissell (University of Alabama, Department of Journalism); Josh Boyd (Purdue University, Department of Communication); Robert S. Brown (Daniel Webster University, School of Business and Management, Department of Sport Management); Adam C. Earnheardt (Youngstown State University, Department of Communication); Linda K. Fuller (Worcester State College, Department of Communications); Walter Gantz (Indiana University, Department of Telecommunications); Paul Gullifor (Bradley University, Department of Communication); Marie Hardin (Penn State University, Department of Journalism); Karen L. Hartman (Ashland University, Department of Communication Arts); Bob Krizek (Saint Louis University, Department of Communication); Kurt Lindemann (San Diego State University, Department of Communication); R. Pierre Rodgers (George Mason University, School of Recreation, Health & Tourism); Raymond I. Schuck (Bowling Green State University, School of Communication Studies); and James R. Walker (Saint Xavier University, Department of Communication).

Third, our institutions/organizations (Clemson University, Bowling Green State University, and the South Dakota Board of Regents) have allowed us the leeway to pursue this project in the timeframe we wished, and for that we are thankful. In particular, we had the capable assistance of two graduate students from BGSU: Cory Hillman and Erin Paun. Cory and Erin gathered sources that we incorporated into our reviews of literature and they also helped us select appropriate images among the thousands archived on numerous stock photo websites. These tasks were made much more manageable because of their hard work. Finally, we must also note that we all are approximately in the same life stage, meaning that we have young children and understanding wives that accommodate our schedules, which often became demanding near various deadlines. The confluence of events and supporters has resulted in a text of which we are proud, and we thank all of the people in our lives that allowed for it to happen.

Andrew C. Billings
Michael L. Butterworth
Paul D. Turman

About the Authors

Andrew C. Billings (PhD, Indiana University) is Professor of Communication Studies and Director of the Pearce Center for Professional Communication at Clemson University. He has published six books and more than 40 journal articles and book chapters related to the intersecting roles of sport, media, and the negotiation of meaning in society. He has taught three different undergraduate courses in communication and sport, consulted and worked with constituencies such as NBC Sports, FOX Sports, and the Ladies Professional Golf Association, and led initiatives on communication and sport scholarship, including chairing the 2010 Broadcast Education Association Research Symposium: *Sports Media: Transformation, Integration, Consumption.*

Michael L. Butterworth (PhD, Indiana University) is an Assistant Professor in the Department of Communication at Bowling Green State University. He has taught the survey communication and sport course, as well as courses on baseball mythology and sports history and myth and a graduate seminar on sport and resistance. He is the author of *Baseball and Rhetorics of Purity: The National Pastime and American Identity During the War on Terror* (University of Alabama, 2010). He has also published scholarly essays in journals such as *Communication and Critical/Cultural Studies, Communication, Culture & Critique, Critical Studies in Media Communication,* and the *Western Journal of Communication.*

Paul D. Turman (PhD, University of Nebraska) is the Associate Vice President for Academic Affairs South Dakota Board of Regents. His scholarly research focuses on the role of communication in the coach–athlete and parent–child relationship within a sport context. Prior to his time with the Board of Regents, he taught a graduate seminar entitled Communication and Sport at the University of Northern Iowa. He has published scholarly essays in journals such as *Communication Education,* the *Journal of Applied Communication Research,* the *Journal of Family Communication,* and *Communication Studies.*

CHAPTER 1

Introduction to Communication and Sport

Imagine, for a moment, a world without sports. For some of you, this might be a welcome development. But for the overwhelming majority of Americans, sports occupy a key, if not central, place in their daily lives. The reasons for this are many. Sports, after all, are usually fun. Whether we play or watch, sports provide an expression of the human body's physical, and sometimes mental, possibilities. They are also educational. Millions of children participate in youth sports because we have come to believe that they provide life-long lessons about teamwork, discipline, and perseverance. Sports can foster unity. Consider the instant bonds formed between strangers who wear the same team's jersey, or the patriotic spirit on display during international events such as the Olympics. Finally, sports are among the most vital and diverse industries in the United States. They generate billions of dollars in revenue and provide a wide range of professional opportunities. To imagine a world without sports would be to alter the conditions of everyday life in the United States.

To understand the impact sports have in American life, let us be more specific. Youth sports, for example, are among the most common activities for boys and girls throughout their childhoods. More than 17.5 million children play organized soccer, more than 260,000 play Pop Warner football, and 2.2 million annually participate in Little League Baseball (Hilgers, 2006). While these numbers provide us with some appreciation for the extent to which sports are important, they cannot fully describe the range of sports in which young people participate or the ways children play sports informally. Sports are also significant because they provide models of leadership for

Colors divided at UCLA/USC football game

young people, environments to develop interpersonal and conflict-resolution skills, and stories of inspiration when children use sports to develop their individual skills and character. All of which is to say that *communication* is central to how we play, watch, interpret, and evaluate sports.

Of course, youth sports beget other forms of sport. A quick glance at your college classmates offers an appropriate example. How many of them wear a sweatshirt or hat that features their favorite team? Perhaps your own wardrobe has these articles of clothing? Indeed, a positive affiliation with sports is one way that college students construct and communicate identity. Many students even choose where to attend college based on a campus culture organized around sports (Sperber, 2000). And, as a recent ESPN advertising campaign called "Never Graduate" illustrates, many of us maintain our allegiances to the colleges we attended. Using familiar rivalries such as Michigan–Ohio State or North Carolina–Duke, the ESPN commercials depicted adults who continue to be loyal to their undergraduate institutions. At the heart of the campaign was the idea that our college affiliation—*understood primarily as a sports affiliation*—communicates something essential about our identity.

Case Study: Cozart's Community

To truly understand the overwhelming impact that sport can have in the lives of athletes and fans, you only need to look as far as your own community. For instance, it's likely that you have developed a following for a local sports team (high school, collegiate, or professional) that has the potential to bridge generations regardless of the sport type. Such is the case for the wrestling program for Brandon High School in Brandon, Florida, which had held one of the longest-standing winning streaks in all of high school sports. In February of 1973, the team began a dual-meet winning streak that lasted until 2008. When the streak began, Russ Cozart was a wrestler on the team; he later became the coach in 1980. Since that time, he went on to win an additional 384 straight dual victories with wrestlers that he helped develop in the town's youth wrestling program. He raised three sons who also wrestled for him, winning multiple individual state championship titles. Athletes he coached in his first few years at Brandon remained in town and then encouraged their own children to compete and train under the tutelage of one of the most successful high school coaches of all time.

As the streak continued throughout the next three decades, Cozart created a following in the town as the streak itself began to take on a life of its own. Young wrestlers indicated they dreamed of one day competing for Cozart with the hopes that, with the streak on the line, they would be asked to step up and win one to ensure that the streak remained intact. Brandon relished in the success of its wrestling program as the team was invited to tournaments throughout the country. After more than 27 years and 459 straight victories, Cozart lead his team into the championship match in the tournament he had created called "Beat the Streak," where he invited the best teams around the region to compete for a chance to beat his highly rated team. Coming down to the second to the last match of the evening, one of Cozart's most talented wrestlers was defeated, which cost the team it 460th straight win. Afterward, Cozart commented that "what this streak has done for this town and this school is give it a cornerstone, a gem, a diamond to look at and to hold up. I hope they keep it that way." In the weeks that followed, Cozart coached his team to his 18th state championship, producing four individual champions. The community has set its sights on beginning the streak all over again in the years to come.

1. What factors help cause a community to gravitate to its sport programs?

2. Can you think of sport franchises where fans continue to support their team despite a history of losing?

3. What are the communicative elements that are an integral part of the success of this program?

The stakes for understanding communicative practices may be even greater at the professional level. Especially because professional sports are inextricably linked to the media that broadcast, report, and opine about the games, it is next to impossible to escape the influence of professional sports. Consider that leagues such as Major League Baseball and the National Football League routinely set attendance records during the 2000s, or that the expansion of digital services makes consuming live sporting events more available through satellite providers and Internet feeds, or that fantasy sports have produced an entire industry that is dependent on, but also separate from, sports themselves, or that community officials often insist that the key to urban development or city pride is to invest in a professional sports franchise and/or arena, or that player salaries continue to rise, often driving up the cost of attendance along with them. There are many other features to add to this list. What is critical, once again, is that communication practices are essential to the success of professional sports—from expressions of collective identity found at live events to the images produced by sports media to the importance granted to sports in the vitality of a community.

Across all levels of competition, and through the media that cover these events, the very language of sports has become commonplace in American culture. As early as 1959, when Tannenbaum and Noah coined the phrase "sportsugese," there has been an acknowledgement that sports influence how we think and talk. Inspired by both his experience as a sportswriter and the prevalence of sports language in the speeches of President Richard Nixon, Robert Lipsyte (1975) termed this phenomenon "sportspeak." Indeed, as Segrave (2000) has pointed out, sports metaphors are commonly used to communicate ideas and feelings about politics, war, business, and sex. For instance, during the 2008 presidential campaign, both Democrat John Edwards and Republican Mike Huckabee compared themselves to the racehorse Seabiscuit, evidently because they embodied similar qualities of determination that characterized the 1930s thoroughbred. During the 1991 Persian Gulf War, General Norman Schwarzkopf famously referred to a military strategy as a "Hail Mary pass," a familiar football reference. Meanwhile, business meetings are routinely punctuated with platitudes such as "this ad campaign is a slam dunk." As for sex, American adolescence is commonly described through the quest to "get to first base" or "hit a home run."

While language use is one indicator of sport's prominent role in American culture, it is also worth noting that as an industry, commercial sport is the tenth largest in the United States (Zirin, 2005). Street & Smith's *Sports Business Journal* estimates that the American sports industry is worth around $213 billion. Meanwhile, we should point out that sport's ability to generate media interest is almost unparalleled. The two most-watched television events in the world are international sporting events—the Olympics and soccer's World Cup (Tomlinson, 2005). With that popularity, television networks eagerly pay astronomical sums for the rights to broadcast sports. In 1999, for example, CBS paid the National Collegiate Athletic Association (NCAA) $6 billion for an 11-year contract to broadcast the NCAA men's basketball tournament ("CBS Renews"). For the right to broadcast the 2010 Winter Olympics and 2012 Summer Olympics, NBC paid the International Olympic Committee $2.2 billion (Wilson, 2003). All of this demonstrates that the immense popularity generated by sports makes them among the most desirable commodities in the media industry.

Interview: Bob Costas, NBC Sports, and MLB Network

Q: What is the greatest contribution sport provides to modern society?

A: Sports are still the ultimate shared experience. Sport draws the attention of people from all walks of life in ways that few other things can. People now receive information and entertainment from niche outlets on television, radio, the Internet, and more, but big sports events are still much broader based. For all its flaws and issues, sports at its best can still be a shared experience that bonds individuals, groups, and even nations.

Q: How has the consumption of sport changed since you entered the business 30 years ago?

A: There is just so much more of it, even from the traditional formats. Add all of the ESPN networks, all of the regional Fox Sports networks, and the Internet and the mass of it has grown exponentially. Even if the coverage hadn't changed, the sheer amount available would change sports tremendously. Of course, the coverage *has* changed—it is more highlight driven because of the presumed shorter attention spans of today's fans. We are barraged with information—which is sometimes good and sometimes overdone. In fairness, much of the event coverage is technically superb and very well crafted, and truly journalistic efforts like HBO's *Real Sports* and ESPN's *Outside the Lines* stand out. On the other hand, in many areas the tone is mindlessly negative—even abusive. The worst of sports talk radio and the sports blogosphere do not just appeal to the least common denominator, they redefine it.

(Continued)

(Continued)

Q: What is the impact of the evolving relationship between athlete, organization, and fan?

A: Athletes are more protected now by layers of agents and advisors. Some may think, "Well, the money is so great, what good does it do me to be all that accommodating to the media? Is it necessary to let the media present my image or can I control it myself?" Add to that a press corps that is generally more critical and snide and you can understand why many athletes are more guarded.

Q: How do you see the participation in and consumption of sports changing in the next several decades?

A: In ways we can't fully predict! Over the next decade I'm sure new technologies will leave our present high-definition televisions, mobile phone videos, and Internet links outdated. If you want it and are willing to pay for it, you will have access to just about anything at just about any time. I would also expect at least some American sports to become more global, particularly baseball and basketball. We can't know all the specifics, but it is fair to speculate that the future of sports will be bigger and more elaborate in virtually every way.

COMMUNICATION AND SPORT

What should be clear by now is that we are interested in sports primarily as phenomena of *communication*. Other academic publications and textbooks have studied sports through other perspectives. Indeed, the disciplines of anthropology, history, kinesiology, psychology, and sociology have contributed greatly to our understanding of how and why people participate in sports. However, they tend to do so without emphasizing the communicative practices that precede and frame the ways people participate in sport. Kassing and colleagues (2004) suggest that people enact, produce, consume, and organize sport primarily as a communicative activity. Thus, our focus in this text is to explore how and why sport can be understood and studied specifically from the perspective of communication, a field with a far-ranging set of interests and applications.

This is not to suggest that the field of communication hasn't benefited from other academic disciplines. Sociology, in fact, is likely the academic field that has done the most to promote the serious study of sports. In 1978, the North American Society for the Sociology of Sport was founded, which led to the publication of the *Sociology of Sport Journal* (*SSJ*). Just a few years later, scholar Richard Lapchick founded the Center for the Study of Sport in Society, housed at Boston's Northeastern University. This led to the publication of the *Journal of Sport & Social Issues,* which alongside *SSJ* publishes the leading scholarship on the sociology of sport. Meanwhile, other academic fields cultivated the study of sport through publications such as the *Journal of Sport Behavior,* the *Journal of Sport Management,* and *Sport in History.*

The field of communication developed its interest in sport around the same time period. In 1975, Michael Real published a study of the Super Bowl called "Super Bowl: Mythic Spectacle." In that article, Real explained that the televised broadcast of the Super Bowl was arranged to emphasize the mythology of football as a ritualized expression of American identity. That sport could be used to communicate—and thus affirm and extend—American values became one of the early themes of communication and sport scholarship. Other early studies in mass communication confirmed the importance of sports. Trujillo and Ekdom (1985), for example, analyzed sportswriters' accounts of the 1984 Chicago Cubs to reveal how journalism is a means by which "American cultural values are displayed, affirmed and integrated" (p. 264). Meanwhile, Farrell (1989) recognized that the mediated production of the Olympic Games used international politics to create dramatic narratives that fostered national identity. By the time that Wenner's *Media, Sport, & Society* was published in 1989, it was clear that there was much to be gained through the communicative study of sport. These early studies were significant not only because they demonstrated the significance of sport but also because they blurred the traditional divisions of communication scholarship, therefore making the study of communication and sport a truly interdisciplinary endeavor.

The relationship between communication and sport further developed in the 1990s with studies that featured an increasingly diverse set of topics and scholarly methods. As Trujillo (2003) notes, "[D]uring the 1990s, communication students and scholars became very serious about studying sport" (p. xiii). This attitude stood in contrast to previous decades, during which many academics dismissed the study of sport as being trivial, much like the traditional view in news media that ridiculed the sports page as a "toy department" (Rowe, 2007). By the turn of the century, this seriousness prompted a robust interest in communication and sport that now cuts across virtually every area of inquiry in the discipline. Throughout the 2000s, communication scholars found new avenues for engaging in sport-based research, resulting in numerous conferences and publications, including several special issues of communication journals dedicated exclusively to sport. The growth in communication and sport scholarship has provided invaluable resources for students and teachers alike. Until now, however, no one has done what we attempt to do here: to provide a comprehensive summary of the avenues for studying the relationship between communication and sport.

Before we continue, then, we should clarify what this book is *not*. First, it is not a reproduction of the sport sociology or history textbooks that have been widely used, even by communication scholars. Although we cover some of the same categories—media or identity, for example—we do so with a different set of intellectual assumptions. For example, whereas a sociologist might examine data that show a correlation between sport participation and success in business, a communication scholar is apt to investigate which communicative behaviors learned in and through sport enable or disable business success. Or, if a sport historian wants to reveal that baseball was invented in cities and not (as myth suggests) in the countryside, a communication scholar hopes to reveal why contemporary use of the myth retains symbolic significance. Thus, even for those of you familiar with studies of sport in other disciplines, this book should offer something new.

Second, it is not a handbook for practitioners. We know that many of you are interested in careers in "sport communication," perhaps working for the marketing department for a sports franchise or in communications at a university athletic department. We make relevant connections to these professional interests throughout this text. However, primarily we take up how communication and sport can be studied and what they can tell us about one another. With this in mind, but before we offer an overview of the material covered in this book, let us turn our attention to some matters of definition.

Communication

It is virtually impossible to find a definition of **communication** that everyone can agree upon. If you have taken a public speaking course or an introduction to communication theory, you've likely encountered some of the more common definitions of this term. These definitions involve key concepts such as *sender*, *message*, and *receiver*, all of which emerged from telecommunications research in the 1940s (Shannon & Weaver, 1948). Communication scholars have used these simple concepts to develop increasingly sophisticated models of communicative practices. Today, communication is largely understood as a process wherein meaning is constructed and exchanged through a variety of symbols and media. Thinking of communication as a *process* instead of a *product* allows researchers to examine more than the content of the "message" or the intention of the "sender." Instead, scholarship may examine message construction, interpersonal influence, small-group dynamics, mass media, rhetoric and persuasion, and the performance of identity. Accordingly, in this book we adopt a broad and inclusive approach to communication, recognizing that different definitions and methods allow for greater understanding. Thus, if there is any single definition we would endorse, it is one in the spirit of Alberts, Nakayama, and Martin (2010), who define communication as "a transactional process in which people generate meaning through the exchange of verbal and nonverbal messages in specific contexts, influenced by individual and societal forces and embedded in culture" (p. 17).

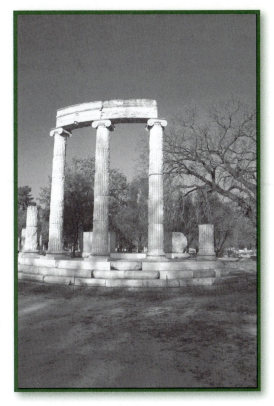

World Heritage Site in Olympia, Greece

Sport

If it is important that we have a shared basis for understanding of the term **communication,** then it is equally important to define **sport.** You may have noticed by now that although the word *sports* is used in the opening pages of this book, we have chosen *sport* for the title. Before we explain this distinction, let us first settle on what makes something a sport in the first place. Guttmann's *From Ritual to Record* (1978) is written in the sociological tradition of sport scholarship. Nevertheless, it provides a typology that helps define and delimit the scope of sport. Guttmann wants to distinguish between four levels of activity: play, games, contests, and sports. Play, he suggests, is "nonutilitarian physical or intellectual activity pursued for its own sake" (p. 3). When that play becomes organized, we have "games," and when games have winners and losers, we have "contests." Not all contests are games, however. As Guttmann notes, a war is a contest with winners and losers, but it is most certainly not a game.

Are all contests sports, then? Guttmann doesn't think so. For example, he notes that just because *Sports Illustrated* writes about it, it doesn't mean chess is a sport. Thirty years later, we could amend this to say that just because ESPN televises it, it doesn't mean poker is a sport. What is required, Guttmann claims, is that sports involve a *physical* component. Therefore, sports are defined as "'playful' physical contests, that is, as nonutilitarian contests which include an important measure of physical as well as intellectual skill" (p. 7). Following this definition, when we talk of specific contests such as basketball or golf, we will likely use the term *sports*. However, and much more frequently, when we refer to the institutional arrangement of leagues, teams, officials, players, fans, and media, we will use the term *sport*. With this in mind, we might also think in terms of Bell's (1987) definition, which states, "Sport is a repeatable, regulated, physical contest producing a clear winner" (p. 2).

PERSPECTIVES AND APPROACHES

In their foundational essay, "Communication in the Community of Sport," Kassing and colleagues (2004) outlined four research areas that have defined communication and sport scholarship. That essay's focus on processes of enacting, producing, consuming, and organizing sport helped carve out an audience for a book such as this one. In this book, we wish to expand the terrain outlined by Kassing and company by casting a broader net. Specifically, we arrange the following chapters in four sections: Community and Sport Foundations, Negotiating Identity in Sport, Relational Issues in Sport, and Emerging Trends in Communication and Sport. Let us now provide an overview of the chapters to follow.

Community and Sport Foundations

Sport is a central feature of life in countries around the world. Our focus in this textbook, however, is primarily on the United States and the study of how Americans participate in the community of sport. With that in mind, what does it mean to study the "community of sport"? Bob Krizek (2008), who is interviewed in Chapter 2, states that it "is a diverse community with often disparate interests that compel us to employ a wide variety of research practices and theoretical frameworks" (p. 105). Thus, on the one hand, the "community of sport" is about those who study it from perspectives as varied as interpersonal influence, mass media effects, organizational behavior, political economy, and rhetorical criticism. However, this community is less about communication scholars and more about those who are invested more directly in the community of sport. Accordingly, in Chapter 2 we examine how this community is constituted by participants, organizations, media, and fans. For example, think about the discussion that took place in early 2010 that led to the expansion of the National Collegiate Athletic Association's (NCAA) men's basketball tournament (from 65 to 68 teams). This decision had an impact on all of the four groups noted above. Expansion would mean more opportunities for players and coaches (participants) to advance to the tournament. The NCAA itself (organizations) would generate millions of dollars in additional revenue. CBS, which televises the event, along with numerous other television stations, newspapers, and Internet sites (media), stood to extend their reach and advertising dollars. Finally, followers of college basketball (fans) were either ecstatic at the prospect of more games to watch or worried that altering the format of the tournament would ruin an ideal sporting event. In this case, all four groups represent different interests in the community of sport. But significantly, those interests overlap, revealing the interdependence of participants, organizations, media, and fans.

The community of sport is also about understanding how sport constructs, maintains, or even threatens the communities in which we live. Fans often tell us a great deal about sport's impact on community. Thus, we turn our attention more specifically to Sports Fan Cultures in Chapter 3. As an example, consider how the connections between sports and the city of New Orleans were on display after the tragic effects of Hurricane Katrina in 2005. Because the Louisiana Superdome was the most visible symbol of the storm's aftermath, it also was seen as vital to the city's revitalization efforts. Even as much of New Orleans struggled to recover, the Saints' *Monday Night Football* victory in 2006 offered beleaguered residents something to be excited about. Such a portrayal was not without its problems—it tended to gloss over ongoing struggles and inequities—but it nevertheless exemplified the connections fans often feel to their teams and cities. This is only one view of fanship, however. In Chapter 3 we examine various forms of fan behavior, including the motivations that guide fans to identify with certain sports or teams as well as the technological changes that have altered the terrain of sport spectatorship and consumption.

The Louisiana Superdome

Connections to the community of sport are commonly cultivated through mythologies that link fans with their communities or sports in particular ways. As we discuss in Chapter 4, myths are stories that are not necessarily true, but their communicative effect is that they feel true. Thus, they provide order and guidance for how people should navigate their worlds. Some myths are local. O'Rourke (2003), for example, revealed how fans of the Cleveland Browns developed an identification with their team based on the perception that the players embodied the blue-collar, industrial ethic that characterized the mythological working-class American. Other myths are national. Consider, for instance, the deeply ingrained belief that baseball, as the "national pastime," is somehow representative of America itself. Or myths may transcend such communities by taking on more cosmological, or religious, significance. Hence, some of the more pervasive sport myths are those that equate sports with religion: the "church of baseball" or the idea that the Super Bowl is a "religious festival" (Price, 1992). In each case, myths depend on heroic figures and universal values to impart their lessons. As a result, when we subscribe to a myth's lessons there are substantial consequences to our attitudes, beliefs, and actions.

Negotiating Identity in Sport

Communication scholars have revealed that sport is one of the primary sites for the construction, maintenance, and contestation of identity. In the second section of the book, therefore, we turn our attention to the relationships between sport and both individual and collective identities. We begin in Chapter 5 with a discussion of gender and sport. As organized sport was institutionalized in the mid to late 19th century, it was largely preserved as a male-only domain. Gradually, and at times painfully, women have challenged and conquered the world of sport. It should be clear that when girls and young women see female athletes excel, that success communicates important messages about identity and self-esteem. Indeed, since the passage of the 1972 Educational Amendments, which included the landmark Title IX, sport has increasingly become a positive force in the lives of women. That is why many celebrated the victory of the U.S. women's soccer team in the 1999 World Cup as not only a triumph for the nation but specifically for Title IX as well.

These gains have not come without resistance, however, and in Chapter 5 we also address problematic representations of female athletes, especially through the media. Overt expressions of sexism are increasingly rare; however, many more subtle iterations of sexism remain. This includes the tendency to provide different coverage to men's sports over women's sports (Billings, 2007), the need to define women first as "feminine" and second as "athletic" (Shugart, 2003), and the all-too-common emphasis on female appearance over other characteristics. Although it is true that many male athletes are also featured for their appearance—New England Patriots quarterback Tom Brady, for instance—it is rare that appearance is the *defining* feature for men. In other words, Brady will always be a quarterback first, a sex symbol second. Can the same be said of racecar driver Danica Patrick?

The previous point also invites us to clarify that *gender* is not a synonym for *women*. Although the role of women in sport is perhaps the most central focus of communication and sport scholarship, we must also attend to sport's role in the construction of masculinity and sexuality. The concept of *hegemonic masculinity*, for example, helps explain the dominant features of masculinity for a given culture. These features are often based on power, strength, and control and frequently come at the expense of women or gay men (Trujillo, 1991). Thus, in Chapter 5 we are careful to acknowledge the multiple identity positions that are implicated by the concept of gender.

If the media has been guilty of sexism with respect to representations of women, then a similar problem arises with respect to race and ethnicity. On the one hand, sport has been the rare institution in American history where racial minorities or non–U.S. natives have been visible, successful, and celebrated. A century ago, when African American Jack Johnson claimed the heavyweight boxing championship, the victory touched off nationwide riots and precipitated cultural anxieties about the diminishment of white cultural authority. Today, American sport is an arena of diverse races, ethnicities, and nationalities. Indeed, often the most beloved stars—LeBron James, Derek Jeter, Tiger Woods—are racial minorities.

The presence of these athletes, however, does not mean that Americans have transcended racial biases or even reached an understanding of what *race* means. Is race equitable with skin color? Ethnicity? Blood? Questions such as these can threaten the harmony that sport has the potential to cultivate. Meanwhile, despite the apparent

Jack Johnson

level playing field offered by sport, racial minorities are often subjected to questionable portrayals and remain marginal participants in managerial and ownership ranks. Meanwhile, what is communicated by a sport like college football, which consistently fields teams comprised largely of African Americans yet rarely coached by them? Or that in major league baseball, where players of Latin American and Asian descent are now commonplace, but the overwhelming majority of owners remain white? These kinds of questions, and many others, characterize our approach to Chapter 6.

Moving from the individual identity positions of the previous two chapters, Chapter 7 evaluates the mutual influence between sport and politics and nationalism. One of the most deeply held misconceptions about sport is that it is "apolitical," or that it offers *only* an escape from the "real world" concerns of politics. However, if you have ever attended a live sporting event in the United States, you have likely participated in a political ritual that few of us would question. Specifically, most of us take for granted that the performance of the national anthem before a game is simply standard procedure, and few of us would think of it as "political." Yet consider the uproar that has been caused over the years when someone dares to threaten the sanctity of the ritual. Jose Feliciano, for example, was widely reviled after he delivered what is believed to be the first nontraditional rendering of the anthem at Game One of the 1968 World Series. Years later, Division III basketball player Toni Smith attracted much criticism for her refusal to face the American flag during the anthem ceremony during the 2002–2003 season.

Both Feliciano and Smith earned scorn for "politicizing" sport. This charge does not stop elected officials from hoping to exploit sport for their own purposes, however. Presidents routinely throw out pitches at baseball games, invite championship teams to the White House, and appear for interviews during broadcasts in order to foster identification with American citizens. This can generate great favor—President George W. Bush was widely praised when he threw out the first pitch at Game Three of the 2001 World Series, just weeks after 9/11—or result in embarrassment—such as presidential candidate John Kerry's attempt to bond with Wisconsin residents by referring to Green Bay's storied Lambeau Field as "Lambert" Field. The international community is also aware of how U.S. politicians communicate through sport. When President Bush used the Olympic success of the Iraqi national soccer team as a symbol of his own leadership during the 2004 presidential campaign, it was seen by many as exploitative and disrespectful (Butterworth, 2007). In most cases, the mixing of sport and politics often sparks controversy about the degree to which they should remain apart from one another.

In the cases of gender, race, and nationality, the construction of identity is often produced, or at least guided, by the media, sports organizations, or

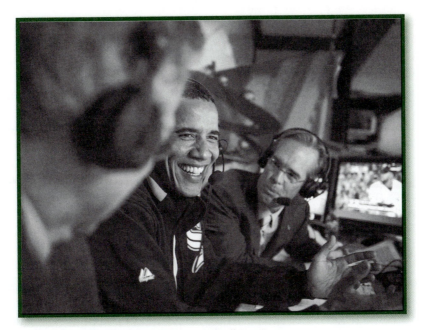

Barack Obama at the Major League Baseball All-Star Game

politicians. Because *athletes* are also part of this process, we turn our attention in Chapter 8 to the *performance* of identity in sport. What this means is that participation in sports is often a means for individuals to express who they believe themselves to be or to challenge conventional expectations about identity that they wish to change. The average sports fan, for example, assumes (probably unconsciously) that athletes are *exceptional* physical specimens and that athletic performance requires a fully able body. Disabled athletes challenge this assumption through their participation in sport. Golfer Casey Martin, for instance, garnered significant attention in 1997 when he sued the Professional Golfers Association (PGA) for the right to use a cart on the tour. Martin had a degenerative leg condition that limited his mobility. The PGA insisted that his request undermined the integrity of its rules, but the Supreme Court ruled in Martin's favor. Although his leg condition ultimately prevented him from pursuing a long-term career in professional golf—he is now the head coach of golf at the University of Oregon—the case helped redefine what it means to be an "athlete."

Sexuality can also be understood as a matter of performance. Scholars influenced by the academic field of cultural studies view terms such as *gender* or *sexuality* on a continuum, meaning that there is no such thing as pure "masculinity" or "femininity," but rather people *perform* their identities in more or less masculine or feminine ways. Performances can take many forms, from choosing types of clothing to using specific words to participating in one sport over another. What is communicated, for example, when a teenage boy opts for figure skating over hockey? As we noted above, one of the common expectations about sport is that it privileges hegemonic masculinity, through which men are expected to be strong, tough, and heterosexual. Thus, the presence of a gay male in sport represents a challenge to the conventions of gender and sexuality. Perhaps this helps to explain why no male athlete while active in a major professional team sport in the United States has publicly stated he is gay. A discussion of the extent to which our performances reinforce or redefine identities, therefore, concludes our focus on negotiating identity in sport.

Relational Issues in Sport

Sport is often celebrated for its ability to foster relationships, develop teamwork skills, and find creative outlets for resolving conflict. Our attention to these issues begins in Chapter 9 with a discussion of parent–child relationships in sports. As participation in youth sports continues to climb, its impact on the family takes on growing importance. For many, sports are seen as means to socialize children. Kremer-Sadlik and Kim (2007), for example, revealed that family interactions during sports activities promote the idea that sport communicates and develops important cultural values. Meanwhile, sport also leads to more troubling phenomena, such as parents who identify too strongly with their children's athletic achievements. The emergence of the so-called "helicopter parent" can arguably be traced to parental involvement in sports, as parents have long obsessed over issues such as playing time or the treatment their children receive from their coaches. For some, the stereotypical figure of the overly demanding father as depicted in the film *The Bad News Bears* remains a cautionary tale about the line between support and pressure.

If parental pressure is a significant issue, so too is the problem of the few but high-profile instances of violence committed by parents. Perhaps the most infamous incident came in 2000, when 44-year-old Thomas Junta beat and killed 40-year-old Michael Costin in a fight prompted by an incident between their sons in a youth hockey game. The case, along with other, less violent incidents, sparked discussions about parental behavior around youth sports. Many communities adopted codes of conduct that required parents to pledge they would maintain good behavior. That parents sometimes become the focus of youth sports invites communication scholars to consider how and why we invest as much in sport as we do.

In some ways, the relationship between players and coaches mirrors the relationship between children and parents. Coaches are often surrogate parental figures, and they are charged with communicating lessons about discipline and hard work even as they are expected to lead their teams to victory. Accordingly, communication scholarship has attended to the ability of coaches to motivate players, including an assessment of different motivation strategies. Although stereotypical portrayals of coaches in television shows and movies—such as the *Bad News Bears* portrayal we referenced earlier—tend to emphasize the role of anger and punishment, Kassing and Infante (1999) discovered that aggressive behaviors commonly lead to unfavorable perceptions of coaches, which leads to weaker performances. In Chapter 10, we explore coaching communication strategies, as well as the significance of the "coach" as a model for organizational leadership.

Coaches can affect the team environment as well. Communication scholars emphasize the term *small groups* over *teams*, but the terms share many traits. Teams are relatively small units that depend on organization and the distribution of tasks across the group's membership. In this way, team sports are appropriate metaphors for understanding small-group communication processes that are found in organizations of every kind. Chapter 11 evaluates various issues related to teams, including cohesion, leadership, and organization. Turman (2003), for example, showed that coaches were instrumental in fostering team cohesion. Meanwhile, Hawkins and Tolzin (2002) concluded that baseball teams provide exemplary models of leadership for postmodern organizations.

Small-group communication is typically considered a part of organizational communication studies. In Chapter 12, we shift our attention to organizations and the specific set of issues prompted by crises. A crisis can occur at multiple levels—it can be macro-level, such as the national crisis in the United States precipitated by 9/11—or it can be micro-level, such as the Formula One racing industry's response to a tire controversy. Brown (2004) addressed the first kind of crisis in his study of the role played by sports leagues in the healing process after terrorists attacked the United States. Organizations such as Major League Baseball or the National Football League, Brown suggests, served as positive and unifying forces for Americans shocked by the tragedy. Pfahl and Bates (2008), by contrast, analyzed the various responses from Formula One teams, the Indianapolis Motor Speedway, Michelin, and others when a dispute over tires threatened to discredit the sport. Their study offers models for communication students and scholars to see how sport provides both positive and negative examples of image-repair strategies. Similarly, in our chapter we seek to understand crisis communication both for what it does well and for the lessons it invites us to consider.

Emerging Trends in Communication and Sport

One challenge in writing a textbook about communication and sport is trying to keep up with changes and new developments. In the final section of the book, we address two particular issues that continue to change the landscape of sport: commodification and fantasy sports. We do not suggest that commodification is entirely new to sport. Despite the contrary claims made by nostalgia buffs, sport has been a commercial enterprise just about from the beginning. Nevertheless, changes to the economy in the late 20th and early 21st centuries have produced new relationships between sport and commerce, which have subsequently altered player contracts, how sports are broadcast, who can afford to attend games in person, and what kind of facilities are built to host sporting events. Even as many are comfortable with these developments in professional sports, there are growing concerns about the increasingly blurred lines between commercialism and amateur sports. Thus, in Chapter 13, we hope to identify the key communication issues that have emerged out of the growing economic reach of sport.

One example of the commercial possibilities of sport can be found in the explosion of fantasy sports. Although many fantasy sports developed in the 1980s, the emergence of the World Wide Web in 1990s made fantasy sports a widespread phenomenon. With fantasy sports now a multibillion-dollar industry, there is little question that it is as much a part of the contemporary landscape as sports themselves. Fantasy sports allow for a new form of fandom and provide an outlet for friends, family, and sometimes complete strangers to communicate and connect with one another. Meanwhile, they also raise questions about addiction or threaten to distract employees who should be working instead of checking their fantasy statistics online. With these issues in mind, we approach Chapter 14 with the intention of viewing fantasy sports as an integral part of the communication and sport relationship.

It should be evident that the relationship between communication and sport is one that requires multiple approaches. The chapters in this book are as comprehensive an overview as is available. Yet we understand that additional topics and questions could be raised. It is our hope that the following chapters provoke you to consider how we might best understand communication and sport. Each chapter incorporates numerous examples and definitions of key terms. We also include three features in all but this and the concluding chapter: an interview with either a communication and sport scholar or a practitioner with experience in sports media, an example that provokes discussion about the role of ethics in communication and sport, and a representative case study that demonstrates the central concepts introduced in the chapter.

At the beginning of this introduction, we asked you to imagine a world without sports. Based on the range of topics included in this book, that is clearly not possible. Neither is it desirable. We are scholars and critics of sport, yes, but we also are fans. We have strong allegiances to our teams, from the Green Bay Packers to the Chicago Cubs to the University of Nebraska Cornhuskers. We played sports as kids and even try to play them as adults. We even participate in fantasy sports. In short, we are invested in the community of communication and sport in multiple ways. Throughout this book, we hope you will join us.

REFERENCES

Alberts, J. K., Nakayama, T. K., & Martin, J. N. (2010). *Human communication in society* (2nd ed.). Upper Saddle River, NJ: Pearson.

Bell, J. B. (1987). *To play the game: An analysis of sports.* New Brunswick, NJ: Transaction Press.

Billings, A. C. (2007). From diving boards to pole vaults: Gendered athlete portrayals in the "big four" sports at the 2004 Athens Summer Olympics. *Southern Communication Journal, 72,* 329–244.

Brown, R. S. (2004). Sport and healing in America. *Society, 42,* 37–41.

Butterworth, M. L. (2007). The politics of the pitch: Claiming and contesting democracy through the Iraqi national soccer team. *Communication and Critical/Cultural Studies, 4,* 184–203.

CBS renews NCAA b'ball. (1999, November 18). CNNMoney. Retrieved March 15, 2009, from http://money.cnn.com/1999/11/18/news/ncaa/.

Farrell, T. B. (1989). Media rhetoric as social drama: The Winter Olympics of 1984. *Critical Studies in Mass Communication, 6,* 158–182.

Guttmann, A. (1978). *From ritual to record: The nature of modern sports.* New York: Columbia University Press.

Hawkins, K., & Tolzin, A. (2002). Examining the team/leader interface: Baseball teams as exemplars of postmodern organizations. *Group and Organization Management, 27,* 97–112.

Hilgers, L. (2006, July 5). Youth sports drawing more than ever. CNN.com. Retrieved March 15, 2009, from http://www.cnn.com/2006/US/07/03/rise.kids.sports/index.html.

Kassing, J. W., Billings, A. C., Brown, R. S., Halone, K. K., Harrison, K., Krizek, B., Meân, L. J., & Turman, P. D. (2004). Communication in the community of sport: The process of enacting, (re)producing, consuming, and organizing sport. *Communication Yearbook, 28,* 373–409.

Kassing, J. W., & Infante, D. A. (1999). Aggressive communication in the coach–athlete relationship. *Communication Research Reports, 16,* 110–120.

Kremer-Sadlik, L., & Kim, J. L. (2007). Lessons from sports: Children's socialization to values through family interaction during sports activities. *Discourse & Society, 18,* 35–52.

Krizek, B. (2008). Introduction: Communication and the community of sport. *Western Journal of Communication, 72,* 103–106.

Lipsyte, R. (1975). *SportsWorld: An American dreamland.* New York: Quadrangle.

O'Rourke, D. J. (2003). The talk of the town: A rhetorical analysis of the Browns' departure from and return to Cleveland. In R. S. Brown and D. J. O'Rourke (Eds.), *Case studies in sport communication* (pp. 63–79). Westport, CT: Praeger.

Pfahl, M. E., & Bates, B. R. (2008). This is not a race, this is a farce: Formula One and the Indianapolis Motor Speedway tire crisis. *Public Relations Review, 34,* 135–144.

Price, J. (1992). The Super Bowl as religious festival. In S. J. Hoffman (Ed.), *Sport and religion* (pp. 13–15). Champaign, IL: Human Kinetics.

Real, M. (1975). Super Bowl: Mythic spectacle. *Journal of Communication, 25,* 31–43.

Rowe, D. (2007). Sports journalism: Still the "toy department" of the news media? *Journalism, 8,* 385–405.

Segrave, J. O. (2000). The sports metaphor in American cultural discourse. *Culture, Sport, and Society, 3,* 48–60.

Shannon, C., & Weaver, W. (1948). *The mathematical theory of communication.* Urbana: University of Illinois Press.

Shugart, H. A. (2003). She shoots, she scores: Mediated constructions of contemporary female athletes in coverage of the 1999 US women's soccer team. *Western Journal of Communication, 67,* 1–31.

Sperber, M. (2000). *Beer and circus: How big-time college sports is crippling undergraduate education.* New York: Holt.

Tomlinson, A. (2005). *Sport and leisure cultures.* Minneapolis, MN: University of Minnesota Press.

Trujillo, N. (1991). Hegemonic masculinity on the mound: Media representations of Nolan Ryan and American sports culture. *Critical Studies in Mass Communication, 8,* 290–308.

Trujillo, N. (2003). Introduction. In R. S. Brown and D. J. O'Rourke (Eds.), *Case studies in sport communication* (pp. xi–xv). Westport, CT: Praeger.

Trujillo, N., & Ekdom, L. R. (1985). Sportswriting and American cultural values: The 1984 Chicago Cubs. *Critical Studies in Mass Communication, 2,* 262–281.

Turman, P. D. (2003). Coaches and cohesion: The impact of coaching techniques on team cohesion in the small group sport setting. *Journal of Sport Behavior, 26,* 86–104.

Wenner, L. A. (Ed.). (1989). *Media, sports, & society.* Newbury Park, CA: Sage.

Wilson, S. (2003, June 7). NBC gets 2010, 2012 Olympics for $2.2 billion. *Pittsburgh Post-Gazette.* Retrieved March 15, 2009, from http://www.post-gazette.com/tv/20030607tvrights0607p4.asp.

Zirin, D. (2005). *What's my name, fool? Sports and resistance in the United States.* Chicago: Haymarket Books.

CHAPTER 2

Community in Sport

No major part of everyday life is left untouched by sport. We join bowling leagues with our coworkers. We play softball with church members against teams representing other denominations. Our schools hold pep sessions to support teams that bear the same school logo and nickname. We attend horseraces by the thousands. In many ways, the topic of this chapter—the community of sport—would be easier to canvass if one were to discuss what does *not* constitute the community of sport. Within American society (and most of the modern world), sport impacts the very manner in which our typical day unfolds. Moreover, it always unfolds within a communicative context. It could involve the interpersonal communication between coach and player, parent and child, or producer and director. It could incorporate the rhetoric of a radio announcer or the bombastic nature of a coach's halftime speech. It could involve intercultural communicative notions of in-groups and out-groups and certainly can be embedded in notions of communication theories that deal with silenced or muted groups or with violations of social expectancies.

Communication informs, persuades, and permeates how we play, how we consume, and how we incorporate notions of sport into our daily lives. The vast ways in which sport permeates virtually all forms of society make it important to recognize who the various "players" within the mingled communication and sport process are. This chapter will outline the major entities that jointly influence the manner in which sport is communicated in the United States and globally. Trujillo (2003) notes that sport is a "billion-dollar industry and an important purveyor of cultural values" (p. xii). Decades ago, a prevailing attitude rendered that sport was a microcosm of society; in the modern day, there are many instances in which the inverse also holds true as society is often a microcosm of sport. This chapter is about how these attitudes, ideas, and behaviors are simultaneously influenced by many crucial "players" who collectively constitute the community of sport. More specifically, we will explore the (a) **participants;** (b) **organizations;** (c) **media entities;** and (d) **fans** that jointly influence sport and society in increasingly conjoined manners.

Interview: Bob Krizek, Communication and Sport Scholar, St. Louis University

Q: What do you feel encompasses the community of sport?

A: The community of sport is a symbolic collective that includes all the people who work in, participate in, are fans of, and /or reporters of sport and sporting events, spanning countries, regions, cities, and schools. It includes everyone who "touches" any aspect of sport and it is larger than any country or single religion. It connects us to the past and helps us anticipate the future. Nonetheless, it is a symbolic community; it exists because we can imagine and talk about it. The community of sport encompasses all that we as humans find meaningful about our forays into the games we play individually and against one another.

Q: How has this community evolved in recent years?

A: Our awareness of it has become much greater. Economic expansion over the last four centuries has provided us with more leisure time, which in turn has allowed the community of sport to develop new ways to experience and define sport. We have introduced "old" sports to new constituencies, as seen in the World Baseball Classic, and legitimized "new" sports such as the X-Games and Ultimate Fighting Championship for all constituencies. The evolution of the community of sport blurs traditional city/state sport boundaries as well as challenges traditional meanings of sport.

Q: In what way do media entities influence this community?

A: The media allows us to be socially present in many places in multiple ways. We can watch the Olympic Games in China while listening to our favorite baseball team play a game in the park of a divisional rival. With exposure comes a tremendous amount of power, including notions about what it takes to succeed and what we should value.

Q: Do you see any dangers in the ways in which people interact within this sporting community?

A: The community of sport and all of its mediated representations is pervasive; therefore, this community may be shaping us in ways we do not truly understand. Because the vast majority of people view the activities that comprise the community of sport as ideologically neutral, we rarely consciously reflect upon what occurs in that community. We concern ourselves with wins and losses and not how the community of sport reproduces dominant ideologies that benefit some and disadvantage others.

Q: What is the biggest misconception about sporting communities?

A: It varies based on the lens in which the person answers. Sport communities are not ideologically free zones. Most people perceive sport as being neutral in regard to politics, gender, culture, and sexual orientation. It is not. The best man not only doesn't always win, sometimes he doesn't even get to play. More often than not, the most talented woman doesn't get recognized for her skills in the same way that her male counterpart does. The community of sport is a privileged place that does not act as a social or political leveler.

Q: To what extent is there a link between community and consumption in sport?

A: In this country, the link is constant and strong. From the sponsors' names on the back of our children's Little League uniforms to the names on our professional sport stadiums, the community of sport encourages us to consume. Even in non-organized neighborhoods in the community of sport, participants in pick-up ballgames don jerseys, headbands, and protective wear that model exactly how the professional and amateur organizations decorate their athletes. The community of sport has a voracious appetite for consuming fed by a constant flow of marketing campaigns and new products.

Q: How do you see the various "players" within the community of sport changing in the years to come?

A: I would hope that as our critical examination of the community of sport gains momentum, a growing body of knowledge gains traction. More realistically, perhaps, I can see the community of sport becoming even more consumer oriented, maybe not to the extent prophesized in the movie *Rollerball*, but certainly more than we currently experience. More positively, more people will actively participate in sport as our life spans increase and as we choose to realign life/work balances.

PLAYER #1: THE PARTICIPANT

We have all played sports—mandatory physical education classes ensure that if nothing else. Games we play range from organized (AAU basketball leagues, school teams, and YMCA clubs) to spontaneous (pick-up basketball games at local parks, throwing a Frisbee with family members in the backyard) games (see Guttman, 1978). As we grow older, the games become more sophisticated and the perceived stakes of participation become higher, allowing for a differentiation between play, games, and sports articulated in Chapter 1 (which is why responses to athletics becoming too intensely serious often involve the rhetoric that "it's just a game"). Relatedly, the decision to continue participation in a given sport is often determined by whether a person is willing to pledge an increased level of commitment. We often hear of the professional player who has forgotten the sheer youthful joy of playing a sport. Thus, to understand our first player, *the participant,* we must begin with childhood play.

Casual Play: Sport as Leisure

By no means is casual play limited to children, but it does represent the formative steps in most people's initiation into the sporting world. Even if children are not indoctrinated into formal types of sports, they naturally create them within the realm of play (such as playing catch with a ball). Four factors influence the degree to which we choose to begin or continue playing sports: personality characteristics (rudimentarily on the continuum of active vs. passive), resources (chances to play and improve via coaching and varied environments), interactions with close contacts (sport-loving parents are more likely to yield sport-loving children), and athletic ability (both inherent and developed in initial experiences). However, variations of these primary four factors occur; for instance, parents who may not overly enjoy sports may nonetheless believe that sport can aid in socializing a child, making the child less likely to participate in delinquent behavior (see Trulson, 1986, for evidence this is true in certain situations). In addition, Chapter 11 will focus on the intergroup dynamics involved in sport that tend to masculinize or feminize the social roles of those who play.

The desire for casual sports play remains for adults, yet the opportunity to participate wanes as life progresses. Whereas children have recess and both informal and structured play-dates and parties, these types of occasions rarely naturally occur for the hyper-kinetic 21st-century adult. When adults do find occasion for casual play, it is most frequently with their children. Regardless of age, casual sports represent a substantial portion of all athletics and communicate many foundational messages: (a) sport should be a vital and healthy part of anyone's life, (b) sport is a primary means for functioning socially, and (c) participation in sport is more likely to yield high character and enhanced opportunity for those involved.

Intramurals: Introductions to Organized Sport

The transition from spontaneously played sport to organized activities comes earlier in a person's life now than ever before. Children begin "smart start" programs as young as age 3 and recreation leagues often feature leagues for preschool children. At this stage, the focus of the sporting activities is on understanding rules and basic levels of sportsmanship. Children are often funneled into these types of structured sporting activities because of the proven correlating benefits between participation in intramural sports and higher grades, lower dropout rates, and greater success in attending and completing college (Lipscomb, 2006). While some experts have been skeptical of these benefits, scholars such as Hartmann and Depro (2006) find positive relationships between activities such as midnight basketball and property crime rates and other forms of deviant behavior. However, research currently has been relegated to finding correlations between intramural activities and positive social benefits; little scholarly attention has been devoted to the communication processes enacted to create this perceived cause-and-effect relationship, making this a ripe area for sport analyses in the future.

Amateur Athletics: Altruism and Idealism

Less than a century ago, being a professional athlete was often equated to being second rate, as the true athletes were the amateurs. They were held in the highest regard largely because they were playing the game because they loved it, not because they needed to in order to make a living. Obviously, the working classes had a much more difficult time staying at the amateur level because of economic realities, so upper classes held to the notions of amateur athletic superiority at least partially because it shut out other classes of people who would be relegated to the professional ranks. For instance, even in the early 1930s, golf's Grand Slam events consisted of the U.S. Open, British Open, U.S. Amateur, and British Amateur Championships, showing just how elevated amateur competition was in comparison to other professional events.

Things have obviously changed since then, as now even the Olympics allows professionals to compete while other sports such as tennis allow players to earn money but place a monetary cap on the amount of prize allotments players can receive while still retaining their amateur status. College athletes do not receive paychecks, yet they receive everything from room and board to tuition waivers to clothing to spending money at college football bowl games in exchange for their participation. Nonetheless, amateurism still is upheld for idealistic and practical reasons, particularly noted within secondary education and university settings. Most athletes participate because they enjoy the competition, yet others do so with their eyes on the ultimate goal of turning professional, with all of the perks that accompany that level of achievement.

Case Study: Bloom's Battle

It isn't unusual for sports to blur the lines between professional and amateur athletics, and the NCAA has established rigid policies that attempt to protect student athletes from the high-stakes game of professional sports. Professional sports can be quite lucrative, and players such as Kobe Bryant and LeBron James are talented NBA players who have found success by opting out of college to obtain the payout that comes from being a professional athlete. While high-profile athletes such as these are fortunate to have the opportunity to make a living at their sports, a small number of amateur athletes are forced to make difficult decisions when confronted with the restrictions placed on collegiate athletes.

For instance, many sport enthusiasts may have never heard of mogul skier Jeremy Bloom, who placed 9th in his event in the 2002 Olympic Games. Skiing is a sport that traditionally doesn't warrant a large paycheck or lucrative contracts, and athletes are required to support themselves by securing sponsorship in order to compete. After finishing his Olympic run, Bloom decided to accept a scholarship offer from the University of Colorado to play college football. His dream was to compete during the season and then continue to pursue skiing during the offseason. However, NCAA regulations limit collegiate athletes from accepting payment of any kind for their athletic abilities, going as far as limiting even their likeness from being used for profit. The fact that Bloom was using the sponsorship money to support his noncollegiate activity did not exclude him from the regulations imposed by the NCAA. He was forced to make a decision: either step down from the Colorado football team or cease accepting sponsorship funding. Both options forced him to give up a sport that he loved for what he perceived to be rules that weighed in favor of the university rather than the student athlete.

As a result, Bloom began to promote the Student Athletes' Bill of Rights, which would allow a student athlete to earn money from outside his or her sport and require institutions to pay athletes a portion of the revenue generated from their competitive efforts. For instance, the NCAA currently sells the television rights to its national tournament each year, for which CBS paid $6 billion to obtain the rights through 2010. More than 94% of the money is distributed back to colleges and universities to support all athletic programs. Yet the athletes responsible for helping to generate this revenue see little of that money beyond the scholarships they receive to attend their institutions. Bloom's Bill of Rights has yet to gather significant support, and he eventually opted to play football throughout the duration of his college career, yet the debate continues to surface each year as the commercialization of the NCAA expands.

1. Do Jeremy Bloom's circumstances warrant an exception to the NCAA policies?

2. Should college athletes be afforded the right to reap the financial benefits from their performances beyond just an athletic scholarship?

3. What potential problems might you foresee if restrictions were eliminated for college athletes?

Professional Athleticism: Style and Substance

Finally, there are those who participate at the perceived highest level of athletics: the professional athletes. Given how jaded some views have become regarding the notion of pure amateurism in the 21st-century, it is no surprise that some have similarly skeptical views about professionalism. Some athletes in high-profile sports can command eight-figure annual salaries, leading fans to feel they cannot relate to the players or that the athletes play not for the love of the game but for a paycheck and the lifestyle that accompanies it. Nevertheless, many professional athletes make much smaller amounts of money, often to the point that they need ancillary jobs to support themselves. For example, until 2009, Home Depot provided part-time, flexible-hour jobs to more than 600 future Olympians because, even though the Olympics now involves professional athletes, most could not fulfill their athletic dreams without outside employment.

Despite economic and celebrity-oriented disparities, one commonality that occurs in professional sports is that athletes are playing the game at the highest level. Perhaps this involves someone making thousands of dollars for each pitch he or she throws, but it also involves professional bowlers;

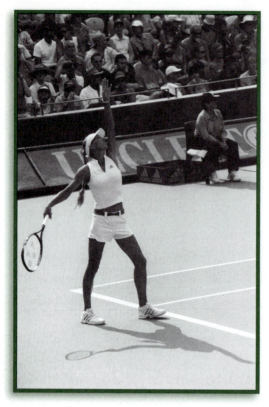

Anna Kournikova

the nation's top bowler may make $200,000 a year while most others make far less. Professional seasons are typically longer than amateur seasons and some notions of athlete welfare are lessened because of the notion that people who earn a living playing a game could (or perhaps even should) endure some hardships in the process. Sports with strong unions are able to ensure some form of equity, but others do not have these bolstered structures in place.

Professionalism involves a ton of talent yet also is about marketability. When a player or sport is marketable, salaries increase along with other sponsorship opportunities. Athletes like BMX biker Dave Mirra make 10 times as much money in outside endorsements and other opportunities as they do for actually playing the game. Athletes such as tennis star Anna Kournikova become famous for their marketability even when they have failed to become one of the best in their sports (Kournikova never won a professional singles title yet cleared millions of dollars in lucrative endorsement deals). Careers of professional athletes tend to be short, and no two ever appear to be alike because of the deviations in talent, health, marketability, and other outside influences.

PLAYER #2: SPORTS ORGANIZATIONS

Of course, these athletes could not begin to participate at these various levels without governing and organizing bodies to oversee these events. *Sports organizations* serve this vital role by coordinating efforts and providing spaces and events that advance opportunities for sport participation. These groups come in all shapes and sizes, ranging from large conglomerates to events coordinated out of a home of a single person. Some types include *recreation clubs* that often serve as a lifeblood of a local community. Some may have ties to formal, structured sports (think YMCA), yet others regard themselves much more as fitness centers where sports are played in the form of pick-up basketball games and other casual events. These games are then supplemented with a heavy dose of activities that represent physical education in a noncompetitive format, such as aerobics classes and public swimming.

Related and yet quite different are *athletic clubs*. Sometimes these organizations function in the same "go to the gym and exercise" manner, yet these also may not involve providing a specific, formal physical space in which sports are played. Instead, the focus is on local (and sometimes state and national) organizing as these groups work with city parks and recreation departments and other entities to use spaces for competitive games. A good example of an athletic club is the AAU (Amateur Athletic Union), as the organization is now so well networked in the United States that AAU coaches can wield more influence on athletes than even their high school coaches. Groups such as these provide opportunities for organized play and regional tournaments.

Another type of sports organization involves *state and national federations*. For instance, each state has an organizing federation to handle high school athletics rules and competitions. These groups facilitate play but also aim to fulfill advocacy roles to ensure athlete equity and welfare. Centralizing national agencies (such as the NCAA) serve similar advocacy functions, intending to offer highly competitive sporting events within the realm of maintaining true amateurism. National groups such as the United States Tennis Association function as federations to promote a certain sport, often by providing youth programs and structures that can aid and help promote sports to those with less access because of their economic or geographic circumstances.

Organizing committees also are integral to the grander sporting events. The biggest sports event of all, the Olympics, has an International Olympic Committee specifically designed to coordinate the Games with a host city. Such a process is so involved for the Olympics that host cities are selected 7 years in advance of the competition after several preceding years of a location vetting process. Yes, these organizing committees sometimes are designed to fulfill advocacy roles in a similar manner to federations, yet this is not always the case. College football bowl games have organizing committees that are centralized around a specific event for a specific sport, yet they do not determine rules or sport governance in any way. Instead, these groups work year-round to promote a game in which the two competing institutions won't even be known until a month before the game is played. Moreover, NCAA Final Four basketball host cities do not know which schools will be participating until one week beforehand.

Finally, there are *team networks.* These types of organizations are not just focused on a specific sport; they are often elaborately designed groups with the intention of promoting a team that plays the sport. All college and professional teams have these types of organizations designed to market and promote a certain team (such as the Atlanta Braves) or institution with multiple teams playing with the same moniker (such as the Arizona State Sun Devils). Branding, media exposure, and the potential for future athletic success are all part and parcel of what these team networks are charged with accomplishing.

PLAYER #3: SPORTS MEDIA ENTITIES

As sports have grown at all levels of society, so too has the plethora of media outlets that now devote substantial time to sport. Aspects of sports media have changed substantially, such as the diminishing opportunities at local sports television networks as a result of increasingly regionalized coverage of sport via regional outlets (Fox Sports Net, New York's YES network). However, parts of *sports media entities* can still be subdivided into visibility jobs and production jobs.

Visibility Jobs

Jim Nantz

First, *visibility jobs* feature media players with which most people are most familiar: Al Michaels commenting on a football game; Jackie MacMullen opining on the Knicks' off-season moves. These players in the sports media empire are well known and often beloved because fans welcome them into their homes on a regular basis. When Chicago Cubs announcer Harry Caray died, millions of people mourned because they had lost a voice with which they had become quite familiar, having listened to his commentary accompany literally thousands of games on WGN television.

In television, multiple visibility roles exist that are now integral to what is consumed at home. The *anchor* often functions as a host. Anchors are typically highly scripted (via teleprompter) even if the words are primarily written themselves (with the help of editors). An anchor's job is often to focus on the significance and scope of sports games and issues; in other words, anchors relay the "big picture." Yes, they may play a role Bob Costas labels a "traffic cop" where the goal is to get people from Point A to Point B (say, from pregame announcers to an injury reporter), yet their primary function is to relay a sense of meaning to their audience (see Billings, 2008). What would a win or loss mean within the overall scheme of things? Why should we be interested in today's starting pitching matchup? Anchors frame all of the discussion that will ensue.

At live televised events, commentary still tends to occur within paired broadcasting combinations of a *play-by-play announcer* and a *color analyst*. The play-by-play announcer describes the athletic contest largely in terms of observable facts ("Albert Pujols is 2–4 tonight with a pair of RBI") while the color analyst interprets the game within a larger context ("The Mavericks are on fire this evening . . . all five starters in double figures"). Several decades ago, a study found that 73% of all television commentary was play-by-play (Bryant, Comiskey, & Zillman, 1977) and this percentage still holds true today, although the strict divisions of who provides which form of commentary are beginning to blur. Even though color commentary represents less than a quarter of all spoken words, color commentators continue to be of extremely high visibility because their dialogue can often be more interesting, memorable, and outside of the box of traditional thinking (consider Dick Vitale's college basketball coverage and his terminology such as a "dipsy-doo dunakaroo" and "diaper dandies").

Television also features another visibility player: the *sideline reporter.* These reporters have been found to be increasingly useful as audience appetite for more "inside" information escalates. More often than not, this role is filled by an attractive female—a topic that will be discussed in greater depth in Chapter 5. Whether it is an interview with the parents of a player, an injury update, or a report on a coach's halftime rant, the sideline reporter offers a form of sports media with an even greater sense of liveness and immediacy.

Beyond television, several of these visibility jobs overlap while others are functionally quite different. For instance, radio sportscasts usually still have play-by-play and color components, yet they are obviously done without video, resulting in even more play-by-play coverage. However, one visibility job that is starkly different than television is the *radio host.* The formats of shows differ, yet the host is rarely considered to be an anchor as much as a facilitator and/or resident expert. Many local shows are defined by a host taking a series of phone calls from fans and then having discussions and assessments of sports happenings. Others feature a group of people who are usually diverse in roles and backgrounds (studied sports enthusiast, former professional athlete, etc.) who jointly engage in sports talk. A few others, such as ESPN Radio's Colin Cowherd, perform more of an anchoring function by taking very few calls and instead providing analysis of "big picture" issues. Still, the large majority of radio shows (local and national) are defined by a host who can create a sense of community (such as Jim Rome and his listeners "the clones," who participate in this radio "jungle;" see Nylund, 2007).

Newspapers and magazines also feature two other forms of visibility players: *print reporters* and *feature columnists*. Comparisons can be drawn as reporters often fulfill play-by-play functions and columnists provide the "color" commentary. Still, the benefit of time and hindsight makes these roles quite different. Print reporters often provide event recaps focusing on the chronology of events ("Down 28–17, the Jets stormed back with two late touchdowns to win, 31–28.") These reporters also can provide "beat" stories, which involve ongoing commentary on full seasons and events (as these reporters often travel with a team or set of athletes continually). Feature columnists, on the other hand, function as color commentators, yet they often have even more freedom as they can seek out a story that perhaps no one has even thought about. For instance, *ESPN Magazine* columnist Rick Reilly often attempts to find a story that arises from a local community yet resonates with the masses about the role of sport within society.

Production Jobs

Because there is less "glamour" in *production jobs* than in visibility jobs, substantially fewer people (often 10 times fewer) seek out these positions in sports media. Nonetheless, these jobs are critical to any sports media entity. Consider the *photographer* who must capture a single shot worthy of encapsulating a 3-hour game or the *producer* who must determine how the storytelling will unfold between the visual, audio, and graphics components. These jobs are no less important but are instead so plentiful that describing each one takes a substantial amount of time. A typical football game requires a television crew of more than 50 people; only a handful of those are visibility players while the rest are directors, camerapersons, technical directors, and so forth who are jointly responsible for airing the contest. Radio certainly operates with fewer people, yet the ratio of visibility to production people still favors production.

One behind-the-scenes area that is critical in all forms of media is the *editorial department*. Many times people consider these people to be strictly focused on streamlining content, such as a newspaper editor who checks a story for accuracy, length, and appropriate emphases. Yet editorial departments also include writers, researchers, and other information gatherers who can make a visibility player's job much easier. For instance, when watching a profile of an Olympic athlete, an anchor or reporter may provide the voice-over, but often the actual writing and certainly production aspects are choices made by a person (or group of persons) in the editorial department.

There are also public relations departments that contribute to behind-the-scenes matters. Years ago, the *sports information director* was charged with most all of these aspects; now, there tend to be separate *marketing, promotion,* and *information* departments. Many sports teams have *media relations specialists* who work to merge promotions (such as public appearances) with relevant information (such as media guides prepared by the sports information department) and marketing to yield a product that the media easily understands and can relay to the masses.

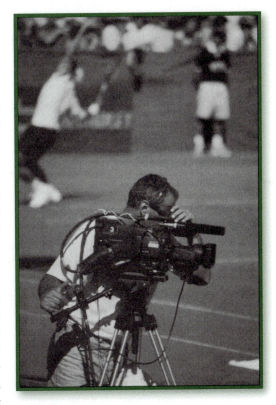

Cameraman at tennis match

Hybrid Jobs

At this point one may wonder why the Internet has been omitted from a section on sports media; this is because new media now often feature new roles and media outlets that are not nearly as established or defined. These are best termed *hybrid jobs* because a single person may contribute to the entire process in a singular fashion. For instance, it is now an expectancy that a print journalist will also work in television and on the Internet. Even prominent sports bloggers often write, present, and produce their own content from their homes; these people are not media entities in any formal sense, yet they contribute to the overall sporting landscape. Other more mainstream forms of the Internet overlap with the roles discussed earlier as a feature columnist often has his or her story on the Internet as well and sports television finds ways to stream a sportscast to essentially make a person's computer into a television. Thus, the principles of sport media hold true, yet the medium changes the way people consume the product in considerably different ways.

PLAYER #4: THE FAN

Motivations for Fandom

Of course, the final "player" of note within the community of sport arguably influences all of the others as an avid *fan* often is motivated to play more sports as well as consume them, allowing sports organizations and media entities to exist and thrive. Raney (2006) probes the psyche of the typical sports fan, noting motivations in the emotional, cognitive, and behavioral domains. These domains, along with much more detail surrounding the communicative nature of fandom, will be discussed in greater detail in the next chapter. However, an overview of the community of sport is not complete without at least a rudimentary articulation of the role millions of fans play.

First, Raney argues that fans are interested in following sports at all levels because of their inherent emotional appeals. These include the (a) desire to be entertained (often watching athletes playing at the highest level and performing physical feats that they cannot begin to do themselves); (b) eustress desires (a form of stress that is actually good for you by providing a sense of fulfillment and achievement); (c) bolstering of self-esteem (for instance, when a person's alma mater wins a national title, he or she may feel pride in selecting and attending that school); and (d) the need to escape from the daily grind of life (one can unwind at the end of a tiring day while consuming a contest that is not a matter of life and death). Collectively, these appeals are very powerful, as sport is used to

Fandom in action

manage moods (see Zillman, 1988) in ways that alter the daily existence of millions of people.

Then there are cognitive motivations for fandom, which Raney divides into the learning and the aesthetic. First, in terms of learning, people glean a great deal of information from following sports at all levels, whether it is about the families involved in a local softball game or the career earned run average of their team's star pitcher. Still, beyond this largely factual level of learning is a higher form of learning, a navigation of a social world. When one watches the Olympics, for instance, a viewer learns about geography (where is Slovenia located?), politics (how did China's government influence the Beijing Games?), and cultural tastes (is table tennis a major sport in Japan?). Even beyond that, issues of identity discussed later in Chapters 5 through 8 are negotiated through fan consumption. Second, aesthetic needs are also fulfilled at a cognitive level. Being a fan often involves being transported to a different place and time. These places tend to be majestic (picture a skiing event in the Alps shown in high definition) and epic (consider more than 100,000 people watching a football game in the Rose Bowl). In sum, the fulfillment of cognitive stimulation facilitates many forms of fandom, from the avid to the sporadic fan.

Finally, there are behavioral motivations, of which Raney lists five: release, companionship, group affiliation, family, and economics. Many of these five action-oriented reasons are interrelated; for instance, people often find companionship with other like-minded souls when attending a game, but they also do this in family formats, witnessed by countless cases of full families tailgating and sharing tickets together for years on end. Similarly, there is an emotional release that arises from being a fan, and sometimes this is manifest economically in the form of sports bets and other ancillary meanings attached to the outcome of the athletic performance(s).

All in all, there are many reasons for fandom and, relatedly, the overemphasis of some of these same motivations provides proof of unhealthy fandom, another topic that will be explored more fully in Chapter 3.

Modes of Fan Consumption

Hugenberg, Haridakis, and Earnheardt (2008) claim that there are macro-levels of sports fandom that include the enactments of identification, motivation, and fan-produced content. Billings (2010) expanded these notions to include four modes of fan consumption (which, admittedly, blend with each other and are not a fully exhaustive list).

The first mode is the *first-person supporter,* who is largely defined not by media consumption but the desire to witness an event first-hand. Season ticket holders for professional and college sporting events certainly fit this criterion, but so do those who stop by a youth sporting event to watch a friend's son or daughter play. First-person supporters often consider themselves to be the "true fans" because they are there in the down times as well as the good. Moreover, they often invest significant funds in booster groups and other agencies in exchange for tickets and VIP treatment.

A direct contrast is found in the second way fans consume sport, the *home-dwelling devotee.* These people also may consume sports in heavy doses but tend to do so using various forms of media (television, radio, etc.) rather than actually attending the game. The motivations for not being a first-person supporter differ, ranging from the economic (lacking the funds to be a season-ticket holder) to the geographic (a Green Bay Packer fan living in the south may find traveling to the game to be quite difficult) to the health oriented (some older fans find the bustle involved in attending games to be overwhelming). Regardless, these people are frequently avid followers, often purchasing television sports packages and better technology to enhance the at-home experience.

Third, there are the *social sports addicts.* These people love sports, but only so far as others help them love the games. The rapid rise in sports bars over the past two decades underscores the need for a place where social sports fans can congregate. For most of these people, watching their team win at home is a hollow experience, but watching the same game with friends (even friends they just met that day) in a social place is highly rewarding. Economics become a crucial factor for these people as well, as people often fit into this category when they have surrendered any notion that they could enjoy some of these sporting events live and in person. Often, they congregate where the resources offer them a relative deal financially, ranging from the sports bar offering games that cost hundreds of dollars in satellite packages to visiting a neighbor who happens to get the channel on which the game is being offered. Some people are social sports addicts because they enjoy it; others are because it is the most practical mode of being a modern sports fan.

Finally, Billings outlines a fourth consumption mode: *virtual world aficionados.* We now have fans without televisions, radios, or season tickets who nonetheless are highly involved not only in watching sporting events online but also in actively creating media themselves, whether this means the creation of one's own blog or commenting on various message boards.

Some virtual-world aficionados are "lurkers" who prefer to consume and not actively participate, but many others seek to become part of the media themselves, and cyberspace provides considerable opportunity for that.

COMMUNITY OF SPORT IN THE 21ST CENTURY: CHANGING "PLAYER" ROLES

The majority of this chapter has segmented out the four major entities of the modern sporting community, yet one must also recognize that these roles are not completely distinct and are constantly changing. The different players are now intermingled more than ever. Most specifically, the role of the fan in the overarching process now alters the other three players through user-generated and 24-hour sports media. Consider the ownership of the Seattle professional soccer team, the Sounders. All season ticket holders (plus anyone who pays $125 annually) become members of the Alliance. This group makes ownership decisions collectively, including a vote every four years on whether to replace the team's general manager. Such decisions are normally left to ownership—the players within the sports organizations discussed previously.

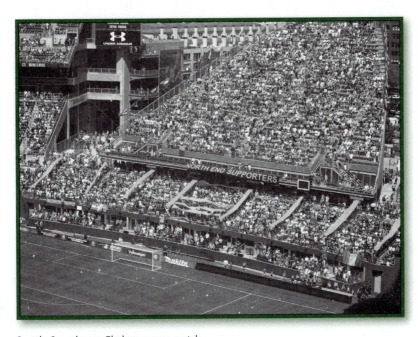

Seattle Sounders v. Chelsea soccer match

A Matter of Ethics: Whose Community?

Since the construction of Baltimore's Oriole Park at Camden Yards in 1992, 19 of the remaining 30 Major League Baseball (MLB) franchises have built new baseball-only stadiums. Many of these new facilities have been labeled "retro ballparks," not only because of architectural features that borrow from the early 20th century, but also because they are often located, as were early-era parks, in city downtowns. In fact, for many cities, baseball (and other sports) stadiums have become anchors in governmental efforts to revitalize urban neighborhoods. Supporters of this strategy argue that ball-parks are magnets for residents and tourists who will come to a game and also visit local restaurants and shopping centers. Accordingly, cities often view a ballpark as the corner-stone of a vibrant entertainment district, such as Baltimore's Inner Harbor or Cleveland's Gateway District. Critics, meanwhile, cite independent research that suggests stadium construction produces only minimal economic benefits to a city's economy. More impor-tant is the possibility that sparkling new stadiums are built to serve more affluent sub-urban residents who visit the city for a ballgame, then promptly return home, and at the expense of local residents who are often poor and are racial minorities.

The tension between entertaining tourists and suburbanites and providing services to local residents was especially evident in Washington, D.C. After the Montreal Expos became the Washington Nationals, the newly relocated franchise planned to build a new, baseball-only facility. Total costs were originally estimated in 2005 at about $395 million. By the time Nationals Stadium opened for play in 2008, it cost the city $611 million. That money came exclusively from public funds, the first time in MLB history such a deal was reached. One baseball executive called it the "sweetest of sweetheart deals." Meanwhile, many District residents objected to locating the sta-dium along the Anacostia River, in a poor, mostly African American neighborhood that lacked sufficient resources for education, health care, or recreation.

1. In light of what you have read about community in sport, to what extent does a major league franchise "symbolize" the local community?

2. Whose interests should be served when new stadiums are constructed?

3. If research is inconclusive about whether new ballparks spark economic growth, should construction move forward?

4. Finally, what does a city's decision to build a sports facility say about its priorities?

Along with these blurred lines between fans and other aspects of sport comes the enhanced bonding that arises in the process. The concept of BIRGing refers to people who "bask in reflected glory" in team triumphs and good times. Fans in New England may have jointly experienced these feelings when major sports teams (Red Sox, Celtics, and Patriots) all won championships within a few years of each other in the 2000s. There is also the concept of CORFing (cutting off reflected failure), which pertains to the inverse feelings fans feel when their teams lose or underperform. The common refrain that "we" won or "they" lost is underscored by these two concepts. New England baseball fans likely felt this until 2004, when the Red Sox finally ended an 86-year drought in winning the World Series. While BIRGing and CORFing have been examined in sport for decades (see Wann & Brascombe, 1990), these fan feelings are exaggerated in recent years, largely because of greater fan investment. It is difficult for fans to put sports in proper perspective when they are increasingly spending thousands of dollars on watching their favorite teams and are constantly consuming messages about sports via sports radio, television, newspapers, magazines, and the Internet. Thus, fans become a part of media and organizations by impacting fan message boards and injecting opinions on radio call-in shows.

The result of all of this interaction between the various players in the community of sport is an enhanced form of identification. There is a feeling of kinship when one spots a person wearing his or her team's logo at the airport or when a community jointly celebrates "its" first championship in decades. Wann (2006) offers three antecedents for sports team identitification—psychological, environmental, and team-related—but then notes that there are myriad forms of antecedents to the point that each person's experience of identification is different. Given the increasingly diverse community of sport, this is not at all surprising. Understanding the players within the community is important, yet equally important is the embrace of change and overlap. Members of sports media are undoubtedly still fans; people within sports organizations are more likely to be players of sport as they have dedicated their careers to advancing the importance of participation in athletics. Society is, indeed, a microcosm of sport and, as we're about to see in Chapter 3, the fan cultures that arise from this deep connection with the public consciousness manifest in ways that represent some of the best and worst that humanity has to offer.

REFERENCES

Billings, A. C. (2008). *Olympic media: Inside the biggest show on television.* London: Routledge.

Billings, A. C. (2010). *Communicating about sports media: Cultures collide.* Barcelona, ESP: Aresta.

Bryant, J., Comisky, P., & Zillman, D. (1977). Drama in sports commentary. *Journal of Communication, 27,* 140–149.

Guttman, A. (1978). *From ritual to record.* New York: Columbia.

Hartmann, D., & Depro, B. (2006). Rethinking sports-based community crime prevention: A preliminary analysis of the relationship between midnight basketball and urban crime rates. *Journal of Sport and Social Issues, 30*(2), 180–196.

Hugenberg, L. W., Haridakis, P. M., & Earnheardt, A. C. (Eds.). (2008). *Sports mania: Essays on fandom and the media in the 21st Century.* Jefferson, NC: McFarland.

Lipscomb, S. (2006). Secondary school extracurricular involvement and academic achievement: A fixed effects approach. *Economics of Education Review, 26*(5), 463–472.

Nylund, D. (2007). *Beer, babes, and balls: Masculinity and sports talk radio.* Albany, NY: SUNY.

Raney, A. A. (2006). Why we watch and enjoy mediated sports. In A. Raney and J. Bryant (Eds.), *Handbook of sport and media* (pp. 313–329). Mahwah, NJ: LEA.

Trujillo, N. (2003). Introduction. In Brown, R. S., & O'Rourke, D. J. (Eds.). (2003). *Case studies in sport communication.* Westport, CT: Praeger.

Trulson, M. E. (1986). Martial arts training: A novel "cure" for juvenile delinquency. *Human Relations, 39,* 1131–1140.

Wann, D. L. (2006). The causes and consequences of sports team identification. In A. Raney and J. Bryant (Eds.), *Handbook of sport and media* (pp. 331–352). Mahwah, NJ: LEA.

Wann, D. L., & Branscombe, N. R. (1990). Die-hard and fair-weather fans: Effects of identification on BIRGing and CORFing tendencies. *Journal of Sport & Social Issues, 14*(2), 103–117.

Zillmann, D. (1988). Mood management through communication choices. *American Behavioral Scientist, 31*(3), 327–341.

SUGGESTED ADDITIONAL READING

Bernstein, A., & Blain, N. (Eds.). (2003). *Sport, media, culture: Global and local dimensions.* Portland, OR: Frank Cass.

Rein, I., Kotler, P., & Shields, B. (2006). *The elusive fan: Reinventing sports in a crowded marketplace.* New York: McGraw-Hill.

Schultz, B. (2005). *Sports media: Reporting, producing, and planning.* New York: Focal Press.

Sullivan, P. A. (2003). *Team sports, gymnastics, and dance in community settings: A guide for teachers, coaches, and parents.* Champagne, IL: Human Kinetics.

Torr, J. D. (Ed.). (2003). *Professional sports: Examining pop culture.* Farmington Hills, MI: Greenhaven.

Wenner, L. A., & Gantz, W. (1998). Watching sports on television: Audience experience, gender, fanship, and marriage. In L. A. Wenner (Ed.), *MediaSport* (pp. 233–251). London: Routledge.

CHAPTER 3

Sports Fan Cultures

S port fan cultures are an ever-changing phenomenon, with each sport creating a variety of unique opportunities that help define what it means to be a fan in today's global sport environment. Sport viewing and spectatorship continues to be a growing leisure activity, producing more than $20 billion in revenue each year in the United States alone (e.g., ticket sales, pay-per-view, sport merchandise, etc.). Within this environment, fans are provided unlimited access to information or *points of contact* and at times direct exposure to the sport, teams, and athletes they follow. Through these opportunities, fans are now just as likely to become connected to the sport franchise itself as they are the players or teams that had once served as the center of the fan's allegiance (Oates, 2009).

Sport fan cultures are likely to evolve and develop dependent on the sport type and level at which it is played, and these factors influence the communicative aspects that drive how fans enact and consume sports. To highlight this feature of sport fan behavior, we present you with two competing sport contexts to demonstrate the divergent perspectives that can exist across sports. First, the National Association for Stock Car Auto Racing (NASCAR) is a sport that has developed more recently, with humble beginnings as a competition between moonshiners testing their driving skills in the late 1950s and '60s. Since this time, the sport has flourished into a multibillion-dollar-a-year franchise. Its total fan base is estimated at more than 80 million fans, and it has grown into one of the largest spectator sports. While NASCAR events can generate a considerable television audience, NASCAR is recognized more as the nation's largest spectator sport because of its ability to accommodate as many as 250,000 spectators at major events. Fans from this sport are also unique in that they have been recognized for their unrelenting loyalty to sponsors—or even to particular car brands—rather than to the drivers themselves. As a result, sponsors

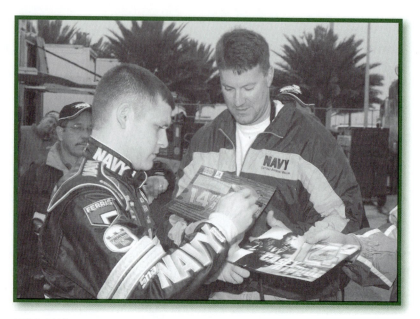

NASCAR driver Casey Atwood signs an autograph

spend as much as $500,000 per race on their respective teams to help build and sustain their fan bases.

Second, at the turn of the century, the National Football League (NFL) developed along similar lines as a sport designed primarily to tap into the commercial success of college football. Despite a number of fledgling leagues, over the past half-century, the NFL has emerged as one of the most dominant sports in the United States, receiving considerable amounts of media coverage. For example, when comparing the most highly ranked television programs in our nation's history, the Super Bowl represents 21 of the top 50 programs of all time and has become an informal national holiday in the United States (Martin & Reeves, 2001). The American Institute of Food Distribution (2004) reports that more products are purchased and consumed during Super Bowl weekend than any other holiday except Thanksgiving. As technology has developed, NFL fans are now given even more opportunities to participate in viewing and responding to league drafts, serving as managers in fantasy football leagues, and even performing simulated play with video games such as the Madden Football series, which has become one of the most successful video games in the world (popular enough that it has spawned a television series on ESPN where viewers watch players compete against each other playing the game).

Case Study: Feeding the Desire for an Undisputed Champion

Since its inception, college football has been dominated by a lucrative bowl system with significant economic potential for participating colleges and universities and their respective bowl sponsors. To date, as a direct result of the bowl system, Division I college football is one of only a handful of sports (collegiate or professional) that does not implement a playoff system to determine a national champion on the field of competition. As sport fans find themselves motivated by a sense of achievement and drama, there is perceived benefit to a system that allows for the top two teams in the country to decide their fate on the field rather than in a poll where coaches and media representatives make the final decision.

With growing pressure to resolve the existing bowl structure, significant change was implemented in 1992 when the Bowl Coalition was established to further ensure a matchup between the top two teams in the country. Prior to this time, the number-one- and -two-ranked teams had only met in a bowl game nine times since 1945. In its first year, the Bowl Coalition system worked effectively to match number-one-ranked Miami and number-two-ranked Alabama to produce what was described as a "true national champion." The same result occurred during the four succeeding years until a joint national championship was awarded to the University of Nebraska and the University of Michigan in 1997. The following year, the commissioner of the SEC established the Bowl Championship Series in an attempt to eliminate the likelihood of future ties. A computer ranking system was created that would ensure the number one and two teams in the country would play in a bowl game that would rotate across four different bowls: Fiesta, Orange, Sugar, and Rose. This practice produced a unanimous national champion until the 2003 season, when a split decision between the coaches and associated press polls awarded titles to both Louisiana State University and the University of Southern California. During the past few years, a number of teams from smaller conferences have gone undefeated (Boise State University, University of Utah) but have been unable to secure enough points in the computer ranking to warrant an opportunity to compete in the championship game.

With these outcomes, coaches, the media, and, more importantly, fans have continued to voice their opposition to this structure by pushing for a playoff system for college football. The issue even surfaced during the 2008 presidential campaign, when Barack Obama voiced his frustration with the current system, speculating that he may push Congress to enact legislation to address the issue. However, despite the ongoing debate about the matchups for the championship game, the creation of

(Continued)

(Continued)

the Bowl Championship Series (BCS) has been both successful and lucrative for college football. For the 2003–2004 bowl games, the four BCS bowls produced an average TV rating share of 11.82 compared with a share of 2.99 for the remaining 24 bowls.

1. Does the fan experience suffer because a definitive national championship is not awarded?

2. Are football fan rituals likely to change if a playoff system were implemented?

3. What are the potential fan benefits that come from a system that does not allow for a true national champion to be assigned?

With the range of sport cultures in mind, as well as ever-changing fan bases, we set our sights in this chapter on exploring the communicative aspects that drive sport fan cultures that exist today. We start by exploring the distinctions between the various types of fans that you are likely to encounter and noting the differences between fans and spectators, and as we present these fan types, we expect that you may even begin to recast your own perception of where you might fit on the sport fandom continuum. The change in the way that fans can experience live and mediated coverage of sports has also had a significant impact on the way that sport fan cultures evolve, along with the rituals that are performed in these two contexts. Within this framework, we attempt to explore the range of motives that drive sport fan cultures by examining the rationales behind fan interest in sport, the by-products they receive, and how these vary by sport types. These motives are linked with what many define as sport identification, suggesting that the relationship between sport and identity (self-esteem or personal identity) can affect a large range of variables outside the sport context. Finally, as the NASCAR and NFL examples demonstrate, sport continues to evolve as we are finding that new technologies continue to provide innovative ways not only of engaging fans with their sports, teams, or athletes but also of affording fans an opportunity to shape the very nature of sport itself. With this broader framework in mind, we begin by exploring the various sport fan types that exist.

SPORT FAN TYPES

In Chapter 2, we explored how fans serve an important role in the community of sport, noting the differences between modes of fan consumption of sport. Here we seek to explore fan types based on the cultures and rituals that are likely to emerge, and the difference between fans and spectators is

Michigan celebrates a basketball victory over Duke

worth establishing at the start of this section. Some use the term sport *spectator* to describe those who simply watch and observe, while the term *fan* (stemming from the term *fanatic*) is more commonly used to depict those who experience a greater sense of devotion to the sport they follow (Trail, Robinson, Dick, & Gillentine, 2003). Fan types often fall somewhere on a continuum between *fair-weather* (those who only display rejuvenated waning interest in their sport or franchise when it is winning) or *die-hard*. You may know a number of people who become excited about college basketball in March each year as the NCAA basketball tournament arrives. Office pools help add to the excitement of the games as the tournament unfolds, but many of those who participate in such events are unlikely to follow the sport beyond this time frame (e.g., college recruitment efforts in the off-season, player early entry into the NBA, etc.). Others become enamored with their local franchise only after it has won a championship yet quickly lose interest shortly after the team's success fades away. *Die-hard* fans, on the other hand, are a different story altogether. They look forward to the upcoming season with great anticipation, often transforming into different people as they are overcome by the successes and failures of their teams.

Sutton, McDonald, Miline, and Cimperman (1997) have classified three types of fans. The first would fall closer to the fair-weather end of the continuum, which they described as the *social fan* (see Figure 3.1). This individual has a limited sense of identification with a particular team, sport, or athlete and sees sport fandom primarily as a socializing opportunity. The outcome itself is less important than the experience gained from participating. The lived experience of the live event or social gatherings connected with sports is what drives social fans' ongoing interest. The *focused fan* has moderate levels of identification, with some form of invested interest in/affiliation with the team he or she follows: "I'm from Denver, which means that I support the Broncos, Rockies, Nuggets, and Avalanche." Focused fans might have a sense of civic engagement whereby they provide their general support to the city, town, or community sport teams. Finally, the *vested fan* is a die-hard fan with high levels of emotional attachment and identification to the teams he or she supports. Team outcomes are of critical import and in many cases, self-esteem and identity of vested fans will be connected to contest outcomes. Not being able to work the day after the Cubs are eliminated from the playoffs might be what you can expect from a vested fan. They have invested time, money, and energy into the support they provide. Advances in technology and the growth of media coverage have had a significant impact on these fan types. More importantly, such changes have created a distinction for fans who attend the live sporting event.

Figure 3.1 Sport Fan Continuum

Sport Interest	Social	Focused	Vested	Emotional Attachment

→

Fan Type	Description	Example
Social	Those individuals whose interest in a sport is driven more for the ability to connect with others. The sport itself is peripheral or secondary to the pleasure obtained from sharing the experience with other fans.	Coworker who takes part in an office pool for the NCAA basketball tournament despite having not followed college basketball the entire regular season.
Focused	Individuals with moderate investment in a particular team, sport, or community who spend considerable time following outcomes.	Dallas native who is vested in seeing the Cowboys and Rangers perform well throughout their respective seasons.
Vested	Sport fans with significant emotional attachment to the success/failure of the teams or sports they support.	Snowboarding enthusiast who attends all national events and makes resevations to attend the Olympics every four years to support the sport.

LIVE VS. MEDIATED FANDOM

In Chapter 9, we will provide greater detail on the transition that has occurred for sport participants as we have transitioned from a game to a sport culture. A similar transition is also unfolding in contemporary sports, as fandom is no longer defined by our physical presence at the actual sporting event. There are a variety of reasons why fans make a conscious choice to attend the live event. First is the ability to serve as a vicarious participant in the event, because it provides an opportunity to engage in retrospective recall after the event. Weed (2007) noted that participants at the live event "have some kind of experience of 'otherness' that will set them aside from their peers on their return" (p. 406). You are able to recount not only the specifics about the event but also what transpired in the historical significance of the event itself. Stating that "I was at the bottom of the course when Lindsey Vonn won the gold for the USA Olympic ski team during the 2010 Winter Olympics" garners more attention than the simple recall for those of us who must rely upon the replay of the event. Second, fans feel a need to participate in the live event because

it serves as an opportunity to collect mementos, but, most importantly, the ability to retell the experience as an intangible outcome of the lived experience. Others have noted the desire for fans to experience the physical connection that comes from being in close proximity to others who are also simultaneously living the event. Being a part of this type of sporting event is one of the enduring features of the lived sport experience. Traditionalists still contend that going to the ballpark is a fundamental feature of the baseball experience, but they have also frowned upon the fact that sport franchises have had to develop a more lucrative experience to stimulate fan interest at these venues. Rushin (2004) noted that MLB attendance, for example, has grown because of the additional amenities that "going to the ballpark" can provide. Wi-fi access, ferris wheels, and picnic areas have become common

The ferris wheel and other amusements at Comerica Park

amenities at these venues, causing the sport or competition to become secondary to the social environment that is fostered.

Rituals (sets of actions or behaviors performed to serve a symbolic purpose) have expanded beyond just the context of viewing the event in person. *Sports Illustrated* noted a number of years ago that with advances in media and game coverage, sport fans are able to obtain a better experience by watching the event in alternate locations. For example, tailgating has become a popular ritual that fans engage in prior to the start of each event, with considerable revenue generated each year by companies that develop a wide range of products that can support this presport experience. Some teams have even begun to view tailgating as a revenue-generating opportunity, by which tailgating and the sporting event itself have been joined in ways that may have never been intended. For instance, in 2008, the front office for a number of NFL teams implemented a policy requiring that fans involved in tailgating activities also have game tickets if they anticipated staying in the parking lot during the game. Weed (2007) observed that in Great Britain, the pub has become a legitimate venue for soccer fans to experience events, noting that more people watch live events in bars or restaurants than those who participate as actual spectators of the event. Three features seem to be influencing this particular trend, including the (a) availability of technology for displaying digital-quality pictures; (b) safety of sport stadiums and negative fan behavior or hooliganism; and (c) increased coverage of all sporting events on television. Regardless of whether a fan takes part in the actual event, a set of rituals often helps to reinforce how fans experience sports.

FAN RITUALS

Rituals produce a permanent change or transformation in an individual or group and represent important rites of passage (Schechner, 2002). Sport is one such situation that is structured around transformational rites of passage for both spectators (e.g., tailgating, cheers, etc.) and participants (e.g., pregame warm-up, athlete superstitions, etc.). Playful performance is an important part of our everyday life experiences, and sport fans are offered a lasting refuge where playful public performance still exists in the patterns and rituals that define sporting events. Fans often paint their faces and wear common attire or even elaborate costumes as a way to show support or allegiance to their sport teams. A number of scholars have examined the role of ritual on sport spectators. Using an ethnographic approach, Carbaugh (1996) assumed the role as a participant observer at 40 college basketball games. His analysis uncovered five important rituals consistent at both the professional and college levels: the warm-up, the salutation, the introductions, game talk, and the dissipation. These stages of fan performance were distinguished by the manner of talk (transition from cooperative to competitive as the game started) and the style of talk (low intensity to high intensity) as the contest approached. The purpose of viewing the sporting event live allowed the fan to live vicariously through his/her team and partake in the highly expressive public discourse.

A source of concern regarding the ritual of sport has been the way sport fans use performance to assist in the perpetuation of racial stereotypes. Miller (1999) contended that the difficulty associated with restricting the use of Native American mascots for professional and college teams resulted from the parallels between stereotypical views and how people assumed the role as "sport fan" for their teams. Dressing up in costumes, wearing sentimental team paraphernalia, and performing game rituals and taunting were essential features of their sport experience. These important rituals were difficult for fans to let go, and we explore this at greater length in Chapter 8.

Research has also examined the impact sport venues have on the performance of these sport rituals. During the closing day of the 1991 baseball season, Krizek (1992) assessed the impact the demolition of Comiskey Park (home of the Chicago White Sox) had on fans. Participants reflected upon their memories of the park, which formed important rituals bonding fathers, sons, and families as well as connections with the past. The ritual of going to the ballpark as children had encouraged fans to make pilgrimages from around the country to be a part of the facilities' final hours. The park also helped to encompass a number of other important rituals in the lives of these

Avid Raiders fan

individuals, most notably weddings and bachelor parties, a final slice of life before going off to war, and relationships formed between fans as they cheered for their beloved team. In a number of ways, these rituals have a direct impact on the factors that motivate fan connection and identification with the sport, teams, and athletes they follow, which we discuss in the following section.

MOTIVES OF SPORT SPECTATORS

Research has identified six primary motives that drive fans' connection to the sports they follow. First, fans who are interested primarily in *aesthetic beauty* are drawn to the sport to see it played to its perfection. Having played a sport as a young child and understanding the difficulties associated with performing at the highest level can be a significant motive for some fans. Baseball fanatics are inspired by the perfect double play, a manager's ability to strategize, or the potential for a perfect game. Someone who could never dunk a basketball may be motivated to follow the sport because he or she experiences a greater sense of appreciation for what professional athletes can accomplish.

Second, *achievement* is a motive that is fulfilled when one obtains a sense of accomplishment after a team or athlete wins. This motive can cause a fan to attend every game or contest as research has shown that highly identified fans have an innate belief that their presence at a sporting event has a direct impact on the competition's outcome. Many sport franchises fuel this belief in their fans. For example, in football, a number of teams emphasize the "12th man," suggesting that the fans can serve as an additional player who influences the game's outcome. Findings from Wann, Peterson, Cothran, and Dykes (1999) suggest that fans will go to great lengths to support their team's outcome, even indicating a willingness to cause harm to (break a leg, trip) the rival players and coaches. They observed that "because their teams'

Texas A&M's 12th Man

performance has relevance to their self-concept, they become more willing to assist the team by acting violently . . . Apparently many sport fans believe that they would go to great (and illegal) lengths to assist their teams" (p. 601). The sense of achievement one experiences after the win (not just for the team but for one's own contribution) can have a direct effect on such behavior.

Third, fans are also drawn to the *drama* of sports as they experience enjoyment that comes from the thrill of watching the game unfold. A last-second shot, a takedown at the edge of the mat, or a quarterback's ability to march his team down the field in the last 2 minutes each provide a heightened sense of drama that motivates individuals. You watch because you don't want to miss out on what could be a memorable sporting event or moment.

Michael Jordan memorabilia

A Matter of Ethics: Bertuzzi's Brutality

Perhaps you've seen the 1977 film *Slapshot* starring Paul Newman? For many, the most memorable characters from the film are the Hanson brothers, three unassuming minor league hockey players who, when finally given a chance to take the ice in a live game, respond by assaulting nearly every member of the opposing team. Their debut makes for a brutal but funny scene. It works, at least in part, because the image of the "hockey goon" is familiar to even the most casual of sports fans.

Fast forward many years later to 2004, when Vancouver Canucks player Todd Bertuzzi punched Steve Moore of the Colorado Avalanche from behind, driving him face-forward into the ice. Moore left the ice on a stretcher with numerous injuries, the most serious of which were three broken vertebrae in his neck. Although Bertuzzi was suspended and missed 17 months of action from the National Hockey League (NHL), Moore's career was ended and his health permanently altered. This was no movie.

The Bertuzzi–Moore incident is perhaps the most recognizable and shocking consequence of the violence that is common in professional hockey. Surely you have heard a version of the famous joke "I went to the fight and a hockey game broke out." For many fans, this is exactly as it should be, as hockey is a violent sport that *requires* the occasional fight to keep order among the chaos of the game. And in our ESPN-driven sports culture, who hasn't seen *SportsCenter* highlights that are little more than a

(Continued)

(Continued)

summation of goals scored and punches thrown? All of this leads critics to call for fighting to be banned in professional hockey. If it can work in amateur and international competition, they insist, why not in the NHL?

1. What would it mean for professional hockey if fights were banned?

2. Would this, as some insist, cause fans to abandon the sport? Or would it open space for new fans for whom fighting is a detriment to the game?

3. Would a ban on fights make *you* more or less of a hockey fan?

Fourth, *escape* is a motive for sport fans when they experience a level of relief from the stress in their day-to-day world. This has been one of the most heavily cited motives, whereby the sporting context provides an important diversion from the negative aspects of one's daily routines (i.e., work, family, college experience) that can be repressed by temporary immersion in sporting events (Wann, Allen, & Rochelle, 2004). Sport offers a distraction for fans as they are allowed to get caught up in something that has less impact on their day-to-day existence. Others suggest it simultaneously serves as an important source of release from overstimulation.

Fifth, fans can also be motivated by *knowledge*, as they gain insight into how the sport is played by viewing it. Watching a television analysis break down the technique involved in a successful double play can assist young athletes as well as youth coaches who are attempting to instill the same technique into their kids.

Finally, sport fans are motivated by the *social connection* that sport can provide. The desire to interact with others who have similar affiliations for sport can help manage friendships and relationships (Wann, Royalty, & Rochelle, 2002). For example, females are more likely to be motivated by increased family time that comes from sport spectating. Each of these motives is influential in determining the level of identification that fans experience.

SPORT IDENTIFICATION AND FANDOM

Many fans are likely to make connections with athletes and teams they support, and a body of research has used sport identification (the psychological connection fans experience to their team, sport, or athletes) to describe the extent to which fans are connected to sport. Highly identified fans are more likely to experience stronger postgame affect (both positive and negative, depending on the team's performance), and studies have also observed positive correlations between team identification and collective self-esteem, psychological well-being, optimism for the team's future performance (Wann et al., 2002), and academic success, while being negatively correlated with loneliness and alienation (Branscombe & Wann, 1991). For example, college and university graduates who attend their institutions' sporting events have been found to have higher GPA, retention, and graduation rates (Wann & Robinson, 2002). Positive impressions of an

Table 3.1 Typology of Fan Motives for Sport Spectatorship

Fan Motives	Definition	Example
Aesthetic Beauty	Drawn to the sport because one appreciates the way it is played or performed.	Enjoying the sport of motocross because of the unique skill necessary to perform the range of jumps or tricks required to win judge approval.
Achievement	Internal sense of accomplishment that comes from the success of the team one is supporting.	Sense of joy experienced by a New Orleans Saints fan after their team finally won the Super Bowl in 2010 just 4 years after Hurricane Katrina almost destroyed their city.
Drama	Thrill obtained from a heated rivalry or key matchup between marquee athletes or teams.	Watching the final round of Wimbledon as Roger Federer and Rafael Nadal compete for a Grand Slam win.
Escape	Following a team to experience a sense of departure from the day-to-day world around us.	Watching the 1980 Olympic hockey team win the gold helped the American public forget about difficult economic times.
Knowledge	Monitoring how the sport is performed to increase one's understanding for how it should be played.	A parent watching the slow-motion coverage of an ice dancing routine in the hopes of further refining the technique employed by her daughter during future competitions.
Social Connection	Ability to interact with friends, family members, or colleagues with sport serving as a background or rationale for supporting the relationship.	Mother and daughter taking a trip to watch the NCAA women's field hockey championship as a way to bond.

institution's sport program increase the likelihood that a college student will persist or be retained at the campus and have also been found to serve as a critical factor in the decision for freshman to return to their institutions a second year. Smith and Schwarz (2003) measured perceived similarity among college students during important rivalries, noting that perceived similarity decreased for the opponents but increased among students at the home school.

The sense of identification fans experience is likely to be affected by the business-oriented model that drives professional sports today. Consider the emotional turmoil that a highly identified fan experiences when his/her favorite team relocates or a star athlete demands to be traded. Fan feeling about Brett Favre is a prime example of the tension fans are likely to experience. Favre, a future Hall of Fame quarterback who played the majority of his career for the Green Bay Packers, retired, only to return to the NFL the following season to play for the New York Jets. After a successful year with the Jets, Favre again retired but then signed with the Minnesota Vikings the following season (division rivals in the NFC North division). Deep-seated rivalries between these two division opponents made it difficult for Packer fans to support their long-time quarterback. Such a move also created a tension for Viking fans who had experienced numerous defeats at the hands of Favre during his time with the Packers.

Brett Favre banner outside the Metrodome

Similar experiences are likely to occur when a sport franchise decides to relocate, leaving fans behind to question their loyalty to their respective teams. For example, the Hartford Whalers moved from Hartford, Connecticut, during the 1997–98 season to become the Carolina Hurricanes. Fans of the franchise described their loss using terms like *death* and *divorce*. Many of the former Whaler fans noted that they no longer support a particular NHL hockey team, with many indicating that the move forced them to lose interest and faith in all professional sports

(Hyatt, 2007). A number of prominent sport teams with strong affiliations with their cities have made the decision to relocate in the NFL (Cleveland Browns, Houston Oilers), the MLB (Brooklyn Dodgers, Milwaukee Braves), and the NBA (New Orleans Jazz, Vancouver Grizzlies). Overall, identification has the potential to invoke a variety of emotional responses, which can be further enhanced as advancing technologies provide fans with new opportunities for interacting with athletes and their teams.

IMPACT OF NEW TECHNOLOGIES ON SPORT FANDOM

By allowing authors a vehicle for providing commentary on sports of all kinds, Internet blogs have become an increasingly common way for sports fans to further identify with their sports. As the relevance of blogs continues to grow, numerous news outlets have devoted segments in their daily newscasts to reporters that track and comment on popular websites. This practice has aided in establishing the blog as a potentially credible source of information, although much of the discussion that flows from these sources represents simple assertions, opinions, and conjecture with limited journalistic quality. In the past, news coverage was reported almost exclusively by seasoned journalists who served as the voice of record. Put simply, "In this digital age, however, we can all be real-time observers, and opinion often trumps fact. Which is to say, for those uninterested in actual reporting, the print media have almost become an afterthought" (Ballard, 2006, p. 58). Some have used the term *reclinerporting* to describe the quality of the growing number of blogs that allow commentary with little to no direct contact with the individuals involved and that is written for an audience with a desire for bias toward their favorite teams or athletes. Sports at all levels have expanded into this growing media outlet. For instance, many professional sports teams have gone as far as allowing fans the opportunity to set up fan profiles on their websites, write blogs, and interact with other fans (Elliot, 2007). Blogs have become an increasingly relevant feature of the sports landscape, so much so that a number of outlets, including the *Sporting News*, have devoted sections of their publications to tracking the most memorable quotes from numerous sport blogs. There is little doubt among seasoned reporters and legitimate news outlets that fan websites are increasingly making and breaking news in a way that is transforming the relationship between fans, athletes, coaches, and organizations (Layden, 2003).

Interview: Jennings Bryant, Emeritus Sports Media Scholar, The University of Alabama

Q: How has the typical sports fan evolved (or devolved) over the past several decades?

A: Fans continue to find fresh ways to express their fanaticism, thereby continuing to push the limits of sportsfanship. Some of these approaches to strengthening identity with favorite teams and players are decidedly low tech, such as developing and institutionalizing fan-section cultures in local stadia and arenas (e.g., Cameron Crazies), escalating fandemonium demonstrations at *Game Day*–type media events, and flooding local talk-radio programs with orchestrated blitzes to support one's cause de jour. Other approaches reside on the back of the digital explosion of the recent era and include huge advances in fan sites, blogs, electronic scoreboards, and the like.

Q: What is the relationship between fandom and notions of ritual and tradition?

A: Rituals permit instant identification across generational, ethnic, socioeconomic, and many other divides, and they provide portals via which one can effortlessly enter into the legions of devoted fans. Anyone can participate in the "Tiger Walk," and by doing so you connect with many generations of the faithful who have gone before you, as well as with your legacy that will follow.

Q: Entertainment has become a trillion-dollar-a-year industry and sport constitutes a major portion of those dollars. How does entertainment theory ground work in the area of sports fandom?

A: Many of the essential principles, concepts, and theories in the entertainment-theory bailiwick are essential to understanding sports fandom. These include disposition theory, selective exposure, excitation-transfer theory, and social-identification theory, among many others. Moreover, several brand-name theories of sportsfanship are special cases of generic entertainment theories (e.g., BIRGing is an extension of disposition theory).

Q: Sport used to be a place where people of all different economic statuses would gather and share a common experience. New sporting financial models have made this less possible. How is the fan's experience changing because of these economic realities?

A: Several major shifts are happening because sportsfanship is getting pricier and pricier. First, a larger portion of the income of lower-income fans is going into the individual and family sports-entertainment budget. We have been studying the

sacrifices some fans make to keep attending increasingly expensive college and professional sporting events; we have found a remarkably large number of poorer fans
giving each other season tickets for Christmas, knowingly cutting back on their gro-
cery budget to allow the family to attend the big game, deferring purchase of that
new minivan or SUV for yet another year, etc., in order to maintain their prior level of
involvement with the team. Secondly, mediated sporting events in off-stadia venues
(e.g., sports bars) with game viewing shared by rooms full of fans have become
popular lower-cost alternatives to live participation. The expansion of regional sports
networks delivered via satellite sports packages helps maintain fan loyalty, albeit
outside of on-site fan participation. This has created home-based "community"
viewing of sporting events in ways similar to India's video parlors of yesteryear.

**Q: How much does the experience of the sports fan transcend national
boundaries? Is there any aspect of fandom that you would deem
uniquely American?**

A: Every culture I have experienced in any depth puts its own special stamp on
sportsfanship, but the differences between cultures pale when compared with the
transnational similarities.

**Q: What changes do you see occurring in the way fans follow sport in the
decades to come?**

A: Each new medium introduced will be rapidly adopted by sportsfans and media entre-
preneurs, because sports communication is almost as important a "killer application"
for the success for new media as is pornography. Also, I suspect that university alumni
groups will use new forms of digital media (e.g., regular daily updates in the form of
texting, video releases for cell phones, etc.) to build more expansive and tight-knit fan
bases. These extant innovations—and many others will emerge—will enable fans to
develop ever-stronger and up-to-date connections with teams, coaches, and players,
increasing the potential for social identification with and between sportsfans.

The socially constructed webspace Wikipedia is an additional source for
fans who are interested in creating a cultural product that represents their
favorite players, sport, or franchise. The collective work of the fans generates a potentially problematic profile through consensus that allows for a
dialogue and historical creation that has never before been possible. Ferriter
(2009) noted that ". . . the relationship between user, structure, and content on Wikipedia set the stage for unique interactive space for those 'in-the-
know' about sports" (p. 129). This imagined community has become an
interesting space where fans and those who are not in the know about a

particular sport can come to celebrate the varied accomplishments of their favorite athletes and teams. Just as *The Baseball Encyclopedia* provides baseball fans with a historical account of Major League Baseball, the Wikipedia site provides a more interpretive formulation of sport history and a uniquely different type of historical account for both the average reader and those who seek to contribute to the narrative.

Lastly, a growing number of social media outlets continue to provide fans with additional opportunities for interacting with teams and athletes. A number of athletes have high-profile Twitter accounts that expose fans to the ongoing activities in their daily lives. MySpace and Facebook pages also afford athletes the opportunity to connect more individually with fans and offer their own interpretations of events that in the past would have been filtered by media outlets. News organizations have also now begun to monitor these sites to assist them in providing commentary on breaking news events. In Chapter 15, we spend time foreshadowing how these outlets will continue to change the communicative function of sport fan cultures.

CONCLUSION

Sport will continue to evoke a range of fan types with varying motives for following the sports, teams, and athletes they have become attached to. As sport continues to define and redefine itself, we are likely to experience ongoing changes to the way that fans can experience sport while also bringing about modifications to those sports that have traditionally held deep-seated fan cultures. In this chapter, we have demonstrated that rituals serve an important function in the sport fan experience, and as fans' identification with sports increases, they find themselves experiencing a host of positive (and potentially negative) outcomes. Just as technology continues to shape how we can experience the spectacle of sport, innovative approaches for sharing the sport experience are likely to draw even more fans in directions that we may never have felt possible. For example, participation in fantasy football leagues (see extended discussion in Chapter 14) has become an important ritual for many sport fans who are just as concerned with individual athlete performance as they are with the outcome of their favorite team. This has shaped television broadcasting of individual athlete highlights and spectator viewing habits as well as generated considerable revenue for sport franchises. What happens when "going to the ball game" becomes meaningless because fans no longer cheer for one respective team and are more concerned about the performance of individual players spread out across 10 or 12 teams throughout the league? The underlying features of devotion still exist in this situation, but the evolving nature of sport and competition puts sport spectatorship at a crossroad for how sport fandom is experienced.

REFERENCES

American Institute of Food Distribution. (2004). *The Food Institute report.* Retrieved September 24, 2004, at http://www.foodinstitute.com/firsample216.pdf.

Ballard, C. (2006). Writing up a storm: The Internet is changing sports coverage. *Sports Illustrated, 104*(3), 58–65.

Branscombe, N. R., & Wann, D. L. (1991). The positive social and self-concept consequences of sports team identification. *Journal of Sport & Social Issues, 15,* 115–127.

Carbaugh, D. (1996). The playful self: Being a fan at college basketball games. In D. Carbaugh, *Situating selves: The communication of social identities in American scenes* (pp. 39–61). Albany: State University of New York Press.

Elliot, S. (2007). The know list 6: Work that net. *Sporting News, 231*(9), 5.

Ferriter, M. M. (2009). "Arguably the greatest": Sport fans and communities at work on Wikipedia. *Sociology of Sport Journal, 26,* 127–154.

Hyatt, C. G., (2007). Who do I root for now? The impact of franchise relocation on the loyal fans left behind: A case study of Hartford Whalers fans. *Journal of Sport Behavior, 30,* 36–56.

Krizek, B. (1992). Remembrances and expectations: The investment of identity in the changing of Comiskey. *Elysian Fields Quarterly, 20,* 30–50.

Layden, T. (2003). Caught in the net: Everyone's a reporter in the world of fan-driven, rumor-mongering college websites, forcing coaches and players to watch their every step. *Sports Illustrated, 98*(2), 46–47.

Martin, C. R., & Reeves, J. L. (2001). The whole world isn't watching (but we thought they were): The Super Bowl and U.S. solipsism. *Culture, Sport Society, 4,* 213–236.

Miller, J. B. (1999). Indians, Braves, and Redskins: A performative struggle for control of an image. *Quarterly Journal of Speech, 85,* 188–202.

Oates, T. P. (2009). New media and repackaging of NFL fandom. *Sociology of Sport Journal, 26,* 31–49.

Rushin, S. (2004). Take me out to the . . . whatever. *Sports Illustrated, 100*(24), p. 15.

Schechner, R. (2002). Performance studies: An introduction. New York: Routledge.

Smith, R. A., & Schwarz, N. (2003). Language, social comparison, and college football: Is your school less similar to the rival school than the rival school is to your school? *Communication Monographs, 70,* 351–360.

Sutton, W. A., McDonald, M. A., Miline, G., & Cimperman, J. (1997). Getting and fostering fan identification in professional sports. *Sports Marketing Quarterly, 6,* 15–22.

Trail, G. T., Robinson, J., Dick, R. L., & Gillentine, A. L. (2003). Motives and points of attachment: Fans versus spectators in intercollegiate athletics. *Sport Marketing Quarterly, 12,* 217–227.

Wann, D. L., Allen, B., & Rochelle, A. R. (2004). Using sport fandom as an escape: Searching for relief from under-stimulation and over-stimulation. *International Sports Journal, 8,* 104–113.

Wann, D. L., Peterson, R. R., Cothran, C., & Dykes, M. (1999). Sport fan aggression and anonymity: The importance of team identification. *Social Behavior and Personality, 27,* 597–602.

Wann, D. L., & Robinson, T. N. (2002). The relationship between sport team identification and integration into and perceptions of a university. *International Sports Journal, 24,* 36–44.

Wann, D. L., Royalty, J. L., & Rochelle, A. L. (2002). Using motivation and team identification to predict sport fans' emotional responses to team performance. *Journal of Sport Behavior, 25,* 207–216.

Weed, M. (2007). The pub as a virtual football fandom venue: An alternative to "being there"? *Soccer & Society, 8,* 399–414.

SUGGESTED ADDITIONAL READING

Aden, R. C. (1994). Back to the garden: Therapeutic place metaphor in *Field of Dreams. Southern Communication Journal, 59,* 307–317.

Butterworth, M. L. (2005). Ritual in the "church of baseball": Suppressing the discourse of democracy after 9/11. *Communication and Critical/Cultural Studies, 2,* 107–129.

Novack, M. (1976). *The joy of sports: End zones, bases, baskets, balls and the consecration of the American spirit.* New York: Basic Books.

Roberts, M. (1974). *Fans! How we go crazy over sports.* Washington, DC: New Republic Book Co.

Wann, D. L., Brewer, K. B., & Royalty, J. L. (1999). Sport fan motivation: Relationships with team identification and emotional reactions to sporting events. *International Sports Journal, 3,* 8–18.

CHAPTER 4

Sports and Mythology

When an unheralded or overmatched athlete or team faces a familiar champion, sports media and fans often refer to the event as a "David vs. Goliath" match-up. Should the underdog emerge with a win, the victory is called a "Cinderella story." When individuals of modest backgrounds achieve greatness, we invoke the rags-to-riches idealism of the "American Dream." Triumphs over adversity offer "redemption," historic accomplishments are considered "heroic," and tests of strength and endurance are performed by "warriors" and "gladiators." Such terminology is so familiar in the world of sports that we have likely forgotten the origins of such references. They are elements of stories, of course, but not merely stories. Rather, they operate as **myths,** providing a compelling lens through which we can view as well as communicate about the importance of athletic achievements and events.

For many of you, the word *mythology* may prompt thoughts about ancient Greek and Roman myths. For example, you may know that the phrase *Achilles' heel* derives from the story of Achilles, whose mother inoculated him from an enemy's attack by dipping him in the river Styx. Because she held him by the heel, however, he was left vulnerable in that lone spot, which subsequently led to his death when he was struck by an arrow. Or you may be familiar with the phrase *Midas touch,* a reference to King Midas, whose touch turned everything to gold. Although contemporary myths sometimes reference these ancient stories or incorporate elements of them, they also draw from historical and cultural conditions of a given time. Thus, mythology is as much about the present as it is about the past.

Rhetorical scholar Walter Fisher (1984) contends that human beings essentially communicate through stories and that the most persuasive stories we tell "are mythic in form" (p. 16). Sports provide especially persuasive people and places for communicating mythology. In this chapter, we explore several of the ways that sports are influenced by myth and how sports affirm myths found in the broader culture. We begin with some important definitions of terms, including **myth, ritual,** and **hero.** Then, we provide examples and discussion of these terms in order to reveal the persuasive power of sports mythology.

DEFINING TERMS

We begin this section with an example most of you probably know something about: the national pastime. This label commonly used to refer to baseball is really shorthand for various expressions of mythology. For example, baseball is said to have been invented in Cooperstown, New York, an idyllic rural village that embodies the virtues of small-town America. Yet this story is an invention, crafted by Albert Spalding, one of baseball's most influential figures in its earliest decades. As the United States became a more mature nation in the late 19th and early 20th centuries, there were those who wanted to prove America's superiority over the "Old World" of Europe. Thus, Spalding commissioned a report designed

National Baseball Hall of Fame and Museum entrance

to find evidence that showed baseball was uniquely American. The result-ing Mills Commission report, issued in 1907, provided "evidence" that Abner Doubleday invented the game in Cooperstown in 1839. This story has been completely discredited, yet it remains central to baseball's mythology. Indeed, Cooperstown serves as the home to the National Baseball Hall of Fame and Museum, which legitimizes the location as the "birthplace" of baseball.

The Hall of Fame's location is about more than baseball's mythic origins. It also serves as repository of baseball's memories and it celebrates the heroes that have contributed the most to the game. In addition, the myth is enacted by the millions of visitors who make the journey to Cooperstown to renew their connection to the national pastime. As Newman (2001) demon-strates, the trip to this small New York village can be understood as a pil-grimage. The idea of the pilgrimage, of course, evokes a parallel to religion and, indeed, many have noted that Cooperstown functions for baseball fans as the Vatican would for Christians or Mecca would for Muslims (Rader, 2002). The ritual of traveling to the Hall of Fame, therefore, dramatizes the overlap between religion and mythology. In sum, Cooperstown symbolizes the **myth** of American exceptionalism, sanctifies the **heroes** of the national pastime, encourages fans to visit the Hall of Fame in **ritual** fashion, all through enactments that are similar to organized **religion.**

Communication scholars examine these features of baseball's history and ask, "Why and how did this mythology develop?" "What does this mythology communicate about us as a people?" and "What needs are served by constructing this myth?" Certainly Americans invest a great deal in the game they call the national pastime. In other words, baseball is more than a sport; it is a cultural institution that claims to be an exemplar of American character. From this standpoint, mythology becomes an essential means for communicating and reinforcing the very identity that binds Americans together. What is interesting about myth, then, is not whether it is true, but to what extent it *feels* true (perhaps, to borrow Stephen Colbert's famous term, myths have "truthiness").

The most basic definition of a myth is that it is a story, which is precisely what its root term, *mythos,* translates to in English (Doty, 1986, p. 3). Yet, as our opening example suggests, myths are about particular kinds of stories. More specifically, they are stories designed to explain the world, or as Hart (1990) puts it, to describe "exceptional people doing exceptional things that serve as a moral guide to proper action" (p. 305). In addition, media and sports scholar Michael Real (1989) notes that "myths arise as community stories that celebrate collective heroes, origins, and identity through expressive rituals" (p. 66). Thus, an especially important element of mythology is that the stories are *shared* and they provide a foundation for a community's identity. This is why baseball's mythic origins continue to resonate long after the Doubleday story itself has been discredited.

Real's definition also includes other important terms for this chapter. **Ritual** can be understood as the means by which myths are enacted or performed. Accepting communion during a Christian religious service and casting a ballot on election day are ritualistic performances that reaffirm the importance of larger purposes—i.e., Christian faith or democratic governance. Meanwhile, **heroes** provide dramatic exemplars by which others may come to understand the "proper action" to which Hart refers. Along with the significance of religious symbolism, these terms provide the foundation for our subsequent discussion of sports and mythology.

SPORTS MYTH

Myths may be either particular or universal. The popular American story about George Washington cutting down his father's cherry tree is an example of a particular myth. It is used, typically with young children, to instill values about truth and honesty. This particular myth might stand on its own, or it might be used as an exemplar of a larger mythology—for instance, as a story that speaks to the United States' commitment to liberty and justice. Sports myth also functions this way. Thus, the celebrated victory of the men's Olympic hockey team over the Soviet Union in 1980 might be a particular expression of the triumph of the underdog, while the universal purpose of the myth communicates the moral superiority of American democracy over Soviet communism.

We begin this section with a discussion of myths that are particular to the world of sports. Sports leagues and organizations are acutely aware of their histories, and they often draw upon the past to create mythological narratives that help guide the present. Consider, for example, the stories that define the modern National Football League (NFL). During the first half of the 20th century, collegiate football was very popular but the professional game still mostly existed at the margins. When the Baltimore Colts defeated the New York Giants on live television to win the 1958 NFL Championship, however, the game began a rapid ascent to become the most popular sport in the United States. More than 50 years later, that contest, which ended in overtime, is commonly referred to as the "Greatest Game Ever Played." It is doubtful that the game is truly the *best* professional football game in history, but that is not important. Rather, its *greatness* lies in the *mythological* character of the game as the genesis of the modern NFL.

Interview: Chris Willis, Head of Research Library, NFL Films

Q: **There is a distinct style to your films. What do you hope that these unique choices will accomplish?**

A: For 45 years, NFL Films has used its distinct style to tell football stories. We want the viewer to be emotionally involved in what they are watching. By using slow-motion footage, powerful music, emotional narration, and the sport's heroes and personalities, we hope to give the viewer a feeling of what these men have accomplished and how they play the game. Each of the unique aspects contributes to telling a great story. For instance, slow-motion footage allows us to show the game in a more artistic and poetic way than what you see on television. Sixteen-millimeter film gives it a Hollywood feel. Music is also critical. Picking out the right music to accompany the footage might be as important a choice for one of our producers than anything. Our shows wouldn't have an emotional feel to them if it weren't for the selection of music combined with slow-motion shots. Finally, I'll mention narration—the producer must write a script that is both clear and entertaining. The narrator then can add the final touch of emotion.

Q: **Nostalgia is certainly at the forefront of what you do. Is it fair to say that NFL Films tends to dwell on the positive aspects of a game, team, or player more than the negative?**

A: Because of our direct affiliation with the NFL, we have always tried to insinuate the positive aspects of the game; we don't try to hide it. Our company exists to promote the game, preserve the history, and tell great football stories. Some people have accused us of being just a propaganda tool of the NFL. This is true, but our business is promoting the game—a game that millions of people live and die with every year. Why not show how great this game is and can be? Sure, we might not focus on issues like arrests or performance-enhancing drugs, but we do show some of the major disappointments the game can reveal. The agony of losing or suffering a career-ending injury can be just as powerful as a game-winning touchdown.

Q: **Baseball is still regarded as the national pastime, but there seems to be something uniquely American about football. Do your products tap into that?**

A: NFL Films (as well as the NFL) definitely has tried to take advantage of its popular and uniquely American game. Baseball still goes by the moniker of the

(Continued)

(Continued)

"National Pastime," but the NFL is known as "America's Game." In 2007, NFL Films produced a series titled "America's Game" to capture the overall spirit and popularity of professional football.

Q: **What do you feel your films, programs, and documentaries collectively contribute to the mythology of football?**

A: NFL Films has contributed mightily to the mythology of football. Our stories have portrayed players, coaches, teams, games, and the Super Bowl in epic form for fans everywhere. Sometimes, we've made these events and people bigger than they actually were or perhaps made certain accomplishments stand out more. Often, the myth is greater than the reality of the actual event (or player). We tell great stories to the best of our abilities.

There are many accomplishments and moments within sports that have achieved mythical status: Babe Ruth's alleged "called shot" during the 1932 World Series, when he supposedly pointed to a spot in the Wrigley Field outfield then delivered a home run to that exact location; Muhammad Ali's "phantom punch" that dropped Sonny Liston in a heavyweight rematch in 1965; Willis Reed's miraculous recovery from a leg injury and re-entry into a playoff game for the New York Knicks in 1970; Keri Strug's final vault to solidify the women's gymnastics gold medal for the United States at the 1996 Summer Olympics; Brandi Chastain's shirt-removal celebration after kicking a penalty shot that secured the women's 1999 World Cup soccer title for the American team. Surely you can identify several other moments. What all of these have in common is that they feature either transcendent athletes or championship moments that persist in our collective sports memories. In this way, sports mythology is a way of preserving the best of our past as we try our best to move forward in the future.

These types of myths often serve a positive function for sports organizations, media, and fans. Yet there is also the possibility that mythology obscures some of the problems found in sports. For example, the National Hockey League (NHL) has long balanced the need for control and order with the excitement generated by the violence of fighting between players. As the familiar cliché says, "I went to a fight and a hockey game broke out." In part, this violence is encouraged and perpetuated by a mythology that equates strength and toughness with hand-to-hand combat. Unfortunately, even as the game's violence may attract some fans, it has the potential to dissuade many others from following what can be an exciting sport. In his study of hockey in Canada, Grant (1998) concludes that "the mythic power of sport is being used to the detriment of sport itself" (p. 58).

Although many myths are contained in the world of sports, many other sporting myths are communicated in the service of broader mythologies. For example, O'Rourke (2003) analyzed the public's response to the announcement that the Cleveland Browns would be leaving the city for Baltimore. In his study, O'Rourke demonstrates the extent to which fan identification with the team was grounded in their mythic identity with their city. As he notes, "Cleveland is a diverse, multicultural urban community that accepted waves of immigrants as labor for heavy industry" (p. 72). As the Browns found success in the 1940s and 1950s, they became associated with

Hockey fight during an NHL game

this diverse, blue-collar ethic. When economic changes in the 1960s and 1970s adversely affected cities like Cleveland—much like similar Rust Belt communities such as Pittsburgh and Detroit—local sports teams, especially the Browns, were viewed as both symbols of past glory and of hope for the future. Thus, when Browns owner Art Modell announced in 1995 that he would relocate the team, local fans reacted as if they were losing a family member. O'Rourke explains that the fans' collective response contributed to the NFL's eventual decision to award an expansion franchise to Cleveland for 1999, a move that also preserved their beloved nickname, Browns.

Even as the above example demonstrates how mythology can positively bind a community around a collective identity, we should also be cautious about myths that threaten communities. Among the most common narratives in sports is the myth of the American Dream in which an athlete of humble origins works hard and achieves greatness on the field or in the arena. Throughout sports in the United States there are athletes who fit this description. Yet the downside to this myth is that it equates success with individual effort and potentially ignores economic, political, and social factors that could prevent someone from achieving success. An excellent example of this concern is found in the critically acclaimed documentary film *Hoop Dreams* (1994). The movie chronicles the lives of two African American boys in Chicago who aspire to be professional basketball players. Over the course of 3 hours, viewers witness the growth of Arthur Agee and William Gates as they move from 8th grade to high school graduation. Although there are many important themes in the film, many observers commented on the hope that basketball provided these two young men and the idea that sports can provide a pathway out of poverty. However, as Cole and King (2003) argue, the film also, perhaps inadvertently, perpetuates stereotypes about urban life in the United States. In particular, *Hoop Dreams* relies on the "already known," meaning that audiences are able to identify with Agee and Gates because they believe they already understand what it means to be African American in the city. Unfortunately, then, the film allows viewers to think positively about the main characters without having to confront the social and economic inequities that serve as the backdrop to the narrative.

Each of these examples demonstrates that myth can perform both a positive and negative function. Because sport is often viewed as an escape or diversion from real social or political problems, we may be less prepared to think about the mythologies that are bolstered by sports narratives. To be sure, some sport myth making is either good fun or provides important links to histories and traditions. Nevertheless, it is important to keep in mind the various levels at which myth functions.

Home game at Nebraska Cornhusker Memorial Stadium

SPORTS AND RITUAL

As we discussed in Chapter 3, **ritual** is an essential element in the enactment of sports mythology. Writing about the culture associated with the University of Nebraska's football team, Deegan and Stein (1989) write, "Extraordinary events—formal rituals—provide the community with an alternate social world to that found in everyday life. Part of the power of these events lies in their ability to evoke symbols and myths relating to the community" (p. 79). That power is evident in Aden's (2008) book, *Huskerville,* which reveals multiple ritual practices that allow Nebraska fans, even those who have moved far from home, to preserve their sense of community. For these fans, "Huskerville" becomes a place that is created not necessarily through physical contact but through symbolic expressions such as wearing team colors or attending team parties, as well as maintaining a commitment to core "rural" values such as working hard and being good neighbors.

Sports rituals are also commonly performed through media. Olsen's (2003) analysis of the National Basketball Association (NBA) draft, for example, illustrates the ritualistic emphasis that sports media place on creating "characters" out of players and exploiting dramatic moments. He explains that various elements of the NBA draft occur regularly throughout the years: Players wait nervously in the green room, they come dressed "in costume" and immediately wear their new team's hat once their name is called, they transition then to the live interview, and so on. As Olsen notes, "Each element of the coverage reinforces the dominant notion of a ritual transformation" (p. 192), meaning that the draft broadcast becomes a sports rite of passage that is shared among media, teams, players, families, and fans.

As is the case with myth more broadly, then, sports rituals can serve communities by providing communicative means of joining people together. Consider, for example, how commonplace songs and chants are among sports crowds. Baseball's 7th-inning

"God Bless America" at a Baltimore Orioles game

stretch would feel incomplete without "Take Me Out to the Ball Game," no self-respecting Ohio State University fan would hear someone shout out "O-H!" without yelling back, "I-O!", And soccer matches buzz with a near-constant soundtrack of "Olé, Olé, Olé," and other songs. In other words, ritual allows us to feel a sense of *belonging*.

Participation in ritual is not always comforting, however. As Rothenbuhler (1998) suggests, "Almost always, rituals are accompanied by a certain social compulsion. The costs that result from choosing not to participate may be such that we do not experience certain rituals as voluntary" (p. 10). This is the point Butterworth (2005) makes in his study of baseball ceremonies that took place after the terrorist attacks of September 11, 2001. As he explains, through repeated performances of "God Bless America" and inclusions of nationalistic imagery, baseball tributes "moved from healing ritual to a potential exercise in ideology that could preserve a privileged interpretation of national identity" (p. 114). Moreover, because of the heightened anxiety felt in the United States after 9/11, any resistance to this ritual was likely to be considered subversive or unpatriotic (see Chapter 7 for more on these ideas).

Case Study: Mythos Surrounding the Miracle on Ice

ABC commentator Al Michaels described the closing seconds of a hockey game that still resonates in the collective memory of many Americans more than 30 years ago in Lake Placid. "Eleven seconds, you've got 10 seconds, the countdown going on right now! Morrow, up to Silk. Five seconds left in the game. Do you believe in miracles? . . . YES!" These closing statements are connected to what has become known as the Miracle on Ice, where a highly underrated USA team defeated the Russian team on its way to Olympic gold during the 1980 Winter Olympics. The David vs. Goliath match-up pitted a group of young amateur players led by now-legendary coach Herb Brooks against a team of Russian veterans (many of whom had been competing together for more than a decade). This game has been solidified as a sporting event that served as a turning point for many Americans who were struggling through a turbulent decade in the 1970s. However, the general mythos that has been generated around the game itself has caused many to forget a number of relevant facts surrounding the team and the gold medal that resulted from the victory.

Although it is accurate that Herb Brooks was able to pull together a group of amateur hockey players to defeat a more "professional" team, the collective talent on the 1980 team was generally stronger than any previous team representing the United States. For instance, of the 20 players on the team, 13 went on to play in the National Hockey League with eight playing 500 or more games in their careers. In fact, Ken Morrow eventually went on to start his career with the New York Islanders and became the first hockey player to win the Olympic gold and the Stanley Cup in the same year. Additionally, many people forget that the team did not win the gold medal after the victory over the Russians. Two days later, the team needed to come from behind against Finland to win. Years after the Miracle on Ice, the structure of the medal round was modified to the single-elimination model that is employed today. Yet in 1980, a round robin was used, whereby it was still mathematically possible for the USA team to be eliminated from medal contention had it lost to Finland two days later. In the locker room before the third and final period, it is reported that Brooks reminded his players that they would "take it to their graves" if they didn't find a way to come from behind to win. Had the team lost, the social significance of the victory over Russia would have ultimately been lost as well, and the team's presence in the mythos of American sport history would have been eliminated despite the fact that the outcome for the event they are most remembered for would have remained the same.

1. What other facts about this particular event tend to get lost in the retelling of the Miracle on Ice?

2. How does the selective recall of sporting events lead many of us to establish our own recollection of the events that transpired?

3. How have the media been influential in depicting the general mythos that has surrounded the 1980 Olympic Hockey team since its win in Lake Placid?

Conformity is a product of ritual's ability to make a myth appear to be normal or "natural" (Barthes, 1972, p. 143). Thus, the more often "God Bless America" is sung at baseball games, the more it becomes the normal state of affairs. This outcome is not restricted to patriotic ceremonies, of course. For instance, Grano (2007) examines the infamous fight that took place between the Detroit Pistons and Indiana Pacers in 2004. The fight, which occurred near the end of a blow-out contest, not only involved players but also spilled into the arena's seats. The subsequent melee between players and fans was viewed by the sports media as "one of the great disasters in American sports history" (p. 446). As Grano explains, there is a ritualistic quality to the unspoken contract between teams and fans wherein each side understands its role in the sporting context—i.e., teams and players *perform* and fans *watch*. That contract was violated the instant that players crossed the boundary between competitive space and spectator space. He concludes that sports rituals are "melodramatic political spectacles" through which fans and media make judgments about athletes' ability to conform to the "expectations of mythic heroism" (p. 449). The public felt the players violated those expectations, he argues, because they abandoned their mythic roles as heroes and turned against the very people who mythologize athletes in the first place. Grano's analysis invites us not only to consider the consequences of ritual but also to examine the connections between ritual and heroism. It is to that topic that we now turn.

SPORTS HEROES

Star athletes are among the most recognized and beloved people in American culture. Their athletic feats produce joy and admiration, they evoke pride among members of the communities in which they play, and they are among the most persuasive spokespeople for commercial products and services. In addition to performing their *jobs* as athletes, they clearly are *entertainers* as well, and consequently, they frequently appear as talk-show guests, at red-carpet openings, and as grist for the tabloid rumor mill. All of which raises an important question for communication and sport scholars: Can athletes be considered *heroes,* or are they simply *celebrities?* Drucker (1994) is one who argues that sports figures are not heroic. Rather, they are media creations, "products of the celebrification of the pro athlete rather than the creation of a hero" (p. 83). Drucker seems to suggest here that celebrities are *manufactured* for the purposes of spectacle, whereas heroes earn public admiration by being *authentic.*

In light of such a critique, it is worth rethinking what it means to call someone a **hero.** Traditionally, the hero is a transcendent individual who faces tests and trials of strength and character. Through such challenges, the hero is transformed, "leaving one condition and finding the source of life to bring forth . . . a richer or mature condition" (Campbell & Moyers, 1988, p. 124). This archetypal image of the hero is designed to provide lessons for others in

Michael Phelps

a culture, using the hero as a model for action and behavior. As Drucker and Cathcart (1994) note, "Heroes transcend ordinary human qualities embodying the divine, the ideal, the quest, the courageous, the virtuous, the superior. All cultures have heroes, but the hero and heroic varies from culture to culture and from time to time" (pp. 1–2). From this view, although Drucker may be correct that sports figures are not heroes in the traditional sense, she and Cathcart acknowledge that in our current time, contemporary figures such as sports stars may meet a redefined standard of heroism. Thus, Vande Berg (1998) maintains, "Sports heroes embody, articulate, and interrogate abstract ideals and cultural values; they highlight social problems, and they proffer hopeful solutions" (p. 152).

The ideal sports hero is one who not only achieves greatness on the field but also is an admirable person off of it. Failure to serve as a role model often earns an athlete public scorn or indifference. Consider the case of Michael Phelps, the American swimmer whose performances during the 2008 Summer Games in Beijing are arguably unparalleled in Olympic history. Phelps won *eight* gold medals and subsequently became the most celebrated American athlete of the moment. Without question, he had achieved heroic status by the time that, in early 2009, he admitted to smoking marijuana at a party in South Carolina. Phelps received a short suspension from international competition and he lost some of his commercial endorsements. Suddenly, because of a relatively minor indiscretion, an Olympic hero was no longer someone worthy of Americans' admiration.

Americans are notorious for their fickle relationships to heroic figures. Nothing is more predictable, it seems, than the cycle of identifying, celebrating, destroying, and then rehabilitating a hero. Accordingly, the case of baseball slugger Mark McGwire provides an ideal example of American sports heroism. McGwire, who began his career with Oakland in 1987, was always a prodigious home run hitter. By the 1998 season, he was regularly the subject of speculation about breaking the single-season home run record held by Roger Maris, who hit 61 home runs in 1961. Playing then for the St. Louis Cardinals, McGwire embarked on the heroic journey toward the record, joined unexpectedly by a then-relatively unknown outfielder for the Chicago Cubs, Sammy Sosa. By the end of the season, McGwire reached 70 home runs (and Sosa had 66) to shatter the record. The "home run race" of 1998 was one of the most compelling sports stories of recent decades, with some sportswriters claiming that the goodwill generated by the pursuit had "saved" baseball after the work stoppage that led to the cancellation of the 1994 World Series. *Time* magazine even went so far as to call McGwire its "Hero of the Year" (Okrent, 1998).

A Matter of Ethics: Wrestling's Dark Side

Sports stars provide us with modern heroes. They are adventurers who seek glory and conquest, warriors who confront their own physical (and mental) limits in the quest for greatness. Ancient Greece had Achilles; modern Americans have Babe Ruth, Michael Jordan, and Brett Favre. To the extent that sports heroes provide us with joy and inspiration and serve as models for achievement, this mythology can be a positive force in our culture. Yet what happens when we push the myth too far?

Professional wrestling may or may not be an "authentic" sport. Yet its popularity depends largely on the same warrior myth that sustains more legitimate sports such as boxing or football. In the latter decades of the 20th century, professional wrestling grew into an enormous entertainment industry unto itself, catapulting performers such as Hulk Hogan, Dwayne "The Rock" Johnson, and John Cena into superstardom. The physical demands of the sport have driven many wrestlers to either narcotics or performance-enhancing drugs (PEDs). In the case of PEDs, the gains in size and strength come with considerable risks to mental and physical health.

At the same time professional wrestling experienced tremendous growth and popularity, an alarming number of former wrestlers were dying at relatively young ages. For those who believed PED use was an underlying cause of these fatalities, Chris Benoit became representative of the problem. In 2007, the 40-year-old Benoit strangled his wife, suffocated his 7-year-old son, and hung himself. Anabolic steroids were found in his home, and speculation linked the abuse of PEDs to his behavior.

In life, Chris Benoit was the embodiment of the warrior myth. In death, he became the symbol of that myth's darker consequences.

1. Should Benoit's death (and the murder of his family) be seen as a manifestation of American culture's obsession with heroes?

2. Do professional wrestling fans share any responsibility for the premature deaths of so many former wrestlers?

3. What, if anything, should be done about the physical demands of professional wrestling?

Although it was largely a "feel-good" story, anointing McGwire as a hero was not without problems. For one, the sports media elevated him to such heights that his fall was almost inevitable. Indeed, when McGwire was called before Congress in 2005 to testify about the presence of performance-enhancing drugs in baseball, his refusal to "discuss the past" meant the "end of Mark McGwire as an American icon" (quoted in Butterworth, 2007). In other words, although his achievements on the field were remarkable, McGwire nevertheless remained human, a simple fact lost in the exaggerated reports of his heroic greatness. Much like Phelps, then, it wasn't a question of *if* McGwire would make a mistake, but *when*. In addition, the coverage also frequently featured McGwire as a "Ruthian" figure, hailing the legacy of Babe Ruth. Meanwhile, reporters relegated Sosa to the role of a "sidekick," often using his Latin American heritage as a point of comic relief. As a result, the portrayal of the two players, unintentionally though it may have been, privileged a white, American hero and diminished the status of a nonwhite, Latin American figure (Butterworth, 2007).

Not all mediated sports heroes are white, of course. However, superstar athletes of color such as Derek Jeter and Jerry Rice are often careful not to disrupt the dominant expectations of the hero's behavior. Indeed, even as their silence on controversial political issues has been criticized by some in the media and by academics, apolitical athletes have profited by crafting public personae that are consistent with heroic ideals. When nonwhite athletes do express viewpoints that are not considered mainstream—Charles Barkley or the Williams sisters, for example—they are criticized either for "playing the race card" or for failing to appreciate their substantial privilege. Thus, as Vande Berg (1998) notes, there is space alongside the sports hero for the antihero, a figure who often disrupts or challenges commonly accepted beliefs and practices that may be oppressive. Minority athletes, women, and gay and lesbian athletes all have the potential to embody the antihero persona. Vande Berg specifically uses examples such as Billie Jean King and Dennis Rodman, athletes who, in different ways, destabilized common interpretations of gender (for more on gender, see Chapter 5). As Grano (2009) illustrates in his analysis of Muhammad Ali, the irony is that antihero athletes are typically reviled in their own time and are "granted heroic status only retrospectively" (p. 192). Indeed, contemporary sports fans may not realize just how despised a figure Ali was—first for converting to Islam and changing his name from Cassius Clay and second for opposing the Vietnam War and refusing to be drafted into the United States Army. Instead of remembering Ali's role in resistance to war and racial oppression, people today tend to associate him with his battle against Parkinson's disease and the inspiration he provided by lighting the torch at the 1996 Summer Olympics in Atlanta.

Thinking of contemporary sports figures as heroes is complicated. They are human beings like anyone else and are thus bound to make mistakes. Although they often provide suitable role models, there are also numerous examples of athletes whose behaviors are indefensible. In 2010, for example, Pittsburgh Steelers quarterback Ben Roethlisberger and golfer Tiger Woods were each implicated in embarrassing scandals involving allegations of sexual assault (Roethlisberger) and chronic marital infidelity (Woods). Nevertheless, in a media-saturated world where sports continue to grow in popularity, there is little doubt that Americans will continue to grant their sports superstars heroic status. And, as cases such as that of Kobe Bryant—who admitted having an extramarital affair in 2003 after he was alleged to have raped a resort employee—illustrate, the community of sport is often eager to welcome back athletes who rehabilitate their images. Thus, it takes little imagination to envision Roethlisberger and Woods successfully leaving their scandals in the past. All of which reminds us, "One of the few places where heroes can still be found is sports" (Vande Berg, 1998, p. 152).

SPORTS AS RELIGION

Because sports fans devote so much passion, loyalty, and faith to their favorite players and teams, it is common to hear sports equated with religion. In particular, as Hoffman (1992) identifies, "The aspect of sport that so invites a comparison with religion is the intense excitement and the spirit of community it generates" (p. 7). It is the emphasis on community found in both sport and religion that suggests we should consider this relationship as a version of mythology. Remember, we are evaluating myth based not on its truth value but on its ability to communicate explanations about the role of human beings in the world and to guide appropriate actions. In this respect, **religion** certainly functions mythologically, as it is principally concerned with molding the beliefs and behaviors of its adherents.

Notre Dame's "Touchdown Jesus"

This orientation to religion focuses less on denominations or organized churches and more on the logic that guides religious practice. Rothenbuhler (1989) takes this approach in his study of the values and symbols that are communicated by the Olympic Games. As he explains, the Olympics can be understood as a kind of religious experience because they bring individuals into community with one another in ritualistic fashion. Moreover, this mass ritual is designed to promote core values, such as pride in one's country (patriotism) and respect for other cultures (internationalism). For American audiences, the Games reaffirm particular ideals about the role of sports in society, including "sportsmanship, friendship between even those who compete, pride in victory, artistry in performance, and the willingness to make personal sacrifices, to submit to training, and to build skills" (p. 152). These values, so often at risk in contemporary commercial sport, are preserved by the religious logic at work during television broadcasts of the Olympics. All of which is to say that an Olympic broadcast can serve as a means to reaffirm one's *faith* in sport itself.

If religious meaning can be found in sports spectatorship, it can also be found in the personal journeys that are inspired by sport. For instance, earlier in this chapter we referenced the idea of the pilgrimage, a journey that is designed to have spiritual significance. This theme is evident in Aden's (1999) discussion of the film *Field of Dreams* and the tourist location of the same name in Dyersville, Iowa. Rooted in the mythology of rural innocence and purity, the story of *Field of Dreams* is one of personal redemption and familial reconciliation. For the millions who visit the ballpark in Iowa, this mythology is bound to the ideals of the nation that have historically been assigned to baseball. Thus, as Aden summarizes, "The fields—both real and reel—are strongly infused with the romantic spiritual elements of community" (p. 222).

Although these religious parallels might help us understand sports' broad appeal, some worry that overstating the case diminishes religion and inflates the importance of sports. Religion may be a powerful metaphor for sports, but the outcome of a game fails to match the gravity of religion's larger purpose. Whether one subscribes to a given religious doctrine or not, it is fair to conclude that religion is about the *transcendental*—that is, about things beyond the grasp of human experience. Sports, meanwhile, are bound to our earthly experience, which is probably as good a reason as any to maintain a distinction between religion and sports.

There might also be reason to be cautious about the influence of religion on sports. Especially during the late 20th and early 21st centuries, religious organizations have gained more and more influence among athletes and teams. Athletes in Action, Baseball Chapel, and the Fellowship of Christian Athletes are just a handful of the groups that view sports as a means for extending the reach of Christianity in American culture. In the 1990s, a group started by a former college football coach gained significant notoriety for trying to merge the purposes of sport and religion. The Promise Keepers sought not only to link religion and sports—their meetings took place in sports arenas, after all—but also to compensate for sociopolitical developments in American culture. As Beal (1997) explains, the movement was largely a response to a perceived feminization or "sissification" of American men. Thus, sport was "used to demonstrate the qualities of masculinity linked with superior leadership" (p. 279).

By weaving political commitments into the relationship between religion and sports, the Promise Keepers earned as much criticism as they did praise. Yet they represent only one iteration of what has become a familiar phenomenon. Baseball fans may now attend promotional events called "Faith Nights," some of which have been sponsored by controversial groups such as Focus on the Family or the Creation Museum. NASCAR driver Bobby Labonte had his car sponsored by *The Passion of the Christ* when that film was released in 2004. University of Florida quarterback and Heisman Trophy winner Tim Tebow was the subject of countless cover stories commending him as much for his missionary work as for his completion percentage. These are but a handful of the religious expressions that are now commonplace, all of which extend the range of ritual and mythology that routinely characterize contemporary sports.

CONCLUSION

In this chapter, we have explored the connections between mythology and sports. Between mythic stories, ritual performances, celebration of heroes, and use of religious metaphors, it should be clear that sports depend on mythology for much of their communicative power. In many cases, this heightens the drama of sports and offers a means for spectators to participate in a larger community. In other cases, sports mythology reproduces troubling practices or restricts the ability of some to participate in such a community. But in all cases, it makes connections between past and present, individuals and groups, and fans and players, all of which makes mythology an essential element in our understanding of communication and sport.

REFERENCES

Aden, R. C. (1999). *Popular stories and promised lands: Fan cultures and symbolic pilgrimages.* Tuscaloosa: University of Alabama Press.

Aden, R. C. (2008). *Huskerville: A story of Nebraska football, fans, and the power of place.* Jefferson, NC: McFarland.

Barthes, R. (1972). *Mythologies* (Trans. A. Lavers). New York: Hill and Wang.

Beal, B. (1997). The Promise Keepers' use of sport in defining "Christlike" masculinity. *Journal of Sport & Social Issues, 21,* 274–284.

Butterworth, M. L. (2005). Ritual in the "church of baseball": Suppressing the discourse of democracy after 9/11. *Communication and Critical/Cultural Studies, 2,* 107–129.

Butterworth, M. L. (2007). Race in "the race": Mark McGwire, Sammy Sosa, and heroic constructions of whiteness. *Critical Studies in Media Communication, 24,* 228–244.

Campbell, J., & Moyers, B. (1988). *The power of myth.* (Ed. Betty Sue Flowers). New York: Doubleday.

Cole, C. L., & King, S. (2003). The new politics of urban consumption: *Hoop Dreams, Clockers,* and "America." In R. C. Wilcox, D. L. Andrews, R. Pitter, & R. L. Irwin (Eds.), *Sporting dystopias: The making and meanings of urban sport cultures* (pp. 221–246). Albany: State University of New York Press.

Deegan, M. J., & Stein, M. (1989). The big red dream machine: Nebraska football. In M. J. Deegan (Ed.), *American ritual dramas: Social rules and cultural meanings* (pp. 77–88). New York: Greenwood Press.

Doty, W. G. (1986). *Mythography: The study of myths and rituals.* Tuscaloosa: University of Alabama Press.

Drucker, S. J. (1994). The mediated sports hero. In S. J. Drucker & R. S. Cathcart (Eds.), *American heroes in a media age* (pp. 82–93). Cresskill, NJ: Hampton.

Drucker, S. J., & Cathcart, R. S. (1994). The hero as a communication phenomenon. In S. J. Drucker & R. S. Cathcart (Eds.), *American heroes in a media age* (pp. 1–11). Cresskill, NJ: Hampton.

Fisher, W. (1984). Narration as a human communication paradigm: The case of moral public argument. *Communication Monographs, 51,* 1–22.

Grano, D. A. (2007). Ritual disorder and the contractual morality of sport: A case study in race, class, and agreement. *Rhetoric & Public Affairs, 10,* 445–474.

Grano, D. A. (2009). Muhammad Ali versus the "modern athlete": On voice in mediated sports culture. *Critical Studies in Media Communication, 26,* 191–211.

Grant, C. (1998). *Myths we live by.* Ottawa: University of Ottawa Press.

Hart, R. (1990). *Modern rhetorical criticism.* Glenview, IL: Scott Foresman.

Hoffman, S. J. (1992). Sport as religion. In S. J. Hoffman (Ed.), *Sport and religion* (pp. 1–12). Champaign, IL: Human Kinetics.

Newman, R. (2001). The American church of baseball and the National Baseball Hall of Fame. *Nine: A Journal of Baseball History and Culture, 10,* 46–63.

Okrent, D. (1998, December 28). A mac for all seasons: Mark McGwire's 70 home runs shattered the most magical record in sports and gave America a much-needed hero. *Time,* pp. 138–144.

Olsen, R. (2003). Fifty-eight American dreams: The NBA draft as mediated ritual. In R. S. Brown & D. J. O'Rourke (Eds.), *Case studies in sport communication* (pp. 171–200). Westport, CT: Praeger.

O'Rourke, D. J. (2003). The talk of the town: A rhetorical analysis of the Browns' departure from and return to Cleveland. In R. S. Brown & D. J. O'Rourke (Eds.), *Case studies in sport communication* (pp. 63–80). Westport, CT: Praeger.

Rader, B. (2002). *Baseball: A history of America's game* (2nd ed.). Urbana: University of Illinois Press.

Real, M. R. (1989). Super media: A cultural studies approach. Newbury Park, CA: Sage.

Rothenbuhler, E. W. (1989). Values and symbols in orientations to the Olympics. *Critical Studies in Mass Communication, 6,* 138–157.

Rothenbuhler, E. W. (1998). *Ritual communication: From everyday conversation to mediated ceremony.* Thousand Oaks, CA: Sage.

Vande Berg, L. R. (1998). The sports hero meets mediated celebrityhood. In L. A. Wenner (Ed.), *Mediasport* (pp. 134–153). London: Routledge.

SUGGESTED ADDITIONAL READING

Chidester, P. J. (2009). "The toy store of life": Myth, sport, and the mediated reconstruction of the American hero in the shadow of the September 11th terrorist attacks. *Southern Journal of Communication, 74,* 352–372.

Collins, S. (2006). National sports and other myths: The failure of U.S. soccer. *Soccer & Society, 7,* 353–363.

Higgs, R. J., & Braswell, M. C. (2004). *An unholy alliance: The sacred and modern sports.* Macon, GA: Mercer University Press.

Roessner, L. A. (2009). Hero crafting in *Sporting Life,* an early baseball journal. *American Journalism, 26,* 39–65.

Scheurer, T. E. (2005). Musical mythopoesis and heroism in film scores of recent sports movies. *Journal of Popular Film & Television, 32,* 157–166.

Trujillo, N., & Ekdom, L. R. (1985). Sportswriting and American cultural values: The 1984 Chicago Cubs. *Critical Studies in Mass Communication, 2,* 262–281.

CHAPTER 5

Gender in Sport

When asked about women's participation in sport, Indy Car driver Lyn St. James once said that "we want to make the world a better place, for women and for everybody, and we do it through sport" (Women's Sports Foundation, 2009a). For centuries, these opportunities have not been widely available to women; now, many more avenues exist (although certainly not the same number as for men in sport). Discussions of women in sport are different than those about **gender** issues in sport; the former is about the struggle for participation, opportunity, and equal treatment for one identity group while the latter is about the power-laden *interaction* between this identity group and those who currently have the access and opportunities—men. Sometimes notions of sex roles and gender identity become intermingled, with sex roles being based on biological differences between men and women and gender roles largely being socially constructed. Thus, sex becomes more binary (either an XX or XY chromosome makeup ends the discussion), whereas notions of gender become far more malleable (indeed, notions of gender change depending on aspects of background, culture, and life experience being exerted upon the binary chromosomal makeup). Put simply, we explore gender issues (since communication is structured through words and other social interactions) through what sport often creates as sex divisions (associations that only allow either men or women to play exclusively). This chapter will explore both feminist and interactive gender issues by (a) surveying the history of women's sport, (b) discussing masculinity under the broader theoretical construct of hegemonic masculinity, (c) assessing the amount of current coverage and exposure afforded to men's and women's sport, (d) addressing gendered language differences in sports media, (e) outlining current opportunities and struggles for women in modern sporting society, and (f) offering gender in sport as a possible agent for social change within an increasingly global society.

A HISTORY OF WOMEN'S SPORTS PARTICIPATION

The history of women's participation in sport is not as long as the history of their desire for inclusion. In fact, records show that even in the 1700s, women were arguing in print that they should be included in athletics (Sandoz & Winans, 1999).

Hargreaves (1994) delineates three distinct time frames for women in sport. She claims the first ranges from the inception of modern sports in 1896 until 1928—an era of overwhelming exclusion and dismissal of any combination of women and sport.

The second spans from 1928 to 1952—a period when primarily "feminine-appropriate" sports received relatively meager forms of societal attention. Kane (1989) outlines the sports that are considered feminine (such as gymnastics and swimming) and also those that society more often regards as not appropriate for women (such as basketball and boxing). Opportunities happened in the sports in which ladies could still behave as they were expected to for the time period. For instance, golf became a mainstream women's sport during Hargreaves's second time span. Hauser (1999) claims that "golf was said to be the 'gentlemen's game,' but it was also the perfect sport for a gentle woman" (p. 81). Women's professional golf (and the Ladies Professional Golf Association, or LPGA) was founded during this time period, as players such as Babe Didrikson Zaharias were respected for their abilities. Sports such as tennis became mainstream for women; Wimbledon hosted its first women's tournament in

Cheerleaders at a football game

1884, just 7 years after the gentlemen's championships began, yet the women's championships became much less of a perceived side-show during this time period. Other sporting opportunities arose as men went to fight in World War II. The rise and fall of the All-American Girls Professional Baseball League is chronicled with a fair dose of historical accuracy in the 1992 film *A League of Their Own*. Opportunities for women in a wider range of sports were still quite limited, however. Of all the athletes participating in the 1948 London Olympics, just 90 women competed (as opposed to nearly 5,000 today). Hargreaves argues that because of increased recognition for women's sporting accomplishments, the standards of skill and international competition accelerated substantially.

The third era provided by Hargreaves ranges from 1952 to the present day, representing decades in which women's sports have been able to conquer some traditional power structures while continuing to challenge long-held stereotypes about women's athleticism. While this third era is certainly progressive in relation to the previous two, women often find their access to facilities, trainers, coaches, and media exposure is still lacking when compared to their male counterparts. As Toohey and Veal (2000) write, there is still a prevailing notion among some segments of society that "women are physically inferior to men and that it is unbecoming for them to indulge in certain activities" (p. 179). Nonetheless, the 1970s brought two tipping points that aided a surge in women's athletics that still escalates today.

Tipping Point #1: Title IX

The most significant change for women's sports in the United States occurred in the early 1970s, when Title IX of the Education Amendments of 1972 made gender equity into law, arguing that "No person in the United States shall, on the basis of sex, be excluded from participation in, be denied the benefits of, or be subjected to discrimination under any education program or activity receiving Federal financial assistance." Title IX is now largely regarded as an athletic law, but note that sport was not specifically mentioned in the wording of Title IX. Rather, athletics was previously considered the largest violator of this principle, making gender equity in sports the most immediately observable change in American gender policies.

Compliance with Title IX has long been a hotly debated issue (see Staurowsky, 1995), with the three-prong approach of 1979 still being used today (see Carpenter & Acosta, 2005). More specifically, college and high school athletic programs are considered to be in compliance if any of the following three prongs is satisfied:

1. Athletic opportunities are provided that are proportionate to the student enrollment.

2. Athletic opportunities are continually expanded for the underrepresented sex.

3. Athletic interests of the underrepresented sex are fully satisfied.

Most college athletic programs strive for compliance under the first prong but use the other two prongs as a means for demonstrating they are continually striving to provide more opportunities for women's athletics. In 2010, the use of student surveys to register compliance based on student interest was eliminated (Thomas, 2010).

Compliance is becoming increasingly difficult as the percentages of men and women enrolled in college have changed dramatically. At Title IX's inception, men and women attended colleges and universities in roughly equal numbers; by 2005, for every 100 male students there were 133 female students (Marklein, 2005). These demographic shifts cause athletic departments to do one of two things to achieve proportionality compliance: Either they must add more women's sports or end existing men's sports. The fact that Division I football programs are permitted 85 scholarships exacerbates the problems confronting lower-profile men's sports. Men's sports such as wrestling and gymnastics have experienced diminished resources and, in many cases, elimination from athletic programs to balance the scales, causing even greater criticism of the ramification of Title IX within these sporting communities.

Regardless of where one stands on proper implementation of Title IX, the impact on women's athletics has been eye popping. Consider the participation rates for five sports 25 years after Title IX was established (see Table 5.1).

Table 5.1 Women's High School Sports Participation Rates (1972, 2007)

Sport	1972 Participants	2007 Participants	% Change
Soccer	700	337,632	+ 48,133%
Lacrosse	450	54,771	+ 12,071%
Cross Country	1,719	183,376	+ 10,568%
Golf	1,118	66,283	+ 5,829%
Bowling	370	20,931	+ 5,557%

Source: Angel, A., Bella, T., Brady, S., & Brauner, D. (2009, Mar. 23). Lady killers. *ESPN: The Magazine*, p. 34.

Case Study: The Unintended By-product of Title IX

Many have argued that Title IX has had an adverse effect on the sporting landscape throughout the country, suggesting that growth in women's athletics has produced a decline in the number of male sports (especially at the collegiate level). As colleges and universities seek compliance with Title IX legislation, wrestling has been one particular sport that has experienced a significant decline. More than 100 college and university teams have been eliminated since the 1972 legislation was enacted, and many fans in this community place the blame squarely on the need to maintain proportionality within women's athletics. While this move has resulted in deep resentment of women's athletics for individuals highly invested in these programs, an unintended by-product is that the sport of wrestling is slowly beginning to experience rebirth stemming from the decreased opportunities for males.

During the 2008 Beijing Olympics, women's Greco-Roman and freestyle wrestling were introduced, with the U.S. wrestling program producing two female wrestlers who contributed to the country's overall medal count. This opportunity stems from the growth of women's wrestling at the college level during the past two decades. In 1993, the University of Minnesota–Morris introduced the first collegiate women's wrestling team as a varsity sport, and the number of such programs grew to more than 30 throughout the country by 2009, with women competing in tournaments hosted by the Women's College Wrestling Association. Interestingly enough, these colleges and universities have found that promoting opportunities for female wrestlers is a viable solution for leveraging Title IX requirements and maintaining the sport of wrestling. The creation of these programs comes at limited cost to the institution, as athletes from each program have been increasingly likely to share coaches, practice facilities, and travel costs for competition. In all likelihood, wrestling may survive as a sport because of the growth of female participation, since institutions must weigh Title IX compliance when eliminating male and female programs that are linked in this way.

However, despite the growth of female wrestling at the collegiate and international stages, limited change has occurred at the high school level in most states. To date, no state high school activity association has developed girls' wrestling as a unique sporting opportunity for females. While few states limit girls from competing against male wrestlers, few female competitors have achieved success by participating in this environment. For example, a female participant made it to the Minnesota state high school wrestling tournament for the first time in 2009 but failed to place when forced to compete against male athletes.

1. Can you envision other sports where this type of joint participation can assist in meeting the sport interests of female athletes?

2. What are the potential benefits/costs to the expansion of other sports due to Title IX legislation?

3. Why shouldn't providing opportunities for males and females to compete for scholarship spots in the same sport be a viable solution to Title IX?

Tipping Point #2: The Battle of the Sexes

Memorabilia from Billie Jean King versus Bobby Riggs match

Nothing can match the impact of Title IX, but another landmark event of the 1970s still can be regarded as a tipping point for women's opportunities in sport: the 1973 tennis exhibition between former men's #1 player Bobby Riggs and women's superstar Billie Jean King. The 55-year-old Riggs claimed he could still beat the best women's tennis had to offer, and King decided to take him up on this challenge. Most knew beforehand that this match would be part of the history of women's rights in society regardless of the outcome. However, when King won in straight sets, the event took on even greater meaning. While gender equality was resisted in false urban legends that Riggs only got one serve while King got two and that Riggs bet large sums of money against himself to fix the match, the outcome galvanized women athletes seeking a place within the sporting landscape and also, for millions of people, signaled that more equal treatment of women at home and at the workplace would surely follow. Given that the event was nationally televised with great promotional fanfare, the impact of the event was that women's athletics was much more widely considered to at least deserve a place at the sporting table. Whereas Title IX was government-mandated inclusion of women in athletics, the Battle of the Sexes was a direct challenge to men's near-exclusive hold on sport.

Moments of Recent Decades

Augusta National Golf Club

Women's athletics had many highs and lows in the subsequent years. The Women's Professional Basketball League lasted a mere three seasons, folding in 1981. The LPGA continues to struggle for sponsors and media exposure. Still, the first generation of women to benefit from Title IX clearly forged new ground; NBC's Bob Costas refers to the 1996 Atlanta Summer Olympics as the Title IX Games because so many of the American women who took center stage were born close to the advent of the legislation. Progress can be measured in many ways, such as the high rating garnered for the 1999 Women's World Cup soccer final, the fact that all Grand Slam tennis tournaments now pay men's and women's champions equal sums of money, and Annika Sorenstam's valiant effort to make the cut in an all-male PGA event, missing by four shots at the 2003 Colonial tournament. Still, some moments have been bizarre (the highest rating ever for women-oriented sport remains the 1994 Olympic skating of Nancy Kerrigan and Tonya Harding, at least partly inflated by the earlier physical assault on Kerrigan by people close to Harding), while other moments are entrenched in gendered stagnation (protests for Augusta National Golf Club to invite a woman member have, thus far, proven unsuccessful). The history of women in sports has been one of steady progress, with setbacks being outnumbered by advances as women continually seek out new ways to join the community of sport. Nevertheless, women continue to break boundaries in sport, establishing noteworthy firsts such as Kelly Kulick's 2010 win in a Professional Bowling Association (PBA) event.

HEGEMONIC MASCULINITY IN SPORT

Seminal theorists such as Gramsci (1971) have used the concept of hegemony to explain how power becomes entrenched in established beliefs regarding power and myth. As Connell (1987) expresses: "In Western countries . . . images of ideal masculinity are constructed and promoted most systematically through competitive sport" (pp. 84–85). Given the hegemony is not only about power but about winning, it is not surprising that scholars have used **hegemonic masculinity** to explain how male athletes maintain dominance in sport that ranges from access to economics to participation rates to media coverage. More specifically, Trujillo (1991) claimed that hegemonic masculinity "refers to the social ascendancy of a particular version or model of masculinity that, operating on the terrain of 'common sense' and conventional morality, defines 'what it means to be a man'" (p. 291). Using pitcher Nolan Ryan as exemplar, Trujillo articulates five features: (1) physical force and control, (2) occupational achievement, (3) patriarchy, (4) romantic frontiersman/ modern outdoorsman, and (5) heterosexuality; these features jointly reinforce masculine ideals at the expense of other forms of masculinity, homosexual men, and women.

Sport often is defined as who is bigger, faster, and stronger, and yes, males have proven in world records that they are objectively bigger, faster, and stronger because of biological circumstance. Nonetheless, one cannot discount the endless cycle of certain sports (boxing, basketball) that are considered masculine that then results in media coverage that is predominantly masculine, which then embeds discourses to society that reinforce notions that sports are not for all, but for males (see Kane & Greendorfer, 1994). Applying hegemonic masculinity also can explain how male athletes sometimes are typified in more objective manners (again, the bigger, faster, stronger) than the more nuanced and repeatable athletic skills (finesse, touch, control). For instance, mediated basketball coverage on programs such as ESPN's *SportsCenter* is more likely to show powerful men performing slam dunks than talented men executing a spot-on assist for a timely layup.

GENDERED COVERAGE OF SPORT

Regarding media exposure, Adams and Tuggle (2004) report that a typical episode of ESPN's *SportsCenter* devotes just 2% of coverage to women's athletics, echoing concerns previously found within the program, where the National Spelling Bee received more coverage than an entire week's nightly coverage of women's sports (Eastman & Billings, 2000). Duncan (2006) summarizes the gendered sports exposure findings at the turn of the century (see Figure 5.1).

While existing power structures tell a major part of the story, the relative lack of women viewers/readers of sports products is a mitigating factor. Women argue they do not consume as much sports media product as men do because so little of it focuses on women's athletics, yet others counter that women fans do not support their athletes and teams in substantial doses in instances when they are shown. The 2003 folding of the Women's United Soccer Association (WUSA) is a case in point where the majority of the admittedly small viewership was men, a trend found in many other televised women's sports including women's professional tennis and basketball. In fact, the only two major sporting events that draw more women than men viewers are the Olympics and the Kentucky Derby (Helm, 2009). Women's sports are frequently offered on fringe or secondary cable networks, making the events difficult to find, yet more men than women are seeking out these sports media offerings.

Figure 5.1 Proportions of Men's and Women's Sports News Coverage

Source: Duncan, 2006.

Given that women represent the majority of U.S. Olympic viewers, one must wonder whether the coverage highlights women in equal measures. Billings (2008) reported on the gendered clock-time differences in six Olympic telecasts (see Figure 5.2).

As one can witness from the two pie charts, there is near equity in the Summer Olympic telecast, but a substantial gap (when excluding mixed pairs competitions) in the Winter Olympic telecast. One could view at least the Summer Olympic results as substantial progress for women, yet one must also note that women won the majority of the U.S. medals in each of these Games and yet still did not receive even half of the coverage from the U.S. networks. The Olympics demonstrates that media outlets can draw a very high viewership while featuring women athletes, something that was

Figure 5.2

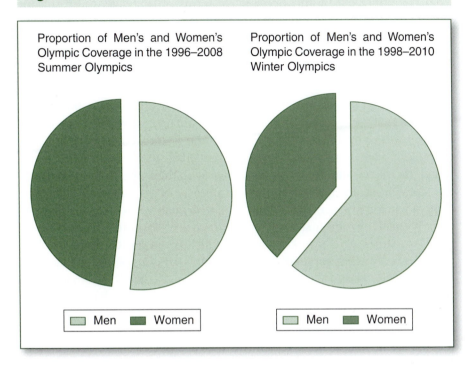

Proportion of Men's and Women's Olympic Coverage in the 1996–2008 Summer Olympics

Proportion of Men's and Women's Olympic Coverage in the 1998–2010 Winter Olympics

☐ Men ■ Women   ☐ Men ■ Women

underscored in the quite surprising 13.3 rating of the 1999 Women's World Cup final between the U.S. and China.

GENDERED LANGUAGE IN SPORT

Males and females may do similar things and even play the same sports, but the notion that they do so in overwhelmingly different ways is still quite prevalent in modern society. As explained in Messner (2002), beliefs that "men are from Mars, and women are from Venus" are "depressing evidence of how a renewed essentialism—the belief that women and men are so naturally and categorically different that they might as well be from different planets" (p. 1). When former Wimbledon Gentlemen's Singles champion Pat Cash said that women's tennis is to men's tennis what horse manure is to thoroughbred racing (*The London Times,* 1999), he received more laughs than admonishment, a sign that women can play sports but are not exempt from being mocked by this decision. In terms of language, the result for women in sport is the diminishment or mitigation of their participation and accomplishments.

Naming Practices

One action that serves to diminish women's sports involves naming practices (see Halbert & Latimer, 1994). To wit, team sports employ qualifiers to women's teams to differentiate them from the "standard" men's teams. For example, a high school may have two basketball teams: the men's team, called the Lakers, and the women's team, called the Lady Lakers. The use of the feminine qualifier (especially in the absence of a men's equivalent) is a form of naming practice. In a similar vein, women athletes are more likely to be referenced by their first names, while men are most often referred to by their last names. Thus, we know that "Annika" was a great women's golfer, but "Watson" was a great men's golfer. In tennis, rivalries persisted matching "Chrissy" and "Martina" (rather than Evert versus Navratilova) while men's rivalries pitted Sampras versus Agassi. It is fair to counter that these practices are occasionally used because women's last names can change when they get married, yet most modern athletes retain their last names, making this impact negligible. Other than the anomaly that occurs when the Williams sisters play tennis (making first names critical for clarification), naming practices impart no gender division that would innately occur, and yet they do. The impact on women who play sport below the professional level can be felt as women often believe that naming practices relegate them to second-class status.

Gender Marking

The feeling that women's sport is substandard to men's is often felt in gender marking, a practice of qualifying which gender is participating in a given sport. Such marking becomes problematic when it is employed for women far more frequently than for men. For instance, one often sees media outlets that refer to two sports: basketball and women's basketball. When the qualifier is not used, the presumed gender is almost always male. Some associations reinforce these markings largely because the men's association was founded first, making the women's organization adopt a new gendered tag. Thus, we have the Ladies Professional Golf Association (LPGA) because the Professional Golf Association (PGA) had already been established for the men; similarly, we have the National Basketball Association (NBA) and then the gender-marked Women's National Basketball Association (WNBA). These qualifiers are then used to ascribe limiting assessments of women's achievement, such as referencing a person as the "best *women's* player in the conference" or "playing well enough to enjoy success on the *women's* tour." One could argue that the qualifier is necessary because men tend to be bigger, faster, and stronger than women at the highest levels of virtually all sports. Still, the notion that we only appreciate the fastest does not appear to apply in car racing, for instance, when the people regarded as the best drivers are ones driving for NASCAR, not Indy Car, which offers substantially more powerful cars. The inverse also doesn't seem to apply in athletics when agility makes women perhaps more innately capable, such as with certain flexibility requirements in gymnastics.

Sexual Disparagement

Gendered language also is used to presumably stigmatize a people through the mislabeling and denunciation of sexual orientations. Female athletes continually battle being labeled as "butch" or lesbian (Caudwell, 1999) when excelling at sports, while homosexual slurs are heaped on males when they fail to perform adequately in sports. Griffin (2007) delineates six ways in which homophobia is manifest in sport: (1) silence—such as the lack of overwhelming outrage when Penn State women's basketball coach Rene Portland enacted a no-lesbian policy (see Hardin, 2009); (2) denial—either claiming not to be gay or claiming that one's private life is not for public discussion; (3) apology—a performance of proper gender roles, particularly in public roles other than during sport; (4) promotion of hetero-sexy image—the LPGA using attractive photo shoots and calendars for promotion (see Hundley & Billings, 2010); (5) attacks on lesbians—badmouthing in recruiting, arguing that other teams have a disproportionate number of gay players; and (6) preferences for male coaches—hiding homosexuality in women's sports through the presence of a male coach. Chapter 8 will reveal much more about how athletes feel pressures to perform in certain ways that match not only their own identity characteristics but also the identity characteristics that they presume are most desirable in society.

Categorical Differences in Gendered Media Dialogue

Decades of study (see Billings, 2009; Blinde, Greendorfer, & Sankner, 1991; Daddario, 1998) have led to a longitudinal understanding of how men and women athletes are depicted using divergent dialogues within the media. One should note that stereotyping is still a notion that is studied within communication scholarship, but the understanding of difference and bias has largely trumped the search for stereotypical behavior. This is largely because both social scientists and critical/cultural scholars have uncovered dialogic differences in sports commentary that may not fit traditional gendered power structures or overt sexism yet nonetheless represent difference in the manner in which we understand men and women athletes. Given that there are biological (e.g., pregnancy or the presence of testosterone) and sociological differences (e.g., unequal opportunities for men and women to compete in youth sports) between the genders that impact athletic performance, some difference is to be expected. Still, one must temper these anticipated differences with notions of dominance and power that also inevitably percolate within these media dialogues. Consider commentary within the 2009 U.S. Open Tennis Tournament, wherein Kim Clijsters was asked over and over again, "How does it feel to win . . . *as a mom?*"

Some terms more likely to be attributed to a male athlete:

Powerful

Conquering

Best in the world

Fearless

Incredible

Some terms more likely to be attributed to a female athlete:

Talented

Dedicated

Best woman in the world

Emotional

Nice

Thus, there are some forms of comments that are more often attributed to men than women athletes. For instance, the most basic trend that has been consistently detected involves the notion that men are inherently superior in terms of athletic skill. This belief has been broken down into subcategories including superior power ("like a runaway locomotive"), touch ("incredible precision in his turns"), and finesse ("one of a handful of people in the world who could perform that dunk").

Beyond this hard-wired trend, male athletes are also more likely to be considered superiorly experienced at their sport of choice. Some of these types of comments may be founded in logic and the sociological differences discussed earlier. For example, sports such as gymnastics typically involve teenaged female gymnasts but men in their 20s. Also, men athletes may truly have more experience (as measured in years rather than amount of practice time) because boys are encouraged to play more organized sports at earlier ages. Even when taking these mitigating factors into account, however, there is still a disproportionate focus on the experience of men athletes when compared to women of similar expertise and backgrounds.

A final trend that is likely to favor men involves perception of superior composure. Media analyses have found that commentary can sometimes regard men athletes as more "ready for the moment." Winners of men's sports events are more likely than winners of women's sports events to have their success attributed to mental toughness and the ability to be unrelenting when faced with an emotional moment.

There are also several areas in which women athletes are more likely to receive comments than men. Perhaps the most unsurprising trend involves a tendency for sports media outlets to concentrate on the overall attractiveness of women athletes. When one considers that the overwhelming majority of sportscasters are male and presumably heterosexual, this may not be much of a shock. However, the types of comments can nonetheless diminish the accomplishments of women athletes (and a discussion of the overt sexualization of women athletes can be found in Chapter 8). Consider the ramifications of watching a telecast where a female gymnast is referred to as an "adorable pixie" or perhaps the self-imposed harm of watching professional volleyball star Gabrielle Reece compete while hearing commentary about her *Playboy* pictorial. Some studies have found that in terms of sheer counts of comments about men's and women's bodies, the numbers could be considered to be relatively equivalent. However, the comments surrounding men athletes tend to be more apt to fall into references to physique ("built like Superman") than the same comments about attractiveness that women players more often receive.

A Matter of Ethics: Exposure Begets Exposure

Swimmer Amanda Beard competed in four Summer Olympic Games for the United States, winning a total of seven medals. In the lead-up to the 2008 Beijing Games, however, Beard received more attention for her appearance in the August 2007 issue of *Playboy*. Knowing that some would be critical of her, Beard justified the decision by stating, "I think, personally, it's showing a wonderful, healthy body." She also acknowledged that the appearance was a "business decision," part of a larger strategy to market herself once her competitive swimming career ended.

In this chapter, you've seen that many female athletes still face either overt discrimination or more subtle forms of sexism, including the expectation that they should remain "feminine" or "pretty" while competing in sports. Increasingly, however, athletes such as Anna Kournikova, Brandi Chastain, and Danica Patrick *choose* to emphasize their physical appearance as a means to increase their marketability. The outcome of these choices is undeniable: Attractive female athletes who pose for publications such as *Maxim* or *FHM* (predominantly read by heterosexual men) generally raise their profiles and collect more, and more lucrative, endorsements.

Critics of these athletes counter that while these overtly sexual images may benefit individual women, they do harm to countless other women who are not able to conform to conventional standards of beauty. In addition, their decision to pose nude (or nearly nude) for an overwhelmingly male audience risks reducing women to simple objects of sexual pleasure, which minimizes the actual *achievements* of women athletes.

1. Do women who pose for these publications have a responsibility to other women?

2. Should an appearance in *Playboy* be understood *only* as a "business decision"? If, as Beard argues, the idea is to show a "healthy body," could there be other means to do so?

3. Why is it still important for female athletes to demonstrate their "femininity"?

4. Are men held to the same expectations as women when it they choose to exploit their own appearance/sexuality?

Beyond an increased focus on looks, women receive more comments than men do about being emotional. Some members of society still argue that women are "too emotional" and "take things personally" in all circumstances, which is then used to argue that women cannot perform effectively at the highest level of the workplace. These same misguided notions have been found to seep into sports media commentary. This is perhaps a corollary to the trend to perceive men's superior composure—men athletes are depicted as succeeding because they do not let emotions override their athletic desires and women athletes are perceived as failing for succumbing to these same obstacles.

A final type of commentary that women athletes are more likely to receive than men athletes involves attri-

Danica Patrick

butions of luck. When a woman succeeds in sport, commentary may attempt to temper these achievements by noting that the player had some breaks go her way. This is often unpacked in communication scholarship as "consonance" or the notion that everything simply comes together at a moment in time to impact the athletic moment. Thus, positive consonance can exact victory (a basketball player who "couldn't miss tonight" or was "on fire") just as negative consonance can result in defeat ("just wasn't his night"). In terms of gender, women are more likely to receive comments about positive consonance than are men. This is especially true when women compete against men in the same competition. For instance, urban legends persist surrounding the Billie Jean King/Bobby Riggs Battle of the Sexes, arguing that King must have won because of luck. When the result couldn't be directly attributable to luck, false claims were made that Riggs only received one serve per point and that King was allowed to hit into the doubles court (both are absolutely untrue). In a similar vein, when Annika Sorenstam competed in a sanctioned PGA tournament, a commentator witnessed a man's shot bouncing from the rough onto the green and noted that it was an "Annika bounce," potentially implying that Sorenstam had a better-than-anticipated score earlier that day because of superior luck.

In all, it is abundantly clear that men and women athletes are described in a variety of media outlets in substantially different manners. Some differences are justified, some are explainable, and others could be judged to arise from personal ignorance. Regardless, the astute communication scholar must understand the dialogic differences involved in the conversations that surround sport at all levels of society.

OPPORTUNITIES FOR MEN AND WOMEN IN SPORT

Mark Twain once observed that "rumors of my demise have been greatly exaggerated," and this appears to be the case when talking about the old-boy network of sports. One cannot talk about opportunities in sport—whether involving jobs or mere access—without talking about power. Social class certainly is a contributing factor, yet gender is critical to the discussion, as men have possessed entrenched power roles throughout the inception and evolution of modern sport. Female sports team owners are still regarded more as anomalies than as trends toward equality. Debates in coaching circles remain over issues such as whether any Division I men's basketball program would offer a head coaching position to a woman such as Tennessee women's coaching legend Pat Summit, who has amassed more than 1,000 victories and eight national championships. Women's access to sportscasting jobs is almost universally relegated to that of sideline reporter or weather prognosticator. These cases are hardly indications that sports structures are providing more access for women.

Interview: Donna de Varona, Olympic Gold Medalist and Award-Winning Sports Journalist

Q: **You were an Olympic gold medalist in an era before Title IX. What opportunities were available to women athletes in your competitive era and how has Title IX changed these opportunities?**

A: In my era, there were few opportunities for women outside of the Olympics. Even then, women only competed for less than a third of the Olympic medals that men did. I began competitive swimming just before my 11th birthday, training with an age-group club swim team because there were no competitive swim team opportunities for women in high school or college and certainly no sports scholarships. However, time, place, and circumstance still put me on a path to success. I was just 13 when I competed on the relay team in the trials but not the finals in Rome.

I held the world record in the 400 individual medley, but while the men already competed in that event in the Olympics, I had to wait 4 more years before my specialty was added. What has changed since then is manifold. There is wide acceptance of the female athlete. Scholarships are offered. There are professional leagues. Tennis players finally earn equal pay. Women are now serving in prominent roles in sports media. There are more professional options available to women.

Q: Can you contrast how people talk about women's athletics today compared to the 1960s?

A: In many areas, women are treated first as sex objects, and that applies to sport as well. However, there are sensitive, educated producers, announcers, and writers who focus on athletic accomplishment above all else. Parents discuss how sport in school is an essential part of education and realize that a sport experience is just as important for females as it is for males.

Q: Much criticism has been levied at women athletes who have promoted a more sexualized image of themselves to be more marketable. Is this criticism fair?

A: I have discussed this issue with many women athletes who feel the pressure. They feel they must not only perform as elite athletes but also compete with idealized images of other famous women they see daily on magazine covers. More exposure can convert into more sponsor dollars, so I am not critical of the athletes but rather of a media culture consumed with pushing images of the impossibly perfect woman.

Q: Beyond being an Olympic gold medalist, you are widely credited with becoming the first female sportscaster in 1965. What was the environment like for a woman in sports media at that time?

A: I am one of the first and certainly the youngest woman to work with a major network covering sports. I was an expert, interviewer, and eventually a host, and Emmy-winning producer and writer. My first assignment was at age 17 for ABC's *Wide World of Sports* telecast when covering the men's swimming championships. Jim McKay hosted. Because he knew little about swimming, I was given quite a

(Continued)

(Continued)

lot of respect. However, when I later expressed a desire to move off the pool deck into larger arenas, I was met with great resistance and doubt about my abilities. Very few women were working behind the camera, but I had mentors like genius former ABC chairman Roone Arledge to support me.

Q: Women sports journalists still sometimes experience a hostile work environment. What can be done to alleviate this atmosphere?

A: Acceptance must come from the executives at the top. Women who work in the industry should be given the same pay and status as the men. Far too often, women are pushed out of the industry just when they have matured as professionals. Women who want to work in sports must be prepared beyond expectations and really know their stuff.

In terms of sheer numbers of jobs, the opportunities for women in sport are growing, but at a very slow rate. The Women's Sports Foundation (2009b) admits that sport is still highly male dominated but argues that five trends are leading to more opportunities for women within the sports marketplace:

1. *The active female consumer.* Women now outpurchase men for items such as athletic shoes and clothing.

2. *Females as spectators of men's and women's sports.* While we have already established that women rarely outnumber men when watching sportscasts, they do represent 40% of all sports consumers—and that proportion is increasing.

3. *Males and females as spectators of women's sports.* Women's professional leagues are struggling financially, yet their mere existence represents progress when compared to past opportunities.

4. *Women's sports being accepted by the sports media.* As Duncan (2006) summarized, the proportions of coverage are meager, yet they are increasing. For instance, the 8.7% of local sports coverage devoted to women in 1999 still represents a 74% increase from the 5.0% of coverage found in 1989.

5. *Corporations using sports to sell to women.* "Athletic" looks are desired within a significant segment of the women consumer population, often more than "sexy" looks. Organizations are hiring women athletes as spokespersons and sponsoring women's sporting events because of this trend.

Some of these postulates could be assessed as mere spin, trying to create a self-fulfilling prophecy, yet all of these trends are, indeed, pointing in the direction of more opportunities for women, even if the scale of these chances is not remotely equivalent to that of men.

Nonetheless, even when given the right to earn a job in sports media, women face many additional hurdles. Hardin and Shain (2005) report that half of women in sports journalism report being verbally abused in conjunction with their jobs. This ranged from sexual comments at the workplace to berating voicemails from readers who belittled their knowledge to locker room hassles with male athletes. The presumptions were that (a) women did not know as much as their men counterparts about the sports they were covering and that (b) they received their jobs either because of their looks or the organizational desire for gender diversity. Women also cited lack of advancement as their top reason for leaving sports journalism, and more women than men dropped out of the field at the early stages of their careers.

GLOBALIZATION AND CHANGE AGENCY

Given the established tendencies that can diminish women in terms of opportunities, representation, and depiction in sport, one could determine that women will always remain in the margins within a larger sporting landscape. However, scholars such as Stephenson (2002) argue for the use of sport to cause social change. Others believe that women athletes are particularly in the position of influencing societal perceptions, political realities, and the overall global treatment of women. As Wulf (2009) writes:

If anything, XX-chromosome games are a truer, more meaningful calling than their XY counterparts. Women often have to compete for nothing more than the joy and the love of sport, not the fame and fortune we heap on the men. They usually have to play for their own rewards. [Consider] Yemeni students, running a relay in Sanaa recently. They're not just girls with exotic wardrobes battling heat and aerodynamics. They're literally racing against time, trying to bring their Islamic traditions of modesty into the modern world of gender equality. (p. 16)

Hopefully, this chapter has underscored more than the negatives for women interested in sport, offering the positive trends and relatively newfound recognition of not just women athletes but also women fans, executives, and consumers that represent a newer and broader way of thinking about sport in society. Gender certainly impacts our understanding of sport at virtually every level, and it is fair to conclude that it remains the most hard-wired and perhaps last bastion of the old-boy network. One could see this as discouraging or could, instead, decide that sport is the venue in which the biggest social change could happen for women in the next generation. Regardless of one's standpoint, gender differences and advancements will continue to be negotiated largely from a communication perspective, whether that is through communication-based media, organizations, or social networks.

REFERENCES

Adams, T., & Tuggle, C. A. (2004). ESPN's *SportsCenter* and coverage of women's athletics: It's a boy's club. *Mass Communication & Society, 7,* 237–248.

Billings, A. C. (2008). Clocking gender differences: Televised Olympic clock-time in the 1996–2006 Summer and Winter Olympics. *Television & New Media, 9*(5), 429–441.

Billings, A. C. (2009). *Communicating about sports media: Cultures collide.* Barcelona, ESP: Aresta.

Blinde, M. E., Greendorfer, S. L., & Sankner, R. J. (1991). Differential media coverage of men's and women's intercollegiate basketball: Reflection of gender ideology. *Journal of Sport and Social Issues, 15,* 98–114.

Carpenter, L. J., & Acosta, R. V. (2005). *Title IX.* Champaign, IL: Human Kinetics.

Caudwell, J. (1999). Women's football in the United Kingdom: Theorizing gender and unpacking the butch lesbian image. *Journal of Sport & Social Issues, 23,* 390–402.

Connell, R. W. (1987). *Gender and power: Society, the person and sexual politics.* Palo Alto, CA: Stanford University Press.

Daddario, G. (1998). *Women's sport and spectacle.* Westport, CT: Praeger.

Duncan, M. C. (2006). Gender warriors in sport. In A. Raney & J. Bryant (Eds.), *Handbook of sports and media* (pp. 231–252). Mahwah, NJ: LEA.

Eastman, S. T., & Billings, A. C. (2000). Sportscasting and sports reporting: The power of gender bias. *Journal of Sport and Social Issues, 24*(1), 192–212.

Gramsci, A. (1971). *Selections from the prison notebooks.* New York: International.

Griffin, P. (2007). Changing the game: Homophobia, sexism, and lesbians in sport. In J. O'Reilly & S. K. Cahn (Eds.), *Women and sports in the United States* (pp. 217–234). Lebanon, NH: Northeastern Univ. Press.

Halbert, C., & Latimer, M. (1994). "Battling" gendered language: An analysis of the language used by sports commentators in a televised coed tennis competition. *Sociology of Sport Journal, 11,* 298–308.

Hardin, M. (2009). The Rene Portland case: New homophobia and heterosexism in women's sport coverage. In H. Hundley & A. C. Billings (Eds.), *Examining identity in sports media.* Thousand Oaks, CA: Sage.

Hardin, M., & Shain, S. (2005). Strength in numbers? The experiences and attitudes of women in sports media careers. *Journalism and Mass Communication Quarterly, 84*(4), 804–819.

Hargreaves, J. A. (1994). *Sporting females: Critical issues in the history and sociology of women's sports.* London: Routledge.

Hauser, M. (1999). Selling their game. In L. Danziger (Ed.), *Nike is a goddess: The history of women in sports.* New York: Atlantic Monthly Press.

Helm, B. (2009, Apr. 29). The race for Kentucky Derby viewers. Retrieved on July 17, 2009, from http://www.businessweek.com/bwdaily/dnflash/content/apr2009/db20090428_323412.htm?chan=top+news_top+news+index+-+temp_news+%2B+analysis.

Hundley, H. L., & Billings, A. C. (2010). *Views from the fairway: Media explorations of identity in golf.* Cresskill, NJ: Hampton Press.

Kane, M. J. (1989). The post-Title IX female athlete in the media: Things are changing, but how much? *Journal of Physical Education, Recreation, and Dance, 60,* 58–62.

Kane, M. J., & Greendorfer, S. L. (1994). The media's role in accommodating and resisting stereotyped images of women in sport. In P. J. Creedon (Ed.), *Women, media, and sport* (pp. 3–27). Thousand Oaks, CA: Sage.

The London Times. (1999, June 20). The spice girls of centre court, p. 1.

Marklein, M. B. (2005, Oct. 19). College gender gap widens: 57% are women. *USA Today,* p. A11.

Messner, M. (2002). *Taking the field: Women, men and sports.* Minneapolis: University of Minnesota Press.

Sandoz, J., & Winans, J. (Eds.). (1999). *Whatever it takes: Women on women's sport.* New York: Farrar, Straus, and Giroux.

Staurowsky, E. J. (1995). Examining the roots of a gendered division of labor in intercollegiate athletics: Insights into the gender equity debate. *Journal of Sport & Social Issues, 19,* 28–44.

Stephenson, D. (2002). Women, sport, and globalization. *Journal of Sport & Social Issues, 26,* 209–225.

Thomas, K. (2010, Apr. 20). NCAA praises change of rule for Title IX compliance. Retrieved on April 22, 2010, from http://www.nytimes.com/2010/04/21/sports/21titleix.html.

Toohey, K., & Veal, A. J. (2000). *The Olympic Games: A social science perspective.* Oxon, UK: Cabi.

Trujillo, N. (1991). Hegemonic masculinity on the mound: Media representations of Nolan Ryan and American sports culture. *Critical Studies in Mass Communication, 9,* 290–308.

Women's Sports Foundation (2009a). Inspirational quotes. Retrieved on July 7, 2009 from http://www.womenssportsfoundation.org/Tips-And-Tools/I-Am-A-Coach-Or-Administrator/Inspirational-Quotes.aspx.

Women's Sports Foundation. (2009b). Sport careers for women. Retrieved on July 17, 2009, from http://www.womenssportsfoundation.org/Content/Articles/Careers/S/Sport-Careers-for-Women.aspx.

Wulf, S. (2009, Mar. 23). Page 2. *ESPN: The Magazine,* p. 16.

SUGGESTED ADDITIONAL READING

Anderson, E. (2005). *In the game: Gay athletes and the cult of masculinity.* Albany: SUNY.

Duncan, M. C., & Brummett, B. (1993). Liberal and radical sources of female empowerment in sport media. *Sociology of Sport Journal, 10*(1), 57–72.

Griffin, P. (1998). *Strong women, deep closets: Lesbians and homophobia in sport.* Champaign, IL: Human Kinetics.

Markula, P. (2009). *Olympic women and the media: International perspectives.* New York: Palgrave Macmillan.

CHAPTER 6

Race and Ethnicity in Sport

Bryant Gumbel once called the combination of race and sport the "third rail of polite discourse . . . a subject sure to burn those who try to deal with it honestly or speak of it truthfully," and he is right that this combination can be perhaps the most difficult of all sports communicative terrain. We can all likely agree that ridiculous comments such as those once spoken by the late NFL player Reggie White to the Wisconsin legislature (i.e., Native Americans excel at "sneaking up on people" and Asians can "turn a television into a watch" [Ford, 2004, p. S6]) are out of bounds and rooted in ignorance. However, much as race itself is not a black/white binary, neither is the discussion of it in sport. Media gatekeepers, athletes, fans, and followers of sport rarely know how to discuss race in sport, resulting in a dropped conversation in which the vast majority finds the issue compelling, yet not compelling enough to risk the penalties of communicating about race in a manner dubbed inappropriate by another person or entity. This chapter will attempt to discuss the presumed dangerous communication cocktail of race, ethnicity, and sport by (a) outlining a history of race and ethnicity in sport, (b) uncovering differences in participation and sport selection rates, (c) identifying the impact of race/ethnicity on sports culture, (d) analyzing differences in media exposure and "stacking" practices, and (e) articulating the ways in which media dialogues differ depending on the race/ethnicity of the athlete being described. We are not pretending to solve racial discord in one simple chapter but rather helping to clarify the current state of the debate that continues regarding the impact of this form of identity on a heavily involved sporting society.

HISTORY OF ETHNICITY IN AMERICAN SPORT

Before we begin this discussion, we must note that race and ethnicity are closely related issues, yet **race** and **ethnicity** should not be regarded as interchangeable synonyms. Debate continues about the ways in which the terms are unpacked, but a general consensus (although hardly a settled one) refers to ethnicity as a person's heritage and culture (e.g., African American) and race as something that can be socially constructed (e.g., hairstyle and dress). Race often gets unpacked by much of the general society as simply a referent of skin color (e.g., black), which can add to the confusion. As Coakley (2009) contrasts, ethnicity refers to "a cultural heritage that people use to identify a particular population while race is when that population of people are *believed to be* [emphasis added] naturally or biologically distinct from other populations" (p. 276). Ways in which ethnicity can be performed will be discussed in more detail in Chapter 8; however, the distinction between the two is worthy of a formative note here with media often referring to race (skin pigment) because it is somewhat easier to explain than a person's detailed cultural heritage. Thus, President Obama becomes "black" rather than of mixed ethnic backgrounds and golfer Vijay Singh is often labeled "black" even though he hails from Fiji.

Almost completely unique to American culture is the ethnic notion of the "one drop rule" (see Sweet, 2005), which posits that if a person has any level of nonwhite heritage, he or she is regarded as a minority. As Langston Hughes (1940) wrote, "There are lots of different kinds of blood in our family. But here in the United States, the word 'Negro' is used to mean anyone who has any Negro blood at all in his veins. In Africa, the word is more pure. It means all Negro, therefore black. I am brown."

Most discussions in sports media do not focus on any notion of one drop or percentages of ethnic backgrounds, instead relying on the visual to provide a streamlined yet ultimately limiting view of race. *Chicago Tribune* journalist Clarence Page (2009) stated, regarding race in the media, that "We are geared toward the visual, not toward the conceptual. We are geared toward conflict, not Kumbaya moments."

We also limit the discussion of race and ethnicity to American sport because a person's human experience varies wildly depending on the nation in which one resides. One's ethnicity, heritage, or skin color is impacted, for instance, by whether one resides in, for instance, Finland, Argentina, or Saudi Arabia. Notions of nationalism, religion, history, hegemony, and culture can enter the equation, making ethnicity in sport far from a monolithic explanation.

In terms of history in the United States, ties between sport and ethnicity began—and remained for quite some time—largely as a white/black dynamic. This was, at least in part, because most other races were just nominally represented in the country's population in the 18th and 19th centuries. Even within the two races with significant populations, participation in sport was highly segregated. Blacks played organized sports very rarely but possessed a deep desire to compete. Slaves were given the very occasional day off and, when this occurred, many opted to play sports from morning to nightfall. The 1834 *Book of Sports* by Robin Carver notes that blacks were playing all sports imaginable during the pre–Civil War time period.

In the past century, advancements for blacks in sports can often be measured by connections with groundbreaking performances and breaking of color barriers. Boxing became one of the earliest places where races competed in the

Jesse Owens

same competitions. Legendary boxer Jack Johnson became the first black heavyweight champion in 1908, albeit surrounded by riots and death threats and capsulated notions of a "Great White Hope" that could defeat him. In the 1936 Berlin Summer Olympics, Jesse Owens won four gold medals in front of the citizens of Nazi Germany, challenging Adolph Hitler's aspiration to showcase Aryan dominance. Blacks participated in organized sports leagues in the early part of the 1900s yet never were afforded the opportunity to move from Negro leagues to white-established professional leagues until 1947, when Jackie Robinson joined the Brooklyn Dodgers. Despite a fair share of teammates and fans who felt racial integration was wrong, Robinson was able to largely win over critics. By 1948, several other black players had joined the ranks of Major League Baseball; when Robinson won the National League MVP award a year later, it was clear that black players would be a fixture in professional baseball from that point forward. Nevertheless, it took until 1959 before every Major League Baseball team was racially integrated.

University athletic programs were still exhibiting segregationist stances years later, but moments like Texas Western's (now the University of Texas at El Paso) 1966 national basketball championship team provided an impetus for changes. As dramatized in the 2006 film *Glory Road,* coach Don Haskins lacked the resources to recruit the top-ranked white high school players and instead opted to recruit players regardless of race. The result was a national basketball title as Haskins's all-black starting lineup defeated the University of Kentucky's all-white starting lineup.

Activism became increasingly prominent in athletics of the 1960s and 1970s. The most resonant example remains the Black Power salute in the 1968 Olympics (see Bass, 2002). After winning medals in the 200 meters in the 1968 Mexico City Games, Americans Tommie Smith and John Carlos received their medals in atypical fashion to bring attention to black heritage (and related American repression of it), including wearing no shoes but black socks (to recognize black poverty), a scarf around Smith's neck (to recognize black pride), and beads around Carlos's neck (to recognize black lynchings). In addition, each wore a black glove and raised his arm (symbolizing black power in America) during the playing of the U.S. national anthem. At the time of the protest, many key Olympic figures reacted quite negatively, but decades later, the image grew in stature to the point that the two men received the 2008 Arthur Ashe Courage Award—even though they have a fair amount of hostility toward each other.

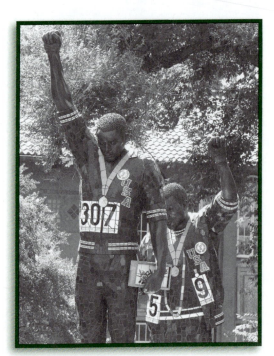

Tommie Smith and John Carlos statue at San Jose State University

Increasingly, organized sports became integrated with not just whites and blacks participating together but with a myriad of other ethnicities represented on the athletic field. The debate shifted to the ability of nonwhite athletes to advocate for broader social change using their visibility and status within professional sport. Considerable criticism has been levied against recent prominent athletes of color, such as Michael Jordan, who have not been nearly as openly activist about racial issues as their predecessors, people such as legendary Cleveland Browns running back Jim Brown and 11-time NBA champion Bill Russell. Jordan opted not to take public stances on political and social issues because, as he was once famously quoted as saying, "Republicans buy sneakers, too." *New York Times* columnist William C. Rhoden wrote of this dilemma in his book, *Forty Million Dollar Slaves* (2006), arguing:

> Occupants of two worlds—the world of the streets and the world of wealth—these athletes can speak from a perch of power and influence . . . [but] contemporary Black athletes have abdicated the responsibility to the community with treasonous vigor. They stand as living, active proof that it does not necessarily follow that if you make a man rich, you make him free. (p. 8)

Interview: Richard Lapchick, Director, The Institute for Diversity and Ethics in Sport (TIDES), University of Central Florida

Q: What are the primary objectives of the TIDES organization?

A: The primary objectives of TIDES are to provide timely information on critical social issues in sport. We publish an average of 18 studies a year on racial and gender hiring practices of Major League Baseball, the NFL, NBA, WNBA, Major League Soccer, and college sport. Every other year we do a report card for the Associated Press. There are two graduation studies for the NCAA, one for bowl-bound football teams in December, and one for the men's and women's basketball tournament teams.

Q: Most people now understand that a discussion of race in sport cannot be a black/white binary; however, to what extent can race be discussed in terms of power—those who have it and those who don't?

A: Most people now understand this discussion. I think the discussion of race and sport was about black and white consistently from the '60s to the '90s, but that discussion has obviously been broadened to include Latinos, Asians, Native Americans, and people from other parts of the globe. It certainly winds up in the Racial and Gender Report Card that the most influential positions are held by white men and, to a lesser degree, white women. It is hopeful that the NCAA, in selecting its new president to replace Myles Brand, will address this issue.

(Continued)

(Continued)

Q: **Because of the pitfalls that can arise when talking about race, many sportscasters have opted to omit the discussion entirely, arguing the preference for colorblindness. Do you agree?**

A: I believe that sportscasters should discuss the racial issue when the situation calls for it. If you talk to any diversity management trainer, they will tell you that nobody is colorblind and that we all see people visually and that is our first impression.

Q: **What are the newest trends in graduation rates and coaching opportunities for minorities?**

A: The newest trend is graduation rates are consistently increasing as well as Academic Progress Rate scores. Coaching opportunities for minorities remain stagnant and will take new tools implemented by the NCAA at the college level to see more progress. Coaching opportunities in pro sport, particularly in the NBA, NFL, and Major League Baseball, are significantly better than they have ever been.

Q: **What can be done to encourage athletes of different races to play sports that are not viewed as traditional within their cultural backgrounds?**

A: The key to encouraging athletes of different races to play sports that are not within their traditional cultural background is to increase opportunities for those young athletes to participate at the youth sport level. There are several positive examples in cities across the country, including opportunities in lacrosse and rowing that have been initiated by former players to serve the cities populated mostly by African American and Latinos.

Q: **You have always been a strong proponent of using sport as a vehicle to make useful social changes. Has this belief wavered or, instead, strengthened over time?**

A: I have become increasingly involved in using sport as a vehicle to make useful social changes. While I think there was a dip in that level of activity of athletes getting involved in the community, Hurricane Katrina opened up opportunities for athletes to visibly and tangibly see the difference they can make. I think that has spread to other areas.

PARTICIPATION AND SPORT SELECTION

America's history of race in sport is one largely of privileging one race at the complete exclusion of others. This is largely not the case today within the majority of organized sports. Instead, races often segregate themselves in self-selected manners similar to those of housing patterns and choices that result in neighborhoods of predominantly similar races. Beliefs that certain races are naturally more gifted at one sport than the other have largely been debunked (see Jarvie, 1991), yet there is no question that certain sports (and even some positions in a given sport) remain highly stereotyped to the point that it appears jarring for many members of society to see an athlete participate in a sport that is different from what is expected for his or her race. For instance, Venus and Serena Williams represented a heavy contrast to the typical racial profile of tennis players participating on the WTA Tour and Shani Davis's gold medal performances in the 2006 Winter Olympics stressed how rare it was to see a black speed skater. Relatedly, professional basketball became so heavily populated by black players that

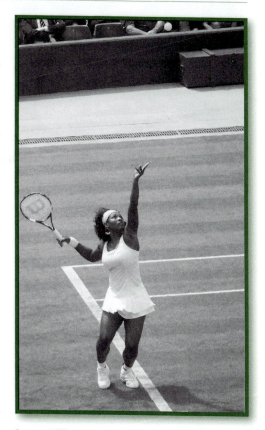

Serena Williams

Larry Bird was regarded by some journalists as the newest example of the mediated Great White Hope, and white wide receivers in football have their defenders who refute their characterizations as "deceptively fast" and "possession receivers."

In sum, sports as a whole are popular for all ethnic groups, but each individual sport brings the reality of differential ethnic expectations. Figure 6.1 on page 113 shows how these expectations are manifested in sport selection rates. Witness the Summer Olympics, which is certainly ethnically diverse, yet it is hard to say we are witnessing ethnicities competing against one another when tuning into a swimming final that is predominantly white and then switching to a sprinting final that is

C. C. Sabathia

predominantly black. Some of these ethnic trends make sense internationally; it makes sense that people like Equatorial Guinea's black swimmer Eric Moussambani was a rarity in the 2000 Summer Olympics when considering that the country only had two swimming pools at the time and both were located inside luxury hotels. However, the manner in which sports segregate athletes by race in the United States is perhaps less explainable. When faced with the opportunity to compete in multiple sports, today's modern athletes often opt for specialization. For instance, Latino players are more likely to opt for baseball; blacks are more likely to choose basketball; whites are more likely to choose golf. This is not because of some biological discrepancy between races that is often espoused by some of the people branded "celebrity racists" in the opening of this chapter. Rather, it is often the case that culture, geography, economics, and heritage jointly influence these choices. For instance, the racial makeup of Major League Baseball has changed substantially since the 1970s with black players constituting 28% of the professional baseball population in the mid-1970s but only 8% in 2008. Black pitcher C. C. Sabathia notes that external influences like college scholarship structures impede black participation because, while basketball and football offer full scholarships, baseball rarely does (see Anderson, 2009). The athletes do not as much choose the sports as the sports (through a confluence of interrelated variables) choose them.

In sports like football, different positions possess different athletic expectations. When these expectancies are violated, people often exhibit cognitive dissonance. In 2003, ESPN hired radio host Rush Limbaugh to participate in its studio show. Limbaugh's inappropriate comments about why the media tends to embrace Philadelphia Eagles quarterback Donovan McNabb (that the media has overplayed his quarterbacking skills because they have been "very desirous to see a black quarterback do well") were indicative of a larger problem with the perception that McNabb and other black quarterbacks were playing the "wrong" position (see Buffington, 2005).

Figure 6.1 2009 Athletic Participation Rates (Reported in Percentages from the TIDES Racial Report Card)

	MLB	NBA	WNBA	NFL	MLS	CFB	MCB	WCB
White	60	18	21	31	62	47	33	43
African American	10	77	65	67	20	46	60	50
Latino	27	3	0	1	16	2	2	1
Asian	2	1	0	2	1	< 1	< 1	1
Other	0	1	0	< 1	1	2	4	4
International	29	18	14	2	32	< 1	< 1	<1

Note: *Percentages do not equal 100 because of rounding and multirace classifications. Abbreviations are as follows: Major League Baseball (MLB); National Basketball Association (NBA); Women's National Basketball Association (WNBA); National Football League (NFL); Major League Soccer (MLS); College Football (CFB); Men's College Basketball (MCB); Women's College Basketball (WCB)

We discuss the apology strategy surrounding these types of statements in Chapter 12. This notion is similar to what used to be the case in 1980s basketball, where white players were expected to be point guards. Even the leader of the Philadelphia National Association for the Advancement of Colored People, J. Whyatt Mondesire, appeared to be ill at ease discussing McNabb. He went as far as to purport that McNabb's temporary decline in play was the result of his becoming a pocket-passer to avoid the image of being an athletic, running quarterback that would befit the black football stereotype (Fitzgerald, 2005).

These variable participation rates are proving to be much more hardwired than many initially believed. When Tiger Woods emerged in the professional golf scene a decade and a half ago, many presumed his success would inevitably lead to a more ethnically diverse professional golf membership. Thus far, this has not been the case, just as 1980s boxer Gerry Cooney did not lead a revival of white boxers and the Williams sisters' participation has not resulted in a substantially more racially integrated professional tennis. People continue to select certain sports at the exclusion of others and there is, no doubt, a racial component to these choices.

MEDIA EXPOSURE AND STACKING

Echoing a theme that is prevalent in this chapter, ethnic diversity in sports media has evolved from outright exclusion of nonwhite participants to selective exclusion of things that may appeal to minority audiences but not mainstream (read: white) viewership. There has been a concerted effort to rework, revamp, and revise the cultures of sports that are currently played by a large number of minorities at the highest level. McDonald (2005) articulates the performance of whiteness, which occurs in sports such as professional basketball. Through the use of enhanced dress codes, the NBA enforces a notion of how a "professional" should present himself. Similarly, when Allen Iverson's tattoos are airbrushed out of a cover photo for NBA's *Hoop* magazine, there is an attempt to reshape the game to make it more marketable for audiences who may not relate to Iverson's cultural background.

While not omitted from the sporting equation entirely, studies have continually found cases of underrepresentation of minority athletes when compared to their relative athletic successes. Longitudinal studies of magazines such as *Sports Illustrated* have found that minority athletes are not only shown less frequently than expected, but that they are also more likely to be shown in ways that are violent, negative, and overtly physical in nature (see Goss, Tyler, & Billings, 2009). Lumpkin and Williams (1991) even found a 30-year gap between the first *SI* cover of an African American female and the second.

Sports on television have exhibited similar underrepresentation and disparities. For instance, college basketball features a majority of players who are black, yet the coverage provides an environment in which they are not only usually orchestrated by a white coach but also are described by white announcers and surrounded by advertisements that only feature black characters 9% of the time (Wonsek, 1992). As King, Leonard, and Kusz (2007) describe, sports media aid the creation of narratives that are intended to present a postracial America, stifling any protest about lingering issues that still persist within race and sport.

The concept of **stacking** enters this equation, although the way it has been unpacked has altered considerably over the years. In a nutshell, stacking relates to the placement of people in roles that closely fit social expectations of identity groups. Some studies have examined stacking from a sense of multiple races playing the same game yet being placed at different positions. For instance, baseball has been found to be racially stacked, with black athletes more likely to play outfield positions, Latino athletes more likely to play in the middle infield, and white athletes more often positioned in corner-infield and catching positions (Margolis & Piliavin, 1999). Other instances of stacking can be viewed as the practice of self-selection mentioned previously in this chapter; athletes of a given race are covertly—and sometimes overtly—told that given sports are or are not for them. Media exposure influences these perceptions by the stacking of newspaper, magazine, television, and even Internet coverage so that white reporters are covering sports played by mostly white participants while black reporters cover sports that are occupied by largely black athletes, and so forth. For instance, when a tennis sportscasting booth is exclusively filled with white sportscasters, a notion that this sport is for white people percolates within our psyches in the same manner that placing a Latino reporter on a soccer newspaper beat relays the subtle message that soccer is not for white people. Sports media become a reflection of sports that are already stacked ethnically, perpetuating differences that are based to a large extent on myth.

MEDIA DIALOGUES

Of course, the language surrounding linguistic choices in sport becomes strained when racial and ethnic difference becomes part of the discussion. Because there is largely a lack of open and honest discussion of perceived racial difference, reliance on embedded stereotypes can seep into media discussions, which then can transfer to everyday conversations about these same issues. Identifying inappropriate comments is relatively easy. When CBS NFL analyst Jimmy "the Greek" Snyder is quoted as saying black athletes are bred to be better because of different bone structures, we know the comment is inappropriate. When Atlanta Braves pitcher John Rocker tells *Sports Illustrated* that riding the 7-train on the New York subway is similar to traveling through Beirut, we rightly understand that backlash will ensue. However, the linguistic choices embedded in dialogic assumptions are much more subtle, asking communication scholars to decipher the difference between stereotypes, biases, and actual demographic trends.

Tiger Woods

A Matter of Ethics: Tiger, Tilghman, and Tough Racial Terrain

Since his arrival on the Professional Golfers Association (PGA) Tour in 1997, Tiger Woods has often been the focal point in conversations about race and ethnicity in sport. In part, this is due to declarations made by his father, Earl, that Woods would become a transformational figure in American society, as well as by an early Nike advertising campaign, one commercial for which that claimed Woods was still prohibited from playing some courses in the United States because of the color of his skin. Despite these early proclamations, Woods himself has mostly deflected any discussion of race, preferring to label himself "Cablinasian" (Caucasian, black, Indian, and Asian; see Nordlinger, 2001). Even when race has explicitly been invoked—such as fellow golfer Fuzzy Zoeller's speculation that Woods might order fried chicken and collard greens (a stereotype of African American cuisine) for the 1998 Masters Champions Dinner—Woods has largely remained silent.

On the one hand, Woods's reluctance to comment about racial issues makes sense. After all, his avoidance of political controversy has contributed to his enormous popularity and widespread marketability. Yet on the other hand, for many engaged in the struggle for racial justice, Woods's silence is regrettable because an athlete of his stature has the ability—not unlike Muhammad Ali or Arthur Ashe in the 1960s and 1970s—to publicize and legitimize important conversations about race in the United States. Thus, even when Woods attempts to avoid making a political statement, his silence itself becomes the subject of political controversy.

This issue resurfaced in early 2008, when Golf Channel anchor Kelly Tilghman suggested that the way young golfers on the PGA Tour could compete with Woods was to "lynch him in a back alley." Although the comment was intended to convey the level of aggressiveness required to compete at the highest level, many reacted strongly to the use of the term *lynch* because it evoked the horrific historical legacy in the United States of African American men being kidnapped and hung to death. Advocates for racial justice condemned the comments and Tilghman apologized, but Woods simply referred to her as a friend and called the comment a "nonissue."

1. In light of continued racial and ethnic discrimination in the United States and the negative connotations of the term *lynch*, how should Woods have reacted?

2. Do you agree with him that Tilghman's comment was a "nonissue"? If not, why not?

3. To what, if any, extent does an athlete of Woods's stature have a responsibility to speak out about politically sensitive issues?

Media outlets often use skin color as a means for classifying race, often indirectly implying that the camera can do the work of telling a full story. In many cases, such as that of Tiger Woods, skin pigment becomes a substitute for more complex ethnic backgrounds. Woods has a lineage that is Caucasian, black, Indian, and Asian, but his skin is black; therefore he is, for all media intents and purposes, black. The classification into larger groups of people dramatically simplifies race, yet communication scholars have found this is not only the case but that media descriptions of athletes diverge based on these essentialist categories of skin color.

One of the most prevalent assumptions in ethnic dialogues is that of the presumed athletic superiority of the black athlete. As renowned sociologist Harry Edwards (1970) notes, so many people bought into this notion that "the White race thus becomes the chief victim of its own myth" (p. 197). Of course, he drew this conclusion decades ago and times certainly have changed. Still, one finding in content analyses of sports media is that there is an increased emphasis on the notion of the innately talented black athlete, the born achiever. In contrast to narratives surrounding other races that overcome great odds to excel through a great deal of hard work and effort, black athletes can sometimes be perceived as succeeding out of a sense of destiny, having a talent at an early age that quickly (and presumably easily) set these athletes apart from their peers. These types of embedded notions are employed to "explain the great number of Black athletes in certain events and sports" (van Sterkenburg & Knoppers, 2004, p. 312). Sailes (1998) offers a history of black athletic stereotypes in sport, ranging from the "dumb jock" to the "brute" or "sambo." Hoberman (2007) references this as the "hardiness doctrine" of sports, which involves the seemingly unrelenting belief that black athletes are "a more primitive human type that is biologically distinct from and physiologically superior to that of civilized man" (p. 213).

In contrast, media dialogues must explain the existence of white athletes who succeed in mainstream sports, and they more often do so through an increased focus on the intellect, leadership, and hard work of a white athlete. Consider Peyton Manning. Consistent narratives exist about him in all of these areas. Without question, he is a tremendous quarterback, but rarely does overt athletic skill become the dominant focus of media discussions. Instead, Manning is discussed as the tactician, the player who is prepping for a game far beyond what others would opt to do. When you put these misguided concepts together, you find an undercurrent of a dialogue in which white athletes succeed through diligence—blood, sweat, and tears—while black athletes have presumably been handed these athletic luxuries by the grace of God.

Black athletes are also expected to play sports in a more aggressive, hypermasculine way. When considering the sports black players are socialized to select, many of the sports naturally lend themselves to power above finesse, strength over composure. Boxing is a classic example in which the hypermasculine black athlete is expected to achieve (see Baker & Boyd, 1997). An interesting storyline in regard to being somehow "true" to the African American ethnicity is in the 1975 epic "Thrilla in Manilla" between Muhammad Ali and Joe Frazier. Ali repeatedly called Frazier an "Uncle Tom" and a "white man's champion," and also labeled him a "gorilla," a primal form of race-baiting. Thus, a classic boxing match between two black men still had racial overtones, pitting Ali's "float like a butterfly, sting like a bee" style against the presumably plodding but powerful Frazier. Decades later, media narratives still hearken back to the days in which Ali and Frazier represented contrasting notions of what being a "true" black champion was supposed to be.

Again in contrast to this aggressive style that is sometimes expected of black athletes, white athletes have been depicted in the media as prototypically heroic. This sometimes occurs because white athletes are more likely to be placed in spotlight leadership roles, such as quarterbacking a football team or starting pitching for a baseball team. However, the notion of what we consider to be heroic is more than just the leader who produces victory. Butterworth (2007) used the 1998 home run chase between white player Mark McGwire and Latino player Sammy Sosa to illustrate the construction of what he termed a "mythological enactment of Whiteness" (p. 228). He notes that heroism in sport has always been connected to a notion of white enactment that rarely allows for other races to be considered prototypical heroes, even when, as was the case for Sosa, he proudly embraced notions of American exceptionalism and patriotism.

Another linguistic characterization that has been found to trend differently based on racial profiles is the notion of deviance. Given the immense white roots of most mainstream sports in America, discourses are often constructed with a sense of history that offers a notion of the "good old days" (which lacked racial diversity) and the current days (which have more racial diversity, coupled with sporting ills such as commercialism, greed, and corruption). The National Basketball Association has felt this tension when black players fail to dress, perform, and talk in the same manners of great past heroes of the game. Media dialogues then reflect that sports are changing largely because of demographic participation changes. ESPN used to have a segment on *SportsCenter* that illustrated this notion perfectly, entitled Old School vs. Nu Skool; a white Skip Bayless debated the "old" way of looking at an issue while a black Stephen A. Smith argued the "nu" way in which we should analyze a current event. Hoberman (2007) notes the ramifications of the increased notion of "street"/urban life that occurs in discourses about sports such as basketball, writing that "the global popularity of the NBA has spread anti-social and dysfunctional images of the African-American athlete around the world" (p. 223).

Such depictions are not meant to excuse cases in which minority athletes are even arrested for crimes, such as Michael Vick's dog fighting crime or Pedro Guerrero's conspiracy to distribute cocaine. Rather, it is important to note the framing of these stories, which is also constructed in a manner of presumed innocence of white athletes and presumed guilt of nonwhite athletes (see Baker & Boyd, 1997). Media have become so aware of this tendency to prejudge minorities that sometimes the presumption of guilt has swung to white defendants as well. The 2006 Duke lacrosse case, in which team members were presumed to be guilty of raping a black exotic dancer, only to be later cleared of all crime and even declared innocent by the North Carolina Attorney General, would be a case in point. The bottom line is that race now tinges discussion of social deviance and crime, altering media discourses in the process.

Dialogues become even more interesting (or, some would argue, convoluted) when race is not as simple to define. For instance, studies have found that attributions for Tiger Woods's successes most closely match that of other white attributions, such as composure and intellect, but that his failures are described in ways more related to black

Chief Osceola

athletic attributions regarding innate skill (see Billings, 2003). Meanwhile, scholars continue to debate whether racial dialogues in the media are getting better (see Byrd & Utsler, 2007) or remain problematic (see Rada & Wulfemeyer, 2005).

Given all of these trends, one could presume that race is largely a black/white binary in America, yet other races are either excluded from discussions at a disproportionate rate or are marginalized and even mocked in other communication portrayals. The clearest example of racial insensitivity conflicting with entrenched postulates about history is the consistently intense debate over offensive team mascots. Many Native Americans, in particular, find some mascot choices quite inflammatory, including the Washington Redskins, the Atlanta Braves' "tomahawk chop" and the Cleveland Indians' cartoonish representation of an American Indian. Some schools have changed nicknames in the wake of increased cultural sensitivity; for instance, the St. Johns University Redmen became the Red Storm in 1995, and the University of Illinois eliminated Chief Illiniwek in 2007. Other teams have resisted such changes, citing close ties and even approval from Native American tribes (such as is the case with the Florida State Seminoles). Others cite branding issues that are too valuable to eliminate in an increasingly commercial sports culture. This subject will be covered at greater length in Chapter 8.

Case Study: What's in a Name?

After a U.S. Commission on Civil Rights declared that American Indian nicknames/mascots were "inappropriate" and "disrespectful," the National Collegiate Athletic Association (NCAA) notified colleges that continued to employ such images that they would no longer be permitted to host NCAA-sponsored tournaments. For events that had already been scheduled, institutions were asked to eliminate images depicting American Indians and remove such images on uniforms during postseason play. This ruling appeared to serve as only a minor appeasement due to the fact that only a handful of colleges and universities had facilities that could host postseason tournaments. It largely excluded Division I football because the NCAA does not manage the bowl game series. The University of Illinois (Fighting Illini), Florida State University (Seminoles), and the University of North Dakota (Fighting Sioux) were three prominent institutions identified as having mascots that were considered to represent hostile representation of American Indians. Shortly after the ruling was announced, the NCAA waived the requirement for

FSU due to the fact that the Seminole Tribe of Florida had officially declared that they did not consider the mascot/nickname to be offensive.

A number of institutions have followed FSU's lead by seeking support from local tribes to validate the use of the nicknames/mascot. Such is the case with the University of North Dakota, which faced considerable backlash from alumni who feel connected to the mascot as a legitimate symbol of the university. They scheduled a vote between the two tribes in the state and claimed that American Indian programs were an essential feature of the campus's mission. However, the primary driver for institutional administration was the high cost associated with covering up images of the Fighting Sioux in their athletic facility. Specifically, former UND hockey player Ralph Engelstad donated more than $100 million to the university to build the sport complex that carries his name. When word of the NCAA ruling emerged, Englestad was influential in pushing a North Dakota Board of Education ruling that the institution's athletic teams must be referred to as the Fighting Sioux. In response, he redesigned the facility currently under construction to prominently display the logo throughout. This includes designs in the bricks on the facility's exterior, incorporated throughout the hardwood, and even embroidered into the leather seating in the hockey area. For UND to be in compliance, the institution would be required to make hundreds of thousands of dollars' worth of restoration to a newly minted facility. To date, the institution has retained its mascot despite growing public backlash in the state and throughout the country.

1. To what degree does the use of mascots/nicknames communicate a lack of understanding that groups might find offensive despite the historical significance they might have for the institution?

2. Should FSU and UND be able to retain their mascot/nicknames even despite gaining support from local American Indian groups?

3. Beyond American Indian mascots/nicknames, what other institutions employ depictions that might communicate a lack of ethnic sensitivity?

In sum, the language that is implemented to describe sport is inevitably shaded by race. This is not all bad as neglecting race as a subject and treating all athletes in a monolithic manner would be to eliminate a sense of narrative, watering down rich stories of heritage and background. Nonetheless, treatment of athletic accomplishments with an equal amount of respect should be the aim of anyone attempting to discuss race and sport in a literate and responsible manner.

CONCLUSION

If there is one lesson to learn from this chapter, it is that there is a responsible way to talk about race and ethnicity in the United States, yet most shy away from doing so because of the ramifications of irresponsible talk. Ignoring differences in participation, media coverage, or language does not ultimately solve the problem. *NBC News* anchor Tom Brokaw once collaborated with author Jon Entine to examine the facts and fictions about black athletes; he felt it was one of the most complicated and difficult processes of his life. In 2000, Entine went on to write a controversial book on the subject: *Taboo: Why Black Athletes Dominate Sports and Why We're Afraid to Talk About It.* He argues that there is a reason why, for instance, Kenyan runners do so well in distance events but not in sprints. The attributions are not about skin color but rather about the combination of science and culture. Some saw this reasoning as an advancement; others saw it still lacking a great deal of nuance. Regardless of where one falls out on these subjects, this chapter, hopefully, provides avenues for conversing about stereotyping vs. bias, self-selection and stacking, and linguistic attribution differences vs. linguistic racism. Understanding the roles of race and ethnicity in sport is vital to gaining a full sense of perspective on issues such as class, sociology, and individual and collective politics. At its core, it helps to explain who plays what sport, why they do so, and to what effect.

REFERENCES

Anderson, T. (2009, Sept. 1). CC Sabathia works to bring more blacks to baseball. Retrieved on April 26, 2010, from http://www.thegrio.com/entertainment/yankee-pitcher-unhappy-with-number-of-blacks-in-mlb-1.php.

Baker, A., & Boyd, T. (1997). *Sports, media, and the politics of identity.* Bloomington: Indiana University Press.

Bass, A. (2002). *Not the triumph but the struggle: The 1968 Olympics and the making of the Black athlete.* Minneapolis: University of Minnesota Press.

Billings, A. C. (2003). Portraying Tiger Woods: Characterizations of a "Black" athlete in a "White" sport. *The Howard Journal of Communications, 14*(1), 29–38.

Buffington, D. (2005). Contesting race on Sundays: Making meaning out of the rise in the number of black quarterbacks. *Sociology of Sport Journal, 21,* 19–37.

Butterworth, M. L. (2007). Race in "the race": Mark McGwire, Sammy Sosa, and heroic constructions of whiteness. *Critical Studies in Media Communication, 24*(3), 228–244.

Byrd, J., & Utsler, M. (2007). Is stereotypical coverage of African-American athletes as "dead as disco"? An analysis of NFL quarterbacks in the pages of *Sports Illustrated. Journal of Sports Media, 2*(1), 1–28.

Carver, R. (1834). *The book of sports.* Boston: Lily, Wait, Colman, & Holden.

Coakley, J. (2009). *Sports in society: Issues and controversies.* New York: McGraw-Hill.

Edwards, H. (1970). *Revolt of the black athlete.* New York: Free Press.

Entine, J. (2000). *Taboo: Why black athletes dominate sports and why we're afraid to talk about it.* New York: Public Affairs.

Fitzgerald, T. (2005, Dec. 16). Philadelphia NAACP head rebuked for McNabb remarks. *Philadelphia Inquirer,* p. 1A.

Ford, B. (2004, Dec. 27). Complex legacy left by White: One of NFL's greatest lineman died yesterday. *The Philadelphia Inquirer*, p. S6.

Goss, B. D., Tyler, A. L., & Billings, A. C. (2009). A content analysis of racial representations of NBA athletes on *Sports Illustrated* magazine covers, 1970–2003. In H. Hundley & A. C. Billings (Eds.), *Examining identity in sports media* (173–194).

Hoberman, J. (2007). Race and athletics in the twenty-first century. In J. A. Hargreaves & P. Vertinsky (Eds.), *Physical culture, power, and the body* (pp. 208–231). London: Routledge.

Hughes, L. (1940). *The big sea: An autobiography.* New York: Knopf.

Jarvie, G. (1991). Sport, racism, and ethnicity. Routledge: New York.

King, C. R., Leonard, D. J., & Kusz, K. K. (2007). White power and sport: An introduction. Journal of Sport & Social Issues, 31, 3–10.

Lumpkin, A., & Williams, L. D. (1991). An analysis of *Sports Illustrated* feature articles, 1954–1987. *Sociology of Sport Journal,* 8, 16–32.

Margolis, B., & Piliavin, J. A. (1999). "Stacking" in Major League Baseball: A multivariate analysis. *Sociology of Sport Journal, 16,* 16–34.

McDonald, M. G. (2005). Mapping whiteness in sport: An introduction. *Sociology of Sport Journal, 22,* 245–255.

Nordlinger, J. (2001, Apr. 30). Tiger time: The wonder of an American hero. *National Review,* p. 8.

Page, C. (2009, July 30). The audacity of hops. On Keith Olbermann's *Countdown* (television).

Rada, J., & Wulfemeyer, K. T. (2005). Color coded: Racial descriptors in television coverage of intercollegiate sports. *Journal of Broadcasting & Electronic Media, 49,* 65–85.

Rhoden, W. C. (2006). *Forty million dollar slaves.* New York: Crown.

Sailes, G. (1998). *African-Americans in sport: Contemporary themes.* New Brunswick, NJ: Transaction.

Sweet, F. W. (2005). *Legal history of the color line: The rise and triumph of the one-drop rule.* Palm Coast, FL: Bakintyme.

van Sterkenburg, J., & Knoppers, A. (2004). Dominant discourses about race/ethnicity and gender in sport practice and performance. *International Review for the Sociology of Sport, 39,* 301–321.

Wonsek, P. L. (1992). College basketball on television: A study of racism in the media. *Media, Culture and Society, 14,* 449–461.

SUGGESTED ADDITIONAL READING

Abdel-Shehid, G. (2007). Welcome to the "sportocracy": Race and sport after innocence. In J. A. Hargreaves & P. Vertinsky (Eds.), *Physical culture, power, and the body.* London: Routledge.

Birrell, S. (1989). Racial relations theories and sport: Suggestions for a more critical analysis. *Sociology of Sport Journal, 6*(3), 212–227.

Carrington, B. (2007). Sport and race. In G. Ritzer (Ed.), *The Blackwell encyclopedia of sociology* (pp. 4686–4690). Oxford: Blackwell.

Davis, L. R., & Harris, O. (1998). Race and ethnicity in U.S. sports media. In L. A. Wenner, *MediaSport* (1st ed., pp. 154–169). New York: Routledge.

King, C. R. (2007). Staging the Winter Olympics, or why sport matters to white power. *Journal of Sport & Social Issues, 31,* 89–94.

Nakayama, T. K., & Martin, J. N. (Eds.). (1999). *Whiteness: The communication of social identity.* Thousand Oaks, CA: Sage.

CHAPTER 7

Politics/Nationality and Sports

As we referenced in Chapter 1, if you have attended a live sporting event in the United States, you have most certainly participated in a ritual that has special resonance in this country. Prior to the beginning of a game or event, officials, players, broadcasters, and fans all stand, face the American flag, and listen to (and sometimes sing along with) the "Star Spangled Banner." The performance of the national anthem serves not only as an expression of national unity but also as an announcement that the action on the field, court, or track is about to begin. Our familiarity with this ritual, in fact, makes it likely that we take it for granted, viewing it simply *as a part of the athletic event itself.*

Is it possible to imagine an American sporting event *without* the anthem? If a *Monday Night Football* game in 2007 is any indication, probably not. Following a severe storm in Pittsburgh that prevented the Dolphins-Steelers game from starting on time, National Football League (NFL) officials decided to cancel the performance of the national anthem so they could avoid any further delay to kickoff. The decision prompted angry responses from fans and organizations like the National Flag Foundation (NFF). A spokesperson for the NFF said, "I think that it's important to sing [the anthem] whenever we have opportunity and certainly as we assemble publicly that certainly is a wonderful opportunity to do that collectively" ("Some Angry," 2007, ¶ 8).

Perhaps you agree that the "Star Spangled Banner" should be sung whenever Americans gather publicly. But *why* do Americans do this and other things like it, and what does it *mean* as a communicative phenomenon within the world of sport? How is it that we've come to expect presidential first pitches and military flyovers at sporting events? And why are so many sports fans uneasy when their favorite athletes talk openly about politics? We open this chapter with these questions to prompt your thinking about the relationship between politics and sport, a relationship that many deny or resist. Ask the average sports fan in the United States if the pre-game performance of the national anthem is *political,* and you're likely to be told that the song is "just patriotic," *not* political. Yet if the anthem is *not* performed, or if someone dares to *challenge* the standards of the ritual, then those acts of transgression are often described as political. During the 2002–03 college basketball season, for example, Manhattanville College player Toni Smith expressed her opposition to U.S. foreign policy by refusing to face the flag during the pregame ceremony. Her actions were seen as especially controversial given that the United States was still reeling from the terrorist attacks of September 11, 2001, and was gearing up for war in Iraq. In this context, public reaction to Smith was overwhelmingly negative, with many claiming that she inappropriately brought politics into a nonpolitical space.

Yet communication and sport scholars would note that politics are present *both* when the anthem is performed *and* when it is challenged. The key is to recognize how and why politics and sport are interrelated and to examine critically the broader significance of sport as a political arena. In the case of the national anthem, its presence is political because it defines a game in terms of nationalism, suggesting that a sporting event is an appropriate place to affirm the principles that bind Americans together as a people. By contrast, its absence, or a protest against its presence, is political because it calls those very principles into question. Politics, then, must be understood in both moments of affirmation and moments of contestation.

The national anthem serves as a specific example of a broader phenomenon. Olympic Games are largely interpreted as competitions between nations. Golf's Ryder Cup and tennis's Davis and Fed Cups are both explicitly designed to highlight national affiliations. More recently, Major League Baseball's (MLB) World Baseball Classic has followed the model of soccer's World Cup, using nationalism as a central theme in advertising and promotion of the event. In spite of these and other examples, many sports fans remain hesitant to acknowledge any presence of politics in sport. They prefer to think of sport as a *diversion,* a place for *escape* from "real-world" issues. On the one hand, this makes sense, for it can indeed be a distraction to go to a game or forget about the world's problems while analyzing fantasy statistics. Yet on the other hand, such a view ignores that sport is a cultural *institution,* one that is inextricably linked with larger economic, political, and social structures. As Wenner (1989) points out, "the symbiotic relationship between politics and sports has yielded both recurring sports themes in politics and recurring political themes in sports" (p. 160). In this chapter, we examine five specific relationships between sport and politics: (a) how sport has been used by elected officials as a political resource; (b) how sport has worked its way into the language of politics, including war; (c) how sport becomes a means of fostering national identity; (d) how sport has dramatized the effects of globalization; and (e) how sport has been used as a site of political resistance. In this chapter, we examine not only how these functions are political but also how they are expressed communicatively.

Before we move forward, it is important that we define what we mean by *politics*. You may have specific images in mind: elected officials, campaign commercials, voting, and so on. Although these certainly are components of politics, it is important to think more broadly. Political theorist Chantal Mouffe (2000) argues that there is an important distinction between the terms **political** and **politics.** The *political*, she maintains, reflects the unavoidable conflicts that are inherent in human relations. *Politics*, meanwhile, encompasses the practices, discourses, and institutions in and through which we seek to address those conflicts and establish order. Politics, therefore, is the means by which we come to terms with conflict and construct collective identities.

Another term that helps us understand the relationship between sport and politics is **ideology.** Ideology can be defined in various ways, but it generally refers to the "system of ideas" of a given class of people (Eagleton, 1991, p. 63). In other words, ideology incorporates the dominant ideas, values, rituals, and history of a group. The more homogeneous a population, the more acceptance there is of a shared ideology. In a populous and diverse country like the United States, there are numerous groups and, thus, numerous ideologies that coexist. Accordingly, many political conflicts are the result of competing ideologies. But not all ideologies operate equally, and it is typically the case that some form of *dominant* ideology exercises greater control. That control might be exercised through formal political institutions such as government, but it also can be found in cultural institutions such as Hollywood cinema or sport. As will become clear below, sport is indeed a prominent institution through which ideology is communicated and politics is engaged and enacted. As we proceed, we want to remind you that our focus in this textbook is on American sport. This does not mean that we believe the relationship between sport and politics is relevant only to a U.S. audience, but this chapter is restricted primarily to an American context.

SPORT AS POLITICAL RESOURCE

In 1971, the American table tennis team unexpectedly received an invitation to visit China and compete against the Chinese team. Since formal relations between the two countries had long been antagonistic, the subsequent trip to China was seen as a positive development for each government. The moment was popularly described as "ping-pong diplomacy," and President Richard Nixon eagerly capitalized on the new spirit of cooperation by using sport as a springboard for his own subsequent visit to the People's Republic. In this way, the U.S. president recognized that sport could be a valuable political resource.

Nixon was, in fact, acutely aware of sport's significance. His CIA codename at one point, after all, was Quarterback. Moreover, he was the president who began the tradition of phoning victorious coaches and players after major championship victories. Decades later, presidents and other elected officials continue to recognize the symbolic importance of sport. For example, it is commonplace for candidates for elected office to attend live sporting events in the effort to build identification with fans. In the years following 9/11, President Bush drew upon his own history in baseball—he had been the managing partner of the Texas Rangers before becoming the governor of Texas—to demonstrate his faith in the national community after the terrorist attacks. Most memorably, he threw out the first pitch during Game 3 of the 2001 World Series in New York, a moment in which many viewed the president favorably.

The use of sport by politicians is risky, however, for fans are quick to interpret such actions either as manipulations of the sporting context or as awkward attempts to invent a likeable persona. As for the former case, President Bush is yet again a suitable example. When the Iraqi national soccer team qualified for the 2004 Summer Olympic Games and later experienced unexpected success, the American president claimed that the team's victories were a direct result of U.S. military actions in the Middle East. As Butterworth (2007) demonstrates, this claim was highly controversial and the majority of the Iraqi players themselves disapproved of Bush's efforts to communicate the triumph of American ideology. Rather than helping to advance American foreign policy, therefore, Bush's use of the Iraqi team instead intensified international criticisms of the president and the U.S. war in Iraq.

Another moment from 2004 shows the awkwardness that can emerge from politicians' efforts to reach the public through sports. President Bush's challenger in the presidential election was Massachusetts Senator John Kerry. When Kerry attended a Boston Red Sox game that summer, he was asked to name his favorite player. Stammering through his answer, the senator replied with a hybrid of superstars David Ortiz and Manny Ramirez: "Manny Ortez." The gaffe was perceived as more than a mere slip of the tongue. Rather, it suggested to many observers that Kerry lacked the necessary authenticity to *communicate* effectively about sports. As you will recall from Chapter 2, sport generates an important sense of *community.* By making such an obvious communicative error, then, Kerry marked himself as an outsider to the community of sport.

Baseball's symbolic importance to the presidency is a product of several rituals, most notable of which is the presidential first pitch. As noted above, President Bush was able to communicate strength and resolve by standing at the center of the diamond in a time of national crisis. In that moment he was calling upon a history dating back to 1910, when William Howard Taft became the first president to toss a ceremonial pitch from the stands of Washington's National Park. Since that time, nearly every president has thrown at least one ceremonial first pitch. Given that baseball has a long history as the national pastime, these presidential appearances are important communicative rituals that reinforce baseball's mythological connection to essential American values (as we discussed in Chapter 4).

These values are often most important at times of crisis, especially when the nation is at war. After the 1941 bombing of Pearl Harbor, MLB Commissioner Kenesaw Mountain Landis wrote to President Franklin D. Roosevelt to ask if the president wanted the league to suspend play during the 1942 season. "I honestly feel," Roosevelt responded, "it would be best for the country to keep baseball going." These words demonstrated the president's belief that playing baseball *communicated* important messages about strength and community. Years later, in the wake of 9/11, President Bush's campaign echoed this theme during the 2004 election. At the Republican National Convention, the party presented a video demonstrating the president's leadership. The most dramatic storyline in the video was the retelling of Bush's first pitch at the World Series in 2001, a gesture that the convention audience was told encouraged Americans to "keep pitching, keep pitching."

President Truman preparing to throw out the first ball at the opening game of the 1951 baseball season, flanked by Washington Senators manager Bucky Harris, Senators president Clark Griffith, and New York Yankees manager Casey Stengel, at Griffith Stadium in Washington

President Obama meets the Pittsburgh Steelers

Presidents also use sport to communicate values when they invite championship teams to visit the White House. Hester (2005) terms these visits "presidential sports encomia," through which presidents "draw attention to examples of athletic achievement that they claim support their visions of national unity and American values" (p. 52). The *encomium* is a classical rhetorical gesture of praise, which points to the fundamentally *communicative* nature of these White House visits. As Hester notes, presidents invite an average of seven sports teams to Washington, D.C., each year, demonstrating the extent to which elected officials recognize sport's symbolic power in American culture.

Case Study: Meeting Mr. President

On average, the President of the United States honors roughly seven championship teams each year with an invitation to visit the White House and celebrate their achievement. This has included high school teams, collegiate athletes, professional franchises, and even Olympic gold medalists, who relish the opportunity to visit with the nation's "number one fan." At the ceremony, the President offers a customary set of remarks about the coach, players, and organization and he is then presented with a #1 jersey from the team's primary representative.

Yet what would happen if a player decided to turn down the invitation by the President? This is actually more common than you would think. For example, after a late-game rally in the fourth quarter of the 2009 Super Bowl, the Pittsburgh Steelers defeated the Arizona Cardinals to win the franchise's sixth Lombardi trophy. An important play during the game occurred at the end of the first half when the Cardinals were within striking distance of the end zone when James Harrison (linebacker for the Steelers) intercepted a pass and returned it for a touchdown as time expired. After taking office, President Barack Obama decided that the Steelers would be the first team he would invite to the White House, and team officials graciously accepted the offer to attend. Arrangements were made and the team was scheduled to attend shortly after President Obama concluded his first 100 days in office.

Shortly after receiving news about the invitation, James Harrison declined to attend. Many questioned why Harrison would refuse to attend the celebration with his teammates. Did he have a political agenda? Was it a political statement against the president's policies? As an African American player, wouldn't he be honored to be the guest of the first African American president? When pushed on the issue, people failed to accept his rationale for declining the offer. He argued that the president wouldn't be interested in meeting him if his team had failed to beat the Cardinals in the closing minutes of the Super Bowl, and he just wasn't interested in making the trip. Losing teams aren't invited, as it would cause serious political repercussions if the American people began to associate losing with the presidency. Upon further review, it became evident that Harrison had also declined to attend a reception hosted by President George W. Bush 3 years earlier after the Steelers had won their fifth Super Bowl. At the time, the media failed to take note, and his record-setting performance during the 2009 Super Bowl had made him stand out this time around.

1. Does the average American make any assumptions about the president based on his affiliation with a sports team?

2. Is it appropriate for an athlete to turn down such an invitation if he or she does have a conflict with the president's political views?

3. In what type of situations would the president be warranted to invite a losing team to the White House?

SPORT AND THE LANGUAGE OF POLITICS AND WAR

Even when sport is not being used overtly by politicians, it is often seen as a metaphor for politics itself. Sport and politics share some obvious features: They involve contests and they usually produce winners and losers. Using sport as a metaphor for politics is problematic, however, as it runs the risk of trivializing serious political issues or short-circuiting substantive debate. Communication scholars, therefore, have focused considerable attention on investigating whether sports metaphors are simply *descriptive* or if they have the capacity to *shape* our understandings of political issues themselves.

At one level, sport is used as description in order to give language added vitality and force. As Segrave (2000) identifies, boxing metaphors have allowed politicians to embody toughness and determination through their language, while baseball metaphors depend on the familiarity of Americans with their national pastime. Meanwhile, media often refer to political campaigns as horse races by emphasizing candidates' positions in the race—"front runner," "long shot," and so forth. Yet with the rise of the NFL as the nation's most popular sport, it is football that has become "the root metaphor of American political discourse" (p. 51).

Football plays a vital role in political language for at least two reasons, Segrave (2000) maintains. First, it is grounded in a set of values that makes teamwork, unity, and respect for authority central to success. The emphasis on "team" is especially important for politicians who seek loyalty and wish to reinforce hierarchy (Bineham, 1991). Second, especially through its mediated production, football cultivates heroic mythologies wherein great men perform great deeds for the benefits of their fellow citizens/fans. These men are great, at least in part, because they are highly specialized at what they do. Thus, the increased specialization found on the football field serves as a metaphor for the technical expertise required of politics and governance.

Left at the level of description, these metaphors provide communicators with colorful figures of speech. Yet communication scholars have noted that metaphors commonly work on a deeper level at which they are capable of shaping how we come to see the world. As Beer and de Landtsheer (2004) contend, "The power of metaphor is the power to understand and impose forms of political order. Metaphors reflect, interpret, and construct politics" (p. 30). Consequently, we should reconsider some of the metaphors noted above to examine how they may construct politics in problematic ways.

Let's begin with the horse race metaphor. The idea that journalists reduce political campaigns to a play-by-play account of who's winning and losing at any given moment has received considerable attention. In a recent study spanning nearly half a century, for example, Benoit, Stein, and Hansen (2005) discovered that the horse race metaphor was *the most common* topic of newspaper coverage of political campaigns. Although it is important to understand where candidates stand in relation to one another during a campaign, the overemphasis on the race comes at the expense of discussions of substantive issues. Thus, when viewers tuned in to the 2008 presidential debates between Barack Obama and John McCain, rather than hearing about policy differences between the two candidates, they were more likely to hear that McCain needed a "game-changing" performance because he was trailing in the polls. In this way, the use of sport as a political metaphor may actually do damage to the political process.

Another concern arises when we revisit the football metaphor. In addition to communicating values of toughness and teamwork, football also is commonly used to describe the military and/or war. Football's emphasis on territorial control, offense and defense, and militaristic language—such as *bombs*, *trenches*, and *blitzes*—has produced an almost seamless relationship between the game and warfare. This metaphor is obvious to anyone familiar with the highlight reels of NFL Films or the pregame narratives that hype big games. Yet if it is familiar to you that war is an apt descriptor for football, you may be surprised to see how often football is used to describe warfare. Therein lies the potential problem.

Especially since the first Persian Gulf War (1991), communication and sport scholars have attended to the use of football language to describe war. Perhaps the most famous reference came from U.S. General Norman Schwarzkopf, who referred to a specific military strategy as an attempt to throw a "Hail Mary pass." Not only does this language choice unwittingly position the strategy as one of desperation—a Hail Mary is an attempt to complete a deep pass for a touchdown as time expires, a play with a very low percentage of success—it also makes the consequences of military action seem no more significant than the outcome of a football play. The idea that sports metaphors trivialize the seriousness of war is one of the strongest criticisms against using this kind of language.

Sports metaphors also risk equating good citizenship with good fanship. If good fans wear their team's colors and root for their favorite players in good times and bad, and despite any questionable decision making, then the language of sport in politics may also position citizens to acquiesce to the decisions of their elected leaders, whether or not these decisions are in the best interests of the people. Writing about the Persian Gulf War, for example, Herbeck (2004) worries that "football metaphors discouraged substantive discussion of alternatives by casting the American public in the subservient role of the fans" (p. 129). Once again, efforts to use sport as a dramatic figure of speech may end up limiting, or even eliminating, the open discussions of policy that are essential to a democratic society.

SPORT AND NATIONAL IDENTITY

One manifestation of politics is the ability to cultivate and maintain a **national identity.** Indeed, because it is often seen as an idealized symbol of a collective identity, sport's relationship to nations and nationalism has attracted the attention of communication and sport scholars. What is a "nation"? Your initial response may be to think in terms of a "country," a place governed by a shared economic and political system with discrete physical borders. In fact, this is the conventional understanding of the "nation-state," a concept that finds its origins in the 17th and 18th centuries. Upon further reflection, however, it may occur to you that the term *nation* is often used to describe alliances of sports fans—for example, "Red Sox Nation" or "NASCAR Nation." Can we understand each use of the word in similar terms? Perhaps, in part because the concept of nationalism is more fluid and dynamic than traditional definitions might allow.

One influential theory of nationalism comes from Anderson (1991), who argues that a nation is a symbolic construct, what he calls an "imagined community." This suggests that national identity is less a product of geography or government and more a product of shared histories, myths, and ideology. You may recall from Chapter 4 that mythology plays a large role in communicating values shared by many Americans. For instance, the idea that the United States is a place where freedom and opportunity are available to an extent that has no precedent in history contributes greatly to the collective identity of its citizenry. In other words, by *imagining* that America fosters a particular kind of *community,* a national identity begins to emerge. Sport is especially important in this process because its shared experience makes it one of the few institutions capable of developing a "collective consciousness" (Rowe, 1999, p. 22).

Allison (2000) argues that "national identity is the most marketable product in sport" (p. 346). A primary reason for this is that when a sporting event has a national appeal, it draws much higher ratings for television. Consequently, when communication scholars examine the relationship between sport and nationalism, they often do so by studying mass media. The Olympic Games provide arguably the most obvious site for researching how television influences our understanding of national identity. As Billings and Eastman (2003) state, "the Olympics represents a mix of nationalism, internationalism, sport, and human drama unmatched by any other event" (p. 569). Their study examined the National Broadcasting Company's (NBC) coverage of the 2002 Winter Olympics in Salt Lake City, Utah. Particularly because the Games followed so soon after 9/11, "NBC created an unabashedly patriotic telecast" (p. 570).

Team USA at 2008 Beijing Summer Olympic opening ceremony

A Matter of Ethics: USA! USA?

Following the September 11, 2001, terrorist attacks, many American sporting events became sites for patriotic ceremonies and celebrations. These collective displays of national unity were mostly greeted with enthusiasm, especially when they occurred within sports unique to the United States. Yet how would such ceremonies be received in an international context?

Such an example emerged during the 2002 Winter Olympic Games, hosted in Salt Lake City, Utah. Both the organization of the Games by the United States Olympic Committee (USOC) and their mediated production by the National Broadcasting Company (NBC) prominently featured storylines and images that emphasized American athletes and symbols. These included frequent references to red, white, and blue, the presentation during the Opening Ceremony of the American flag recovered from the World Trade Center, and introductory comments from President George W. Bush, who appeared in person to "declare open the Games of Salt Lake City."

(Continued)

(Continued)

For some, the 2002 Winter Olympics crossed the line into a clear display of nationalism and jingoism. As one International Olympic Committee (IOC) member said, "This is a show designed to send a message to [9/11 mastermind] Osama bin Laden. President Bush is saying: 'Look at us: you bombed us but you can't stop us going about our normal lives.' But that is not what the Olympic Games are supposed to be about."

1. To what extent is it appropriate for the host nation of an international sporting event to feature nationalistic themes?

2. Why does it matter that the 2002 Games followed only a few months after 9/11?

3. Is there a risk that excessive displays of patriotism might foster negative attitudes and consequences?

4. Is there any way for an international sporting event to avoid altogether these political controversies?

A component of these studies is the use of *framing theory,* an approach to media studies that examines how print and broadcast journalists tell stories so that particular themes or values are featured over others. Delgado (2003) also uses this theory in his study of newspaper coverage of a match between the United States and Iran during the 1998 World Cup finals. Because the two countries had a poor relationship, many sportswriters positioned the match as a symbolic contest over competing ideologies. Even as most players and coaches insisted that they were not interested in (or even aware of) the match's politics, newspaper accounts used political terms to create a dominant frame. Some stories interpreted the match as a diplomatic effort between the U.S. and Iran not unlike the ping-pong diplomacy we discussed at the outset of the chapter. Thus, as Delgado argues, this narrative frame used politics and nationalism as rhetorical strategies to make this sporting event seem important to American sports fans who otherwise largely ignore soccer.

Narrative cinema also is a prominent site for expressing national identity. Movies such as *Seabiscuit* (2003) and *Cinderella Man* (2005) are popular largely because they use historical events to celebrate the core values that comprise American ideology. *Seabiscuit* recalls the story of a thoroughbred racehorse that became a symbol of hope for Americans in the midst of the Great Depression. *Cinderella Man,* meanwhile, is the story of boxer Jim Braddock, who also became a Depression-era symbol of triumph over adversity. In the case of these films, the celebrated values are those of individualism, hard work, and perseverance. The affirmation of contemporary political values was evident in the Disney production *Miracle* (2004), which dramatized the U.S. Olympic men's hockey victory over the heavily favored Soviet Union in 1980. The film is a relatively accurate account of the surprising victory—often called the Miracle on Ice—that was largely understood at the time as a symbolic victory for the United States over the Soviets in the "Cold War." Yet Butterworth (2010) argues that the production is only partially about history and is more symbolically about contemporary political matters. Thus, he concludes that the story of the 1980 hockey team operated as a metaphor for post-9/11 America, where the need to triumph over the "evil" of terrorism replaced the need to triumph over the "evil" of Communism.

Interview: Christine Brennan, *USA Today* Sports Columnist

Q: George Orwell argued that sport is like "war minus the shooting." How true is this statement in international sporting competitions?

A: Pretty true, but I say that with a smile—most of the time. In 1994, Sweden won the Olympic gold medal in men's ice hockey. I was in the press center and we would hear this roar from the offices of Swedish newspapers and news organizations when Sweden would score a goal. For smaller countries that don't win that often, that is one of the great charms of the Olympics.

For me, it was the 1980 Miracle on Ice hockey game. That's the metaphor—war minus the shooting—in this case, Mike Eruzione scoring the winning goal. All of our nation's problems melted away for a few hours and we celebrated as a country. Years later, I was discussing the game with a Russian figure skating coach and she didn't know what I was talking about. The loss didn't resonate for them the same way the win did with us. It's about context.

Q: If assessing nationalism within sports media, to what degree is it still "us versus them"?

A: Certainly in print and on air, the U.S. press never uses *us* or *we*. For me, it may slip in casual conversation, but anything for the record—never. Many other nations don't make the distinction, but the U.S. is so big and wins so many medals, plus, most important, our press is not run by our government, so we avoid it. I understand why South Africa or Nigeria would use *us* or *we*.

(Continued)

(Continued)

The other big point is that major rivalries no longer exist since the fall of the Soviet Union and, to a lesser extent, East Germany. We're glad it's gone; nobody's lamenting the loss of the Soviet Union. Still, we all love the concept of "your team versus the hated enemy." You live for that. China wants to be a player but will never mean to the U.S. what the Soviet Union did. No U.S. citizen can muster the immense dislike and even hatred toward China that we had then.

Q: What role does politics play in events such as the World Cup and the Olympics?

A: I'm amused when people or commentators say there is no place for politics in sports. It's never *just* about sports in international competition. Flags and anthems make it special. Watching such events even helps children learn about geography and other global issues. At the Ryder Cup in 1999, there is a prickly memory because the American golfers celebrated too early before a match was over, but no war started, obviously. If the big battle is who jumped around on the 17th green in Brookline, we're OK.

Q: For women, what impact does an athlete's citizenship have on the opportunities she has within sport?

A: It's about creating role models. For me growing up, I had my own personal Title IX—my father and mother—but for many others, it was about watching your countrywomen and cheering for them. President Obama recently said, "My girls look at the TV when I'm watching *SportsCenter* and they see women staring back. That shows them that they can be champions, too." I can imagine this is even truer for women from other countries.

Q: Thomas Friedman argues that "the world is flat." How true is this in sports?

A: It's true, but with way more advantages than disadvantages. There will be growing pains. We've seen that in the LPGA as they took a lot of criticism for how they were insisting their international players speak English. It was handled poorly, but you need a common language. You can't just go on hand signals; communication is essential.

You also run into this at the U.S. college level, where many international athletes are now taking scholarships at NCAA institutions that could have gone to American student-athletes. Still, the university is a place to come and learn and this is another moment for that. I can see the concern, but are we opening up our world to others or are we not? So, it's not just the world that is flattening, it's also the field of play.

There is a fine line between fostering national unity and cultivating an attitude that either stereotypes or denigrates other identities. Too often, sports narratives overemphasize the "us versus them" storyline to the point of influencing political attitudes (Jhally, 1989). Once again, reactions to 9/11 in the United States provide a useful example for communication scholars. When sports leagues returned to action after the terrorist attacks, they each used their games as a means to show resolve, patriotism, and unity. Brown (2004) notes that "sport can be seen as providing solemn opportunities to mourn the dead, patriotic messages to inspire, salutes to honor the life-saving efforts of all involved, messages to re-enforce unity amongst Americans and remind everyone that life must go on" (p. 41). Yet he also points out that the emphasis on military imagery brought risks of positively associating sport with war. Butterworth (2005) extends this theme by arguing that patriotic ceremonies at baseball games quickly moved from rituals of healing to expressions of militarism and an endorsement of war. The transition was perhaps best illustrated by the inclusion of "God Bless America" as a mandatory performance during the 7th-inning stretch of all baseball games. The song not only guaranteed a nationalistic element would be present at games, but because it was commonly performed by members of the United States Armed Forces, it also conflated national unity with the military. As a result, Butterworth maintains that sport communicated a hostile and belligerent attitude at a time when the United States was engaged in controversial military actions in the Middle East. In each case, these scholars emphasize that sport, far from being a distraction from matters of politics, served the political function of affirming national identity at a time of crisis.

SPORT AND GLOBALIZATION

Because nationalism is frequently on display during international sporting events such as the Olympics, the World Cup, or a Grand Slam tennis tournament, it is also important to think about politics and national identity in the context of **globalization**. Maguire (2006) concludes that globalization can be understood as "the growing network of interdependencies—political, economic, cultural, and social—that bind human beings together, for better and for worse" (p. 436). Although globalization is not a new phenomenon, it has intensified in recent decades. Among the consequences of this development is that individuals are exposed to multiple forms of media, politics, and economics, thus calling their "national identity" into question. Miller, Lawrence, McKay, and Rowe (2001) note that, because of globalization, "what constitutes a national game or a contest between representatives of local, regional, and national identities is subject to constant reformulation" (p. 11).

Representative World Cup soccer ball

One of the central debates regarding globalization has to do with the extent of American influence around the world. Perhaps you are familiar with Barber's (1995) *Jihad vs. McWorld,* in which he describes the global influence of American corporations such as McDonald's or MTV. Critics of such influences are likely to worry that the United States is engaged in a project of "cultural imperialism" wherein the integrity of national identity is threatened by the penetration of U.S. popular culture and ideology into native cultures. The presence of a LeBron James jersey in Spain may sound like good marketing to the National Basketball Association (NBA), but to some Spanish citizens, it could feel invasive.

For an example of how Americans react to the "intrusion" of an unpopular domestic sport, consider the outpouring of criticism against soccer each time it appears the sport may gain exposure in the United States. Perhaps the most dramatic example of this was the attention given to British superstar David Beckham's arrival in the United States to play for Major League Soccer (MLS). Much of the American sporting public felt it was much ado about nothing, while many international fans mocked Beckham's choice to play in a lesser league. Meanwhile, many fans and players have grown resentful of the NFL playing regular-season games in England or MLB playing regular-season games in Japan because these decisions appear to destabilize these sports' central place in the nation. The point here is that globalization does not operate in only one direction. Indeed, the United States *feels* its effects as much as it *produces* them.

Regardless of direction, globalization is seen by some as a threat to national identity. The increase of Japanese ownership of American businesses in the 1980s and 1990s produced cultural anxieties about a perceived loss of identity. When this trend affected ownership of baseball's Seattle Mariners, those anxieties were expressed through a fear that America's pastime was under siege from foreign interests (Ono, 1997). Similarly, British football (soccer) fans were upset when American millionaire Malcolm Glazer purchased the storied Manchester United franchise. Such moments are reminders that our imagined communities place great emphasis on their sports teams as symbols of their identities.

Part of the outcry in these incidents is surely the concerns about commercialization (for more on this, see Chapter 13). Globalization facilitates the exchange of capital and, because sport is a valuable commodity, leagues and players alike seek new opportunities across increasingly fluid geographical, economic, and political borders. An exemplary case of this occurred in 2002, when the New York Yankees reached an agreement with Manchester United to cross-market their franchises. As Miller (2004) explains, "The Yankees are world-renowned but world-unwatched, and Manchester United is no doubt covetous of opening up the wealthiest and most protected market in the world—sport in the United States" (p. 244). Although the agreement ultimately produced little of note, it is indicative of the cross-promotion and synergy strategies that characterize contemporary capitalism.

More than ever, sport is a truly international affair. Nearly 30% of MLB rosters are made up of players born outside the United States. The NBA is wildly popular around the world. ESPN and Fox Sports televise European football (soccer). The biggest stars in tennis come from nearly every corner of the world. Meanwhile, 1.5 billion watch the World Cup finals every four years, and the Olympics remain the "biggest show on television" (Billings, 2008). All of which makes the ideas of "nation" and "nationalism" particularly interesting phenomena for communication and sport scholars. Perhaps most important is to keep in mind that the relationship between sport and globalization reveals important dimensions of international cooperation. As Jarvie (2003) suggests, "the choice between global and local sport" is a false one (p. 549). Instead, contemporary sport is the scene of a developing sense of *internationalism* and *cosmopolitanism*.

SPORT AND RESISTANCE

Even in a democracy, politics entails power. Power may be defined in various ways, but our most common understanding assumes that individuals possess power with which they make decisions about access, opportunity, and resources. Because not everyone will have equal access to power, there will be those who are placed in the margins or even excluded from mainstream society. Consequently, the opposing side to power is **resistance.** More specifically, resistance can be understood in dynamic tension with power, for the ability to resist is itself a form of power (Tomlinson, 1998). Resistance can take many forms, some of which we examine in Chapter 8. In this chapter, we address the ways in which athletes have used sport as a means for resisting governments and/or formal political policies. In particular, we look to exemplars of participation in social movements, through which we can better understand the communicative role of sport in the resistance to power and dominant ideology.

Roberto Clemente, Babe Ruth, and Jackie Robinson stamps

Because sport is public and popular, it can become a site for productive political struggle and social change. For example, consider the legacy of Jackie Robinson, who, in 1947, became the first African American to play major league baseball in the modern era. Robinson's presence on the Brooklyn Dodgers—one of MLB's signature franchises—embodied a form of resistance to the social and cultural inequities of the era. Remember that this moment occurred nearly a decade before the advent of the Civil Rights movement. Given baseball's cultural significance at the time, it is difficult to overestimate the impact Robinson had on affecting American attitudes about race. Thus, sportswriter Bob Ryan (2002) calls the moment "the single most important social happening in American sports history" (¶ 5).

As the Civil Rights movement developed in the 1950s and 1960s, Muhammad Ali (formerly Cassius Clay) used his boxing celebrity as a platform to resist racism and war. When he refused to submit to the draft and serve in Vietnam in 1967, he was stripped of his heavyweight boxing title and banned from the sport for 3 years. A converted Muslim, Ali insisted that war was a violation of his religion, stating, "It is in my consciousness as a Muslim . . . and my own personal convictions that I take my stand in rejecting the call to be inducted in the armed services." Ali had already earned a great many detractors who felt his bravado and showmanship were disrespectful. Yet it was his defiance against the United States military that provoked the greatest controversy. However, there was a shared purpose to his fighting both inside and outside of boxing: Ali used violence inside the ring to promote peace and justice outside of it.

Other athletes of the time embraced similar convictions. Arthur Ashe critiqued the apartheid government of South Africa, while his fellow tennis star Billie Jean King fought for women's equality. Yet perhaps the signature image of protest came from two Americans at the 1968 Olympic Games in Mexico City. After winning the gold and bronze medals in the 200m sprint, Tommie Smith and John Carlos used the medal ceremony to protest racial inequalities within the United States. As the national anthem played, the two men bowed their heads and raised fists clad in black gloves. The protest was largely interpreted as a sign of "Black Power," and it resulted in both sprinters' dismissal from the Olympics. Nevertheless, it was fundamentally a *communicative* gesture, one that "created a moment of resistance and confrontation with dominant and existing forms of racial identity" (Bass, 2002, p. 239). As Hartmann (2003) details, despite the negative impression the protest made on many Americans at the time, people who see the image now typically associate positive values with it. In other words, it was a moment of resistance that has retained significant communicative power, even as social and political conditions have changed over the decades.

The 1960s and 1970s are often remembered as especially turbulent years in American history. During that time, sport was a site for challenging some of the political injustices that had too often been left unexamined. As a result, athletes such as Ali and King were able to use sport as a platform to advocate and advance social movements such as the civil rights movement or second-wave feminism. In the years since, however, fewer athletes have used sport as an outlet for political resistance. The explanation for this, at least in part, likely has something to do with the explosion of electronic sports media and the incredible rise in player income. In the words of sportswriter Robert Lipsyte (2002), "Forget about expressing yourself politically or socially; just wear the shoes; take the money and run" (p. 28). Yet even if it is rare to see athletes resist the status quo, there are those who feel compelled to express themselves politically. Steve Nash of the NBA responded to the American invasion in Iraq in 2003 by wearing a "No War" t-shirt. Carlos Delgado of MLB refused to participate in the orchestrated "God Bless America" ritual in 2004. In 2009, Andy Roddick withdrew from a prominent tennis tournament in the United Arab Emirates because officials refused to allow Israeli player Shahar Peer to enter the women's competition. Although these moments may lack the dramatic effect of Ali's defiance or the visual impact of Smith and Carlos's protest, they nevertheless serve as reminders that, like people in all walks of life, athletes do have the capacity and, at times, opportunity to challenge political power.

Meanwhile, sport organizations may also begin to play a greater role in political resistance. For example, in 2010 the state of Arizona passed new legislation to curtail illegal immigration. Many argued that the law's language encouraged police to profile Latinos and, as a result, was racist. In response to the controversy, Phoenix Suns owner Robert Sarver had his team suit up for a Cinco de Mayo playoff game in jerseys stitched with "Los Suns." Sarver acknowledged his decision was not only to honor the holiday but also as a protest against "a flawed state law." The "Los Suns" jerseys provoked considerable discussion in the community of sport, making it a significant communicative moment for both those in support of and those opposed to the decision. Moreover, the decision overlapped with efforts from national lawmakers to pressure Major League Baseball Commissioner Bud Selig to move the site of the 2011 All-Star Game from Phoenix. In spite of Selig's reluctance, several major league players and managers expressed support for the move, and Adrian Gonzalez, then playing for the San Diego Padres, even declared he would boycott the 2011 game if elected to play. While these efforts may or may not become models for other franchises and players to follow, it is nevertheless a compelling moment that makes real the relationship between politics and sport so often believed not to exist.

CONCLUSION

In this chapter, we have reviewed some of the major contributions of communication scholars interested in sport and politics. The symbolic use of sport by politicians, the interplay of sporting and political language, the cultivation of sporting nationalisms, the relationship between sport and globalization, and the necessity for resistance within sport are key features of this relationship. Despite the common claims that sport and politics should be separate, it should be clear that this is impossible. To return to our example of the national anthem, each performance of the "Star Spangled Banner" is a reminder that politics were necessary to make the song possible in the first place and they will be necessary to determine the song's continued significance. Thus, if indeed politics are about managing conflict and constituting identities, the question isn't about whether or not sport *is* political, it is about *how* sport is political. In the words of sportswriter Dave Zirin, "However you slice and dice it, politics are an enduring, constant, and historic presence in sports" (King, 2008, p. 335).

REFERENCES

Allison, L. (2000). Sport and nationalism. In J. Coakley & E. Dunning (Eds.), *Handbook of sports studies* (pp. 344–355). London: Sage.

Anderson, B. (1991). *Imagined communities: Reflections on the origin and spread of nationalism* (rev. ed.). London: Verso.

Barber, B. (1995). *Jihad vs. McWorld: How the planet is both falling apart and coming together and what this means for democracy.* New York: Crown.

Bass, A. (2002). *Not the triumph but the struggle: The 1968 Olympics and the making of the black athlete.* Minneapolis: University of Minnesota Press.

Beer, F. A., & de Landtsheer, C. (2004). Introduction: Metaphors, politics, and world politics. In F. A. Beer & C. de Landtsheer (Eds.), *Metaphorical world politics* (pp. 5–52). East Lansing: Michigan State University Press.

Benoit, W. L., Stein, K. A., & Hansen, G. J. (2005). *New York Times* coverage of presidential campaigns. *Journalism & Mass Communication Quarterly, 82,* 356–376.

Billings, A. C. (2008). *Olympic media: Inside the biggest show on television.* London: Routledge.

Billings, A. C., & Eastman, S. T. (2003). Framing identities: Gender, ethnic, and national parity in network announcing of the 2002 Winter Olympics. *Journal of Communication, 53,* 569–586.

Bineham, J. L. (1991). Some ethical implications of team sports metaphors in politics. *Communication Reports, 4,* 35–42.

Brown, R. S. (2004). Sport and healing America. *Society, 42,* 37–41.

Butterworth, M. L. (2005). Ritual in the "church of baseball": Suppressing the discourse of democracy after 9/11. *Communication and Critical/Cultural Studies, 2,* 107–129.

Butterworth, M. L. (2007). The politics of the pitch: Claiming and contesting democracy through the Iraqi national soccer team. *Communication and Critical/Cultural Studies, 4,* 184–203.

Butterworth, M. L. (2010). Do you believe in nationalism? American patriotism in *Miracle."* In H. Hundley & A. C. Billings (Eds.), *Examining identity in sports media.* Thousand Oaks, CA: Sage.

Delgado, F. (2003). The fusing of sport and politics: Media constructions of U.S. versus Iran at France '98. *Journal of Sport & Social Issues, 27,* 293–307.

Eagleton, T. (1991). *Ideology: An introduction.* London: Verso.

Hartmann, D. (2003). *Race, culture, and the revolt of the black athlete: 1968 Olympic protests and their aftermath.* Chicago: University of Chicago Press.

Herbeck, D. A. (2004). Sports metaphors and public policy: The football theme in Desert Storm discourse. In F. A. Beer & C. de Landtsheer (Eds.), *Metaphorical world politics* (pp. 121–139). East Lansing: Michigan State University Press.

Hester, M. (2005). *America's #1 fan: A rhetorical analysis of presidential sports encomia and the symbolic power of sports in the articulation of civil religion in the United States.* Unpublished doctoral dissertation. Georgia State University.

Jarvie, G. (2003). Internationalism and sport in the making of nations. *Identities: Global Studies in Culture and Power, 10,* 537–551.

Jhally, S. (1989). Cultural studies and the sports/media complex. In L. A. Wenner (Ed.), *Media, sports, & society* (pp. 70–93). Newbury Park, CA: Sage.

King, C. R. (2008). Toward a radical sport journalism: An interview with Dave Zirin. *Journal of Sport & Social Issues, 32,* 333–344.

Lipsyte, R. (2002). Prophets. In J. Lovinger (Ed.), *The gospel according to ESPN: Saints, saviors & sinners* (pp. 9–58). New York: Hyperion.

Maguire, J. (2006). Sport and globalization: Key issues, phases, and trends. In A. A. Raney & J. Bryant (Eds.), *Handbook of sports and media* (pp. 435–446). Mahwah, NJ: Lawrence Erlbaum.

Miller, T. (2004). Manchester, USA? In D. L. Andrews (Ed.), *Manchester United: A thematic study* (pp. 241–248). London: Routledge.

Miller, T., Lawrence, G., McKay, J., & Rowe, D. (2001). *Globalization and sport: Playing the world.* London: Sage.

Mouffe, C. (2000). *The democratic paradox.* London: Verso.

Ono, K. A. (1997). "America's" apple pie: Baseball, Japan-bashing, and the sexual threat of miscegenation. In A. Baker & T. Boyd (Eds.), *Out of bounds: Sports, media and the politics of identity* (pp. 81–101). Bloomington: Indiana University Press.

Rowe, D. (1999). *Sport, culture, and the media: The unruly trinity.* Buckingham, UK: Open University Press.

Ryan, B. (2002, October 24). Memory serves us better. *Boston Globe*, E5. Retrieved September 2007, from http://web.lexis-nexis.com/universe.

Segrave, J. O. (2000). The sports metaphor in American cultural discourse. *Culture, Sport, Society, 3,* 48–60.

Some angry after officials skipped national anthem (2007, November 27). *KDKA .com.* Retrieved May 20, 2010, from http://kdka.com/topstories/National .Anthem.Football.2.597313.html.

Tomlinson, A. (1998). Power: Domination, negotiation, and resistance in sports cultures. *Journal of Sport & Social Issues, 22,* 235–240.

Wenner, L. A. (1989). The Super Bowl pregame show: Cultural fantasies and political subtext. In L. A. Wenner (Ed.), *Media, sports, & society* (pp. 157–179). Newbury Park, CA: Sage.

SUGGESTED ADDITIONAL READING

Allison, L. (Ed.). (1986). *The politics of sport.* Manchester, UK: Manchester University Press.

Hogan, J. (2003). Staging the nation: Gendered and ethnicized discourses of national identity in Olympic opening ceremonies. *Journal of Sport & Social Issues, 27,* 100–123.

Jansen, S. C., & Sabo, D. (1994). The sport/war metaphor: Hegemonic masculinity, the Persian Gulf War, and the new world order. *Sociology of Sport Journal, 11,* 1–17.

Jarvie, G. (1993). Sport, nationalism, and cultural identity. In L. Allison (Ed.), *The changing politics of sport* (pp. 58–83). Manchester, UK: Manchester University Press.

Riggs, K. E., Eastman, S. T., & Golobic, T. S. (1993). Manufactured conflict in the 1992 Olympics: The discourse of television and politics. *Critical Studies in Mass Communication, 10,* 253–272.

Silk, M. L., Andrews, D. L., & Cole, C. L. (Eds.). (2005). *Sport and corporate nationalisms.* Oxford, UK: Berg.

CHAPTER **8**

Performing
Identity in Sports

W hen we look at athletes, what do we see? Do we see strength and
power? Grit and determination? Or perhaps we see the markers
of identity—the skin color that we associate with race, or the
hair length that signals gender? Although much public and media commentary celebrates the athleticism of sports figures, it is often done without a
conscious awareness of the foundation of that athleticism. In other words,
when we look at athletes, we see **bodies.** These are bodies sculpted and
molded for highly specialized activities, and the fact that they are used in the
pursuit of victory means that we inordinately value the bodies of athletes. As
Houck (2006b) notes, "What sorts of public and commodified bodies showcase health, success, physical desirability, and relational bliss? Almost without exception they are athletic bodies—toned, fit, in control, and active"
(p. 545). Thus, as a culture, we take a great interest in how bodies **perform**
and what those performances *communicate.*

Our idea of performance probably means something different than what
you have in mind. When you think of athletic performance, you likely are
evaluating whether an athlete is successful. In communication scholarship,
however, performance takes on additional levels of meaning. The visual
attention given to bodies, athletic or otherwise, generally operates at the
level of *representation.* Thus, our attention to gender (Chapter 5) or race
and ethnicity (Chapter 6) in this textbook focuses mostly on how athletes are
represented in and by the media. This approach is valuable, yet it does not
account fully for the *presentation of self* that comes through bodily performances. Fenske (2007), who draws from the foundational work of theorist

Judith Butler, suggests that focusing *only* on representation limits the ability of individual people, including athletes, to shape their own identities in accordance with their values and self-concepts.

With this in mind, we turn our attention in this chapter to the performances of identity that occur in and through sport. More specifically, we concentrate on the relationship between sport and the body, which we interpret as a "site of cultural inscription, self-regulation, and resistance" (Patterson & Corning, 1997, p. 7). This demands that we think of athletic performances as having an influence over interpretations of identity categories such as gender or race. Thus, to some extent, this chapter revisits some of the themes discussed elsewhere in this book. However, our focus here is on *performance* rather than *representation,* which allows us to examine additional dimensions of identity. These performative dimensions are significant because they communicate the willingness to either accept or resist the norms and dominant expectations of bodies in our culture. We proceed, then, with discussions of the (a) performance of gender and sexuality; (b) performance of race and ethnicity; and (c) performance of disability.

PERFORMANCE OF GENDER AND SEXUALITY

In the summer of 2009, a little-known South African sprinter won the women's 800-meter event at the track and field world championships. Caster Semenya not only won, she destroyed the field by nearly 2.5 seconds—an enormous margin in elite track competition. Almost as soon as she crossed the finish line, she was confronted by accusations that she was not really a woman. To be sure, her physique resembles characteristics typically understood as "masculine"—thick muscles, a deep voice, and so forth. Moreover, Semenya *performs* masculinity by eschewing conventional displays of femininity—she wears baggy clothing, avoids makeup, and so on. In the midst of growing controversy about her "sex," the International Association of Athletics Federations (IAAF) ordered a "gender test" in order to determine Semenya's eligibility for women's events. In response, media outlets fueled rampant speculation about the test's results, and one tabloid went so far as to discern that an anagram of "Caster Semenya" is "Yes, a secret man." Meanwhile, Semenya herself replied with an appearance on the cover of a South African magazine called *You.* The photo, accompanied by the headline, "Wow, Look at Caster Now," presented her in full makeup and a dress. The message was clear: In order for Semenya to be accepted as a woman, she needed to *perform* like one.

The Caster Semenya case recalls the controversy precipitated by the appearance in 1976 of Renee Richards, a male-to-female transsexual who participated in a professional tennis tournament. Once discovered, Richards indicated her desire to participate in the U.S. Open (one of tennis's four major tournaments). In response, the United States Tennis Association and the Women's Tennis Association (WTA) mandated she take a sex test, which she refused. A 1977 Supreme Court ruling subsequently allowed Richards to play on the WTA tour, which included her participation in the 1977 U.S. Open. Richards lost in the first round, but she continued to play on the tour until 1981. Although she had relatively little success on the court, she provoked significant anxiety in the tennis community, primarily because her performance of gender disrupted cultural expectations about how we communicate what it means to be a man or woman. More specifically, she threatened to cast doubt on the conventional wisdom that insists there are "two apparently natural, mutually exclusive, 'opposite' sexes" (Birrell & Cole, 1990, p. 2).

Semenya and Richards reveal a great deal about how we understand sex and gender, especially as they relate to sport. As you'll recall from Chapter 5, **sex** is most commonly understood as the biological difference between men and women. **Gender,** meanwhile, is a social category, one that emerges and develops in a given culture. Wood (2009) adds that gender "is defined by society and expressed by individuals as they interact with others and media in their society. Further, gender changes over time" (p. 23). As is evident by the IAAF's use of a "gender test" when attempting to determine Semenya's biological attributes—that is, her sex—there is much confusion about how these terms relate to one another. Moreover, because gendered norms change over time, there is additional confusion over what constitutes being a "man" or "woman." This is why Semenya's choice to perform her gender by defaulting to conventional markers of femininity—dresses and makeup—is so revealing. It also is why the physical transformation of Richards from a man to a woman complicates the natural assumptions that one is *either* a man *or* a woman. Thus, these instances remind us that sport is a particularly important site for examining how gender identity is performed and what implications those performances may have on our culture at large.

The idea of gender performance—or, more accurately, performativity—derives from the work of Judith Butler. Butler (1999) contends that gender is not something we *are,* it is something we *do.* In addition, for our actions to be understood as performative, they must be repeated so that they become naturalized. In American culture, for example, women commonly greet one another with a hug using both arms. Men, meanwhile, often opt for a half-hug and slap on the back that serves as an extension of a handshake. It is safe to conclude, then, that if two (heterosexual) men in the United States were to greet each other with a full embrace, they would immediately be seen as performing (if only temporarily) a feminine identity. Thus, the norms of gender are highly regulated by social expectations. In part, those expectations emerge from the institutions of popular culture, including sport. Because sport features such ritualized performances of gender, it is arguably "the most important public arena for the performance of gender as an asymmetrical, oppositional relation based on natural sex differences" (Disch & Kane, 2000, p. 126).

Interview: Marie Hardin, Associate Director for Research, John Curley Center for Sports Journalism, Pennsylvania State University

Q: In what ways do athletes perform their identity roles?

A: Athletes perform roles in regard to gender and sexuality on and off the field. It's easier to point out the ways women do so because their ideal roles require performances at odds with our understanding of sports. Thus, images of female athletes are often marked by *contrast*. For instance, a professional softball player may make a point to wear makeup or a ribbon in her ponytail when she takes the mound; off the field, she may seek an identity tied to fashion or to modeling. We've seen a number of high-profile women do this, from basketball player Lisa Leslie to tennis star Serena Williams. For men, the roles are more about *conformity* to the ideals of sport, which fit idealized masculine identity. Thus, role performance is embedded in the act of sport itself for men—a proposition less charged with *role negotiation* than it is for women.

Q: Can you think of examples where athletes challenged traditional identity assumptions on the field of play?

A: Anytime a female athlete engages in a sport that requires overt displays of strength or speed, she's challenging traditional identity assumptions for women. Think of women boxing, wrestling, weightlifting, or playing rugby. When men engage in sports with a heavy aesthetic, or "pretty" component (say, figure skating or diving), they're defying expectations of men. Generally speaking, we're very uncomfortable with these performances.

Q: "Mandatory heterosexuality" has been argued as the expectation for those who participate in sport. To what degree is this still true?

A: I wish I could suggest differently, but it is still true to an overwhelming degree. The performance of heterosexuality is so important to sport that few athletes dare defy that expectation—witness the number of active professional male athletes in team sports who have identified as gay in the U.S.: zero. I believe the straitjacket is a little looser on female athletes, as we have seen some high-profile female athletes, including Sheryl Swoopes and Amelie Mauresmo, come out in recent years. But the stakes in making such a disclosure are lower for female athletes out of the gate because of the simple fact that they are already considered "suspect" by being active in men's domain (sports).

Q: What potential impact does athletic performance of identity have on societal conceptions of these same issues?

A: It's tremendous. We idealize sport in U.S. culture as teaching work ethic, obedience to authority, perseverance, and character. What it teaches more than anything else is the boundaries of gender: What's ideal, what's acceptable, and what's out of bounds. The "role modeling" athletes do for children and adolescents is in their performance of gender and sexuality. It's so taken-for-granted that it's generally not considered when we debate the ways (for better or worse) athletes influence children's aspirations.

Q: Are sports becoming more inclusive or exclusive in regard to acceptance of athletes who don't fit into traditional power structures?

A: It depends. The Internet and other communication technologies have narrowed the isolation gap for athletes who don't fit the "norm," and that's a good thing. It's easier for communities of participants to develop spaces for all athletes. But high-level spectator sports are another situation altogether. Sports are a pyramid: You have participatory sports, with no potential for spectatorship (in the mediated sense), at the bottom. The greatest room for movement and acceptance is here. As you move up the pyramid, you may be amassing power, but there's considerably less freedom. The top remains a very exclusive—and constraining—place.

There is considerable support for the idea that sport reinforces a male/female, masculine/feminine essentialism. Accordingly, it is in the moments when gender norms are disrupted or challenged that we often find them reinforced most vigorously. Sloop (2005), for example, evaluates the performative dimensions of Deborah Renshaw's presence in auto racing. In 2002, Renshaw was a rising star in the lower division of NASCAR, someone viewed as both a skilled driver inside the car and a marketable personality outside of it. On the one hand, her participation as a professional driver helped redraw the boundaries of what is considered to be properly feminine. However, racing promoters and Renshaw herself were careful to emphasize her attractive appearance and conventional feminine performances when she was not behind the wheel (not unlike the far more famous Danica Patrick). Even more significantly, when she was involved in a crash that led to the death of another driver, many within the racing community argued that Renshaw should never have been allowed on the circuit in the first place. Her intrusion, then, was met with a vigorous "preservation of male space" that sought to re-establish auto racing as a uniquely masculine domain (Sloop, 2005, p. 206).

A similar reaction followed Katie Hnida when she joined the University of Colorado football team as a walk-on placekicker in 1999. Butterworth (2008) notes that Hnida's presence on the team constituted an embodied argument that potentially blurred the lines between masculinity and femininity. Like Renshaw, Hnida was largely viewed as conventionally attractive and feminine away from her sport but as an unnatural intruder within it. Hnida's case made national headlines when it became the focal point in a series of accusations that the football program at Colorado fostered a culture of violence and discrimination toward women. Although Hnida became an eloquent spokesperson on behalf of gender equity, her disruption of acceptable gendered performance led to a substantial amount of hostility that caused her to leave the university. Thus, even though Hnida "provided a model by which we may reconsider what it means to have 'male' or 'female' bodies" (Butterworth, 2008, p. 270), her resistance came with considerable risk to her own well-being.

What is true for women challenging gender norms in sport may be doubly true for gay and lesbian athletes. There are remarkably few openly gay athletes in the United States. Perhaps the most high-profile athlete to come out while still playing is the WNBA's Sheryl Swoopes, who revealed her sexuality in 2005. Meanwhile, no male athlete within mainstream American team sport has ever come out while actively playing. Because gendered expectations are so rigorously reinforced, gay and lesbian athletes most often "pass" as straight in order to avoid being ostracized by their teammates. Former baseball player Billy Bean (Bean & Bull, 2003), for example, writes about the difficulties he faced while hiding his identity within a culture that so openly derided homosexuals. Bean understood that in order to preserve a roster spot in Major League Baseball, he needed to *perform* an acceptable form of masculinity. Similarly, former basketball player John Amaechi (2007) describes the years during which he concealed his identity as a gay man for fear that he would be denied the opportunity to play in the National Basketball Association (NBA). Even in cases where athletes do not feel their playing time is at risk, the pressure to abide by cultural expectations can affect their personal well-being. When Swoopes came out in 2005, for example, she said, "I'm just at a point in my life where I'm tired of having to pretend to be somebody I'm not. I'm tired of having to hide my feelings about the person I care about. About the person I love" (quoted in Granderson, 2005, ¶ 2).

Case Study: Performing Maternity in the WNBA

As this chapter attests, men and women are asked to perform their sport identities in unique and different ways under an unusual set of standards. For example, male soccer players commonly remove their shirts after scoring a goal, yet Brandi Chastain was heavily criticized for performing a similar act during the 1999 Women's World Cup. Most viewed it as an explicit sexual act rather than an individual celebration commonly performed by male athletes in the sport. In women's basketball, Sheryl Swoopes had been a standout collegiate player winning the Sportswoman of the Year honors and a gold medal as a member of the USA women's basketball team during the 1996 Olympic Games. Her appeal to women's basketball led Nike to develop the Nike Swoopes line of shoes and featured her as the prominent female basketball equivalent to Michael Jordan.

Shortly after the Women's National Basketball Association (WNBA) was formed, Swoopes was logically selected as the first-round draft pick by the Houston Comets. Shortly afterward, the league and the team faced a potential setback as it was reported that its premier player would miss the first half of the season. Female athletes are often confronted with the challenge of childbirth in ways that do not interfere with male athletes' ability to perform in sports. Although many female athletes have become pregnant during the course of their athletic careers, Swoopes was required to sit out the first 6 weeks as she recovered from the birth of her first son at a crucial time for a sport league in its infancy. At the time, she felt legitimate concerns that the pregnancy would adversely affect her commercial appeal and that the contract with Nike might be in jeopardy. However, the WNBA saw this as a potential marketing strategy as it embraced her maternity and the distinction that it helped make between the WNBA and the NBA. The notion of performing motherhood on the court aligned with the league's early marketing campaign "We got next," which targeted female sport enthusiasts. The premiere issue of *Sports Illustrated/Women Sports* even displayed her on the cover at the peak of her pregnancy, further establishing the balance between her dual maternal and athletic qualities. After returning to the league, Swoopes went on to win three MVP awards and two additional Olympic gold medals. In 2005, she publicly acknowledged that she was a lesbian after two other prominent WNBA players had also made similar disclosures, noting that in the end, sexuality or motherhood have little to no effect on her on-court performance.

1. Was it appropriate for the WNBA to use Swoopes's pregnancy as a marketing campaign for the league?

2. Why would you suspect that public backlash is less for female athletes who acknowledge they are gay when compared to male athletes?

3. How might male and female athletes overcome the performance standards placed on them for the sports they find themselves engaged in?

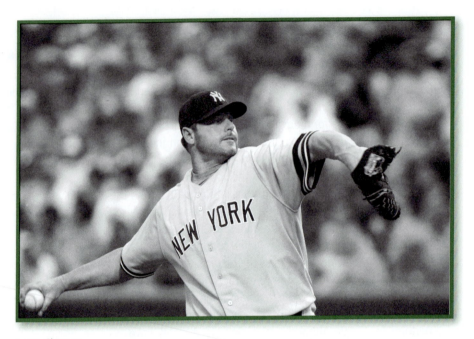

Roger Clemens

Even mere speculation that an athlete might be gay is commonly met with concern or, in some cases, outrage. When New York Mets catcher Mike Piazza was rumored to be romantically involved with a man, he eventually attempted to quell the rumors by holding a press conference to declare he was straight. Piazza was especially vulnerable to these rumors because his "manhood" had been questioned by some who felt he responded inadequately to separate instances of aggressive behavior from rival pitcher Roger Clemens. In the aftermath of the speculation about his sexuality, Piazza suddenly (perhaps coincidentally) began responding more assertively to challenges from opposing pitchers. Meanwhile, he more publicly performed his gender, culminating in his marriage to a former *Playboy* model. As Butterworth (2006) concludes, "Given all the attention paid to Piazza's sexuality, it is reasonable to conclude that his more recent performances were motivated efforts to reconstitute his masculine identity" (p. 150). In fairness to Piazza, he attempted to be respectful of gay men even as he reaffirmed his own heterosexuality. Yet the public nature of his declaration reminds us of the stigma that is associated with being gay, especially within the world of sport.

Part of the issue is perhaps a preoccupation with the "coming out" narrative. Media speculation about whether or not (male) professional sport is ready for a gay athlete is common, but too often coming out is assumed to be the only means of performing a gay or lesbian identity. Iannotta and Kane (2002) argue that an overemphasis on public declarations of identity risks "marginalizing other, more subtle forms of identity performance" (p. 349). In their study of college coaches who are lesbian, they discover that women have multiple options when it comes to performing their gender. For example, interviews revealed that coaches were often "out" without ever explicitly telling anyone. Rather, they simply made their partners a part of their daily lives so that it would be obvious to others around them. Iannotta and Kane emphasize that these more subtle behaviors are just as, if not more, effective than public statements about sexual identity. Most importantly, they demonstrate that gender and gender performance are fluid, dynamic, and ever changing.

PERFORMANCE OF RACE AND ETHNICITY

In Chapter 6, we referenced the dress code installed by the NBA in 2005. Many critics have suggested that this policy was a means of curtailing the excessive performances of African American identity, which are commonly marked by baggy clothing, cornrows, and exposed tattoos. Grano (2007) argues that especially in the aftermath of the infamous brawl between the Detroit Pistons and Indiana Pacers—and the fans in Detroit—the NBA wanted to "restore order and a veneer of professionalism by bringing players' dress into conformity with corporate tastes" (p. 460). The dress policy reveals a tension between interests in the NBA—management and players—and the corresponding attitudes about racial identity. No one in the league office admitted that race was a factor in installing the policy, of course. Yet few could argue that the effect of the dress code was to limit forms of expression that were specifically associated with African American players.

The NBA dress policy illustrates the performative dimensions of racial or ethnic identity that are located in sport. Just as gender identity is dynamic, so too is racial identity. Think no further than golfer Tiger Woods, an athlete often referred to as "African American" despite a heritage that includes African, Asian, and Caucasian ancestry. In an effort to avoid being reduced to a particular identity category, Woods has referred to himself as "Cablanasian"—a merger of multiple categories—or denied the relevance of race altogether (Houck, 2006a). Woods' insistence that he not be reduced to an essential identity speaks to the communicative power of identity performance. By avoiding conventional racial labels, Woods seeks to communicate the importance of valuing someone for his or her character and merit as opposed to race or ethnicity. Critics, meanwhile, suggest that by denying the persistence of racism, Woods's "postracial" identity further marginalizes those who continue to experience racial discrimination and oppression.

As the Woods example demonstrates, performances of racial identity entail risks because of a troubling legacy of racism that associates certain attributes with observable markers of race. Thus, as we discussed in Chapter 6, conventional stereotypes hold that African Americans are physically dominant while white athletes are mentally superior. Similarly, certain performances become associated with different racial and ethnic groups: African American football players make outlandish displays when scoring a touchdown; Latin American baseball players have large swings with little plate discipline; white basketball players are fundamentally sound even if they lack spectacular athleticism, and so on. These characterizations become especially pronounced when an athlete deviates from the expected norm. For example, Larry Fitzgerald is an elite wide receiver in the NFL. He is also African American. It is common to hear television announcers praise Fitzgerald, in near disbelief, for his understated demeanor when he scores a touchdown. Rather than perform an elaborate scripted celebration, he simply hands the ball to the nearest official. Fitzgerald is seen as the exception to the rule, and as Cunningham (2009) points out, much like the NBA's dress policy, the NFL has responded to the excesses of African American players by enacting harsher fines for their touchdown performances.

The assumption that players of a particular race or ethnicity will all behave similarly is problematic in other ways. Carrington (2008) describes his own experiences as a black man raised in London, where soccer (football, as it is called in England) and cricket are popular. As both an athlete and a then-aspiring academic, he was seen simultaneously as an insider and an outsider to the members of a cricket club for whom he began playing. Because the club was predominantly black and working class, Carrington's shared background allowed him to be accepted. However, his pursuit of a college education also marked him as different and prevented him from fully fitting in. Carrington thus emphasizes that although he was able to perform his racial identity in a manner that was consistent with that of his teammates, he was never quite an insider. As he notes, "This highlights one of the problems . . . with much of the [academic] work on race, namely the failure to fully interrogate and deconstruct what we might term the internal hierarchies of racial identity and the porous fault lines of racial boundaries" (p. 436).

Carrington's biographical example is echoed by scholarship that reveals the simultaneously complementary and contradictory nature of racial performance. For example, Schultz (2005) describes how Serena Williams's decision to wear a skin-tight "catsuit" during the 2002 U.S. Open gave voice to common stereotypes about the "animalistic" nature of African American athletes while at the same time challenging conventional thinking about femininity in tennis. After all, in a sport long dominated by images of players such as Chris Evert and Anna Kournikova, Williams's muscular and curvaceous physique provides a striking alternative. Meanwhile, others have noted that racial and ethnic performances can also be enacted when sport is fictionalized. The popular movie *Bend It Like Beckham,* which is about a young Indian woman in London who seeks the approval of her family to play soccer, was widely praised for its portrayal of British-Indian culture. Giardina (2003) expresses concern, however, that the stylized portrayal of a cultural group on the big screen can mislead an audience into believing that they have witnessed some form of "authentic" cultural expression. Because those outside of England will be exposed to so few images of British-Indian culture outside of a film like *Bend It Like Beckham,* the risk is that popular portrayals of sport limit, rather than expand, the acceptable range of racial or ethnic performance.

We also want to point out that performance may be a means of resisting the dominant or oppressive conceptions of racial and ethnic identity. An illustrative example of this can be found among those who object to the use of Native American mascots and imagery for sports teams. Miller (1999) argues that controversies about such mascots are a product of competing versions of how to perform "Indian." As he notes, "While the names and symbols that sports teams adopt are upsetting to many protesters, the primary concern is how those symbols get used or embodied" (p. 189). Thus, when fans of the Atlanta Braves perform the "Tomahawk Chop" or fans of the Washington Redskins come to the game wearing feathered headdresses, actual Native Americans see elements of their culture being taken out of context at best and outright disrespected at worst. Sport is crucial not only because it is a site where Native American imagery is used, but also because it has the power to shape our understanding of race and ethnicity. "Viewing sports as cultural performances," Miller writes, "means acknowledging the power of sporting events to *create* culturally shared beliefs and values" (p. 189).

Protests against Native American mascots must therefore be understood as performances designed to change those beliefs and values. In some cases, they have been successful, especially at the high school or collegiate level. Stanford University was the first to change its name when it went from the "Indians" to the "Cardinal" in 1972. Since then, dozens of others have followed suit, either with entirely new names or with accommodations designed to minimize ongoing controversy. However, no professional teams have yet to take these concerns seriously, and in 2009 the United States Supreme Court refused to hear a case that might have led to a change of name to the Washington Redskins. Fans and teams are reluctant to change, at least in part, because "the stereotypical views of how one performs Indian in mainstream American culture closely parallel the cultural rules about how one performs 'sports fan'" (Miller, 1999, p. 189). In this respect, the performance of identity is, and will continue to be, contested in the arena of sport.

PERFORMANCE OF DISABILITY

Disability studies is a growing area of research across academic disciplines. Because sport features the body in such prominent ways, disability scholars have increasingly turned to sport as a means of examining the practices of **ableism.** As Duncan (2001) explains, ableism is an ideology that assumes "the world should be tailored to those without disabilities" (p. 1). Such a worldview results in diminished visibility and opportunity for people with

5K wheelchair race in Tucson, Arizona

disabilities. Cherney (2003) adds that the spectacular performances within sport reinforce this ableist thinking by "locating ability in the body. [Sport] assumes an ideal of the stable and controllable body as the foundation of ability and as the essential characteristic from which ability derives" (p. 82). As a result, he argues, sport ironically rewards "certain freakish bodies" (p. 84)—those trained "to perfection" (p. 95)—while it marginalizes others— those that are disabled.

Communication scholars of sport and disability recognize that sport provides a space through which ableist practices might be challenged. Over the years, several high-profile examples of athletes with disabilities have given fans the opportunity to reconsider what counts as "able-bodied." Former Major League Baseball pitcher Jim Abbott, for example, had a lengthy and productive career despite being born without a right hand. More recently, South African runner Oscar Pistorius, who had both lower legs amputated when he was just 1 year of age, nearly qualified for the 2008 Summer Olympic Games. The most familiar case, however, is likely that of golfer Casey Martin, who successfully sued the Professional Golf Association (PGA) Tour to be allowed to use a cart during tournaments due to a circulatory problem. Because the case made its way to the Supreme Court, it has arguably generated the most attention and controversy about the Americans with Disabilities Act, which was enacted in 1990 (Cherney, 2003). At the heart of the matter was which bodies were allowed to perform in professional sport and a recognition that "certain bodies enjoy unwarranted privileges created by [sport's] rules, and that the resulting disparity discriminates" (Cherney, 2003, p. 97).

A Matter of Ethics: The Modern Blade Runner

Sport is often assumed to provide a model of meritocracy—that is, it is seen as the "level playing field" that is valued in a democratic culture. That everyone competes with the same rules and constraints guarantees our faith in the excellence of those who are victorious. But what happens when augmentations relevel the playing field?

(Continued)

(Continued)

The history of sport is replete with innovations that have made players more competitive, resilient, and successful. Consider the difference in professional football once players started wearing full pads and helmets or the changes that resulted in tennis when wooden racquets were tossed aside in favor of graphite and other lighter materials. These developments have been welcomed, partly at least, because we assume that all athletes have equal access to them. Yet in the case of disabled athletes, the line between achieving the level playing field and providing a competitive advantage has grown increasingly blurred.

For example, prior to the 2008 Summer Games in Beijing, South African runner Oscar Pistorius appeared ready to become the first disabled athlete to qualify for and compete in the Olympics. However, the 20-year-old double amputee faced criticisms that his artificial lower legs actually provided him with an *advantage* over his able-bodied competitors. Thus, in early 2008, the International Association of Athletics Foundation (IAAF) passed a rule prohibiting "any technical device that incorporates springs, wheels or any other element that provides a user with an advantage over another athlete not using such a device." Later in the year, the Court of Arbitration for Sport reversed this ruling, thereby giving Pistorius a chance to qualify for the South African Olympic team. Despite running well during qualifying, Pistorius finished third and did not make the team.

Although Pistorius did not end up competing in the Olympics, the mere *possibility* that he might do so provoked considerable controversy. At the heart of the matter is whether an artificial limb constitutes a reasonable accommodation or an unequal advantage.

1. Would you have endorsed Pistorius' inclusion in the Olympic Games? Why or why not?

2. How might public conceptions of disability have been affected had Pistorius qualified for the 2008 Olympics?

3. What augmentations do you think are fair?

Despite the discrimination that athletes with disabilities face, there are also opportunities to resist ableist thinking. One of the more dramatic performances of ability, then, occurs through wheelchair rugby, which is often termed *murderball*. Wheelchair rugby began as a form of therapy for individuals who are paralyzed but quickly evolved into a highly competitive sport. Because they take place within sport, the "performances of disability . . . can subvert the stigma associated with physical disability in surprisingly effective ways" (Lindemann, 2008, 113). These performances were brought to life in the critically acclaimed documentary film *Murderball* (2005). As Cherney and Lindemann (2010) suggest, "*Murderball* presents the point of view of the disabled athlete so that the audience views from a perspective that sees the players as powerful and heroic instead of lacking ability and pitiable" (p. 207). In addition, the documentary mostly avoids the common practice of oversentimentalizing these athletes for overcoming physical adversity.

Yet even as *Murderball* recasts popular conceptions of disability, Lindemann (2008) cautions that wheelchair rugby depends on other forms of identity performance that might reinforce ableist thinking. In particular, because the athletes default to conventional performances of aggressive masculinity, murderball could reaffirm "ableist notions of competitiveness, athleticism, and the body" (p. 99). This point reminds us that identity performances are complex, often revealing multiple and, at times, competing visions of the athletic body. What should be clear, however, is that the performances of disability in sport open up new possibilities for how people with disabilities can be seen and understood in public. Given this, what has

2003 Special Olympics opening ceremony

been a relatively recent area of interest in communication and sport scholarship is likely to generate increased interest in the years ahead.

CONCLUSION

As we conclude this chapter, we want to be clear that we have not covered every possible variation of identity. Our discussion of diversity, for example, is limited to examples of athletes with *physical* disabilities. Equally important, however, would be to explore the performative dimensions of athletes with *mental* disabilities. For instance, the Special Olympics provides a showcase for these athletes to challenge stereotypes that restrict the range of activities that are accessible to those with mental disabilities. Not only can the Special Olympics help redefine common perceptions of mental disability, then, they also provide outlets for athletes to alter their perceptions of themselves or even improve communication skills (Lord & Lord, 2000). In addition to disability, we should also acknowledge that identity may be performed through categories such as age or religion. Consider, for example, how assumptions about age were undermined by the performance of 41-year-old swimmer Dara Torres, who won three silver medals during the 2008 Summer Olympic Games in Beijing. Or think about how public affirmations of religious faith—such as those made by former NFL quarterback Kurt Warner—call into question the more traditional practice of keeping religious beliefs private. The willingness of an "old" swimmer to compete or a committed Christian to speak publicly about his faith are important communicative moments, and they remind us of how much of our identities are produced by our performances of them.

In this chapter, we have demonstrated that identity in sport is not always what it appears to be or what it is represented to be. Indeed, through the performances of athletes who challenge dominant expectations of gender, sexuality, race, ethnicity, and physical ability, sports fans are invited to consider the dynamic and multifaceted nature of identity. With this in mind, what will you see when you look at athletes in the future? Will you question norms of masculinity that are enacted in mixed martial arts fights? Will you wonder whether it is appropriate that a white man beats a drum to simulate a Native American ritual during a baseball game in Cleveland? Or will you reconsider what counts as "able-bodied" when watching the performance of an athlete with a disability? Not all athletic performances of identity are designed to challenge norms or promote social change, of course. Nevertheless, the examples from this chapter should demonstrate that such possibilities help make sport a dramatic part of American life.

REFERENCES

Amaechi, J. (2007). *Man in the middle.* New York: ESPN.

Bean, B., & Bull, C. (2003). *Going the other way: Lessons from a life in and out of Major League Baseball.* New York: Marlowe.

Birrell, S., & Cole, C. L. (1990). Double fault: Renee Richards and the construction and naturalization of difference. *Sociology of Sport Journal, 7,* 1–21.

Butler, J. (1999). *Gender trouble: Feminism and the subversion of identity.* New York: Routledge.

Butterworth, M. L. (2006). Pitchers and catchers: Mike Piazza and the discourse of gay identity in the national pastime. *Journal of Sport & Social Issues, 30,* 138–157.

Butterworth, M. L. (2008). "Katie was not only a girl, she was terrible": Katie Hnida, body rhetoric, and football at the University of Colorado. *Communication Studies, 59,* 259–273.

Carrington, B. (2008). "What's the footballer doing here?" Racialized performativity, reflexivity, and identity. *Cultural Studies ⇔ Critical Methodologies, 8,* 423–452.

Cherney, J. L. (2003). Sport, (dis)ability, and public controversy: Ableist rhetoric and *Casey Martin v. PGA Tour, Inc.* In R. S. Brown & D. J. O'Rourke III (Eds.), *Case studies in sport communication* (pp. 81–104). Westport, CT: Praeger.

Cherney, J. L., & Lindemann, K. (2010). Sporting images of disability: *Murderball* and the rehabilitation of masculine identity. In H. L. Hundley & A. C. Billings (Eds.), *Examining identity in sports media* (pp. 195–215). Thousand Oaks, CA: SAGE.

Cunningham, P. L. (2009). "Please don't fine me again!!!!!" Black athletic defiance in the NBA and NFL. *Journal of Sport & Social Issues, 33,* 39–58.

Disch, L. J., & Kane, M. J. (2000). When a looker is really a bitch: Lisa Olson, sport, and the heterosexual matrix. In S. Birrell & M. G. McDonald (Eds.), *Reading sport: Critical essays on power and representation* (pp. 108–143). Boston: Northeastern University Press.

Duncan, M. C. (2001). The sociology of ability and disability in physical activity. *Sociology of Sport Journal, 18,* 1–4.

Fenske, M. (2007). *Tattoos in American visual culture.* New York: Palgrave Macmillan.

Giardina, M. D. (2003). "Bending it like Beckham" in the global popular. *Journal of Sport & Social Issues, 27,* 65–82.

Granderson, L. Z. (2005, October 27). Three-time MVP "tired of having to hide my feelings." *ESPN The Magazine.* Retrieved May 13, 2010, from http://sports.espn.go.com/wnba/news/story?id=2203853.

Grano, D. A. (2007). Ritual disorder and the contractual morality of sport: A case study in race, class, and agreement. *Rhetoric & Public Affairs, 10,* 445–474.

Houck, D. W. (2006a). Crouching Tiger, hidden blackness: Tiger Woods and the disappearance of race. In A. A. Raney & J. Bryant (Eds.), *Handbook of sports and media* (pp. 469–484). Mahwah, NJ: Erlbaum.

Houck, D. W. (2006b). Sporting bodies. In A. A. Raney & J. Bryant (Eds.), *Handbook of sports and media* (pp. 543–558). Mahwah, NJ: Erlbaum.

Iannotta, J. G., & Kane, M. J. (2002). Sexual stories as resistance narratives in women's sports: Reconceptualizing identity performance. *Sociology of Sport Journal, 19,* 347–369.

Lindemann, K. (2008). "I can't be standing up out there": Communicative performances of (dis)ability in wheelchair rugby. *Text and Performance Quarterly, 28,* 98–115.

Lord, M. A., & Lord, Jr., W. J. (2000). Effects of the Special Olympics of Texas *Athletes for Outreach* program on communication competence among individuals with mental retardation. *Communication Education, 49,* 267–283.

Miller, J. B. (1999). "Indians," "Braves," and "Redskins." A performative struggle for control of an image. *Quarterly Journal of Speech, 85,* 188–202.

Patterson, R., & Corning, G. (1997). Researching the body: An annotated bibliography for rhetoric. *Rhetoric Society Quarterly, 27,* 5–29.

Schultz, J. (2005). Reading the catsuit: Serena Williams and the production of blackness at the 2002 U.S. Open. *Journal of Sport and Social Issues, 29,* 338–357.

Sloop, J. M. (2005). Riding in cars between men. *Communication and Critical/Cultural Studies, 2,* 191–213.

Wood, J. T. (2009). *Gendered lives: Communication, gender, and culture* (8th ed.). Boston: Wadsworth.

SUGGESTED ADDITIONAL READING

Clayton, B., & Harris, J. (2009). Sport and metrosexual identity: Sports media and emergent sexualities. In J. Harris & A. Parker (Eds.), *Sport and social identities* (pp. 132–140). New York: Palgrave Macmillan.

Davis, L. R. (1990). Male cheerleaders and the naturalization of gender. In M. Messner & D. Sabo (Eds.), *Sport, men, and the gender order: Critical feminist perspectives* (pp. 153–161). Champaign, IL: Human Kinetics.

DePauw, K. P. (1997). The (in)visibility of disability: Cultural contexts and "sporting bodies." *Quest, 49,* 416–430.

Lindemann, K., & Cherney, J. L. (2008). Communicating in and through 'murderball': Masculinity and disability in wheelchair rugby. *Western Journal of Communication, 72,* 107–125.

Trujillo, N. (1991). Hegemonic masculinity on the mound: Media representations of Nolan Ryan and American sports culture. *Critical Studies in Mass Communication, 8,* 290–308.

Wellard, I. (2002). Men, sport, body performance and the maintenance of "exclusive masculinity." *Leisure Studies, 21,* 235–247.

CHAPTER 9

Communication and Sport in Parent–Child Interactions

Parent:	Brandon, get on the damn bag.
Spectator 1:	Brandon, maybe you should listen to your father and get on the bag, partner.
Spectator 2:	You know what I always tell my son, Nathan, is to go out there and try to have fun.
Parent:	Well, you know, having fun is the name of the game. Hey son. You trying to make an ass out of me? Get on the bag!
Spectator 1:	Brandon, everything is going to be okay. Just do what your father tells you, please.
Parent:	Hey little crybaby, I will downsize your face with a shovel if you don't get on the bag. By the way, does anyone know who I talk to about being a coach next year?

During his time on *Saturday Night Live,* Will Ferrell's performance as a vocal spectator at his son's youth baseball game resulted in a frightening portrayal of a verbally abusive parent. The scene depicts the competing orientations between "having fun" and the ego involvement that many parents confront as they cope with a child's participation in sports. During sport competition, there are numerous opportunities for parents to interact with their children to produce a range of constructive (i.e., encouragement during events, shared experience, etc.) and destructive

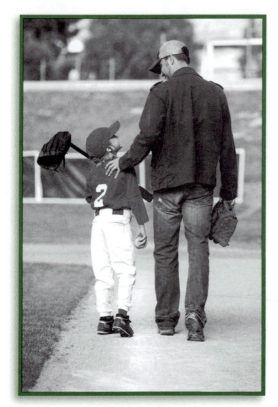

Father and son after a baseball game

outcomes (i.e., verbal abuse, obscene behavior, etc.). For many families, sport consumes a significant portion of their leisure activities, including the enactment, consumption, and performance of sports (Kassing et al., 2004). For larger families with multiple youth athletes, it is not uncommon for sport to constitute a central role in parent–child interaction (i.e., talk about practice and competitive experiences), parent–child time together (i.e., transporting to practice, coaching etc.), and family leisure time (i.e., multiple family members assuming spectator roles). Also included is the financial investment on the part of the parents (club dues, purchasing equipment and uniforms, admissions), which can consume anywhere from 3% to 12% of a family's annual income (Baxter-Jones & Maffulli, 2003). For example, young athletes interested in participating in youth hockey can expect to spend up to $500 for their equipment in addition to the expenses associated with traveling to games, hotel costs for weekend tournaments, and everyday expenditures associated with being on the road.

Parents seek to encourage sports participation because of the valuable socialization function it serves (promoting teamwork, leadership, and sport-specific skills), and fostering such skills represents a direct communicative function that can be fulfilled as a result of a child's sports participation. Unfortunately, a number of underlying motives also exist to foster a heightened level of pressure for athletes at all ages. For instance, a number of parents are likely to push sports on their children as a way to live vicariously through their son's/daughter's accomplishments (Hirschhorn & Loughead, 2000). Parents who failed to achieve their own sports-related dreams/goals are likely to find themselves pressuring their children to meet goals they were unable to attain themselves. In these situations, it becomes difficult for a parent to separate the child's sports identity from his or her own. We can point you to a number of prominent sports families where a parent's identity is inextricably linked with his/her child's athletic prowess. For example, Peyton and Eli Manning's accomplishments in the NFL are often compared in contrast with the success of their father, Archie Manning. After a successful college career at the University of Mississippi, Archie had an obscure career in the NFL because of the fact that he had been drafted by the New Orleans Saints (a team that just recently was able to achieve a Super Bowl appearance and victory). Eli's decision to reject a contract from the San Diego Chargers after his graduation in 2004 was perceived by many to be inspired by his father's experience in the NFL. The resulting trade to the New York Giants helped secure a Super Bowl win in 2008, through which the success of both Eli and Peyton have altered the Manning family's identity. In a similar vein, the careers of professional tennis players Venus and Serena Williams have also been linked with their father, Richard Williams, who has served as both coach and agent and is renowned for his ability to produce two world-class champions whose first exposure to tennis came from the broken-down courts of Compton, CA.

The culture of youth sports in our society continues to evolve in ways that further necessitate the potential for parent–child sports interaction. We would like to open this chapter with a historical overview of the role of parents in the lives of their children's sporting experience as society has shifted from a *game-* to a *sport*-based culture. This transition has further extended the impact factors such as sports rage and socialization are having, as well as the competing perspectives toward sport involvement that have evolved over time. The body of sport socialization research stems more from research conducted in the fields of sports sociology and psychology, yet it emphasizes the important communicative distinctions between parental support and pressure. We introduce you to these two forms for parental sport communication (which emphasizes noticeable gender differences) as

Youth soccer game in Indiana

we examine the discursive behavior of parents in the private family setting and as spectators at sporting events. This chapter includes discussions of: (a) changing sports culture, (b) sport socialization, (c) parent–child sports interaction, and (d) sex difference in parental influence.

CHANGING SPORTS CULTURE: GAME VS. SPORT

When considering the prevalence of sport in our society today, it is evident that sport and competition will continue to evolve. For instance, youth sports is at a crossroads as our society has shifted from a *game culture* (in which children were responsible for the design, maintenance, and development of the games they took part in) to a *sport culture* primarily organized by adults, especially parents. For example, there was a time when there were no organized youth baseball activities in the United States. Kids who enjoyed watching professional teams compete were responsible for organizing their own games as a way to further develop their own skills. This slowly transitioned into the creation of youth baseball leagues with drafts, practice and game schedules, and adult coaches and managers. In our opening chapter, we noted that sports participation in our society has been on the rise, with recent evidence suggesting that 90% of children take part in some form of organized sport(s) between the ages of 5 and 17 (Jellineck & Durant, 2004). As parents have become more involved, the number of youth participants has increased dramatically, yet this has come at a cost. Adult models have been applied to the youth sports enterprises, where skill development and competitiveness have become the norm. For example, traditional youth baseball, soccer, and basketball programs intended to simply introduce athletes to a broad range of opportunities have transitioned into a collection of traveling teams that are becoming more selective. In 2007, the Amateur Athletic Union (AAU) began to sponsor a national youth wrestling dual tournament that requires youth clubs and programs to have wrestle-offs to develop competitive lineups that include athletes as young as 5 years of age.

Interview: Darrell Burnett, Clinical Psychologist and Board Member for Little League of America

Q: **In a sporting context, what is the most important aspect of the parent–child relationship?**

A: If I see my child as an *athlete* who happens to be a kid, I may tend to overreact emotionally to situations involving my child at a youth sports event (not enough playing time; not playing the "right" position; making an error; striking out; losing a game; etc.). My overreactions may also run the risk of communicating to my child that his/her self-worth is somehow tied in solely with his/her athleticism.

If I see my child as a *kid* who happens to be playing sports, I can keep youth sports in perspective. I will not allow my child's athleticism (or lack thereof) to become the definition of my child's self-worth. I will maintain a solid, supportive, positive relationship with my child and situations involving my child in youth sports (not enough playing time, etc.) will not be seen as "catastrophic" or "horrible."

Q: **What is unique about a parent who takes a supportive rather than competitive approach toward his/her child's sport participation?**

A: It is possible to be both supportive and competitive, provided the emphasis is on *process* (skill development) rather than *end product* (winning, statistics, etc.). Parents who see youth sports participation as an ongoing process of learning skills and having fun can be supportive of their children as they continue to participate in the process of playing sports. They can teach their children to compete against themselves, to become the best athletes they can be.

Q: **Some parents are concerned that youth coaches wield too much influence on children. Is this a problem for the Little League of America?**

A: The term "positive coaching" is common in youth sports. Little League International takes pride in making sure that "everybody plays" and that each player, regardless of his/her skill, has a positive experience. Managers and coaches are required to attend coaching workshops with an emphasis on positive coaching. The Positive Coaching Alliance works hand in hand with Little League International to assist the Little League managers and coaches in their efforts to be a positive influence on the players. Managers and coaches are monitored; there are always exceptions (and these exceptions tend to make the 6:00 PM news). However, the vast majority emphasizes fun and skill development.

Q: **What trends are you currently experiencing regarding the pressure parents place on their children to compete? Are there particular approaches that are becoming more detrimental?**

A: There seems to be a movement away from the "carousel" (youth sports as a process with friendly competition) and more movement toward the "brass ring" (youth sports as "big business," with an emphasis on the "prize"). The result is an

(Continued)

(Continued)

increase in parents' decisions to spend more money on their child's sports development (specializing in one sport, individual training, equipment, travel ball, etc.) and a tendency for parents to put the emphasis on the win-at-all cost competition.

Q: **In a recent study, 55% of parents reported that their children dropped out of sports because of hypercompetitiveness. How can this be counteracted?**

A: When children see themselves as competing against *others,* they start comparing themselves to other players on the team ("I can't run as fast as . . .") and the tendency is to drop out. However, if they can be taught to compete with *themselves,* they may continue to participate. If a child can be taught to measure his/her progress in terms of *frequency* (how often), *duration* (how long), and *intensity* (how much energy), and if parents and coaches help the child to see the progress, an emphasis on process overcomes focusing on end product.

Q: **What would you say is different about parental involvement today than it was 20 years ago? Are there benefits in regard to how things have changed?**

A: It's mixed. The good news is that more positive parental involvement creates a sense of validation, especially in younger children. When a child repeatedly yells, "Watch me! watch me!" to his/her parents while trying a trick dive in the swimming pool, it is as though the dive doesn't "count" unless the parents see it. Likewise, if the parents and family "see" the hit, playing time, catch, etc., it "counts" more in the eyes of the child. The bad news is that with more parental involvement comes the possibility of overinvolvement and overreaction.

There was a time when athletes would make a decision about specializing in a sport to increase their chances of competing at collegiate and professional levels; however, more and more athletes are now required to specialize to ensure a spot at even the junior high school level. China has been recently criticized for the emphasis that it places on sport specialization as an opportunity for social mobility. This became an international issue during the 2008 Olympic Games when speculation arose about the age of gymnasts on the Chinese women's gold medal team. International rules require gymnasts to be 16 years of age to compete during international competition. Discrepancies emerged in the reported birth date for a number of the team's gymnasts, resulting in the loss of a bronze medal from a gymnast who had competed on the 2000 women's Olympic team for China. The push to be successful at such a young age should make you consider for a moment your own experiences as an adolescent. What types of opportunities were available to you, and how have those opportunities changed today? Were you encouraged to participate in a variety of sports, or were you pushed into selecting one particular sport to be more competitive? A basketball season used to just be in the winter, but now the game is played year-round; if you

Chinese gymnast Yang Yilin

drop out at any point so you can play another sport, you are perceived as falling behind or lacking commitment. This transformation has taken hold and is beginning to produce a variety of unintended consequences that carry over into the increased likelihood of parents placing a stronger emphasis on athletic competition, which has increased the potential for sports rage.

Sports Rage

Recent statistical accounts indicate that children involved in youth sports find themselves the focus of increasing incidents of pressure and abuse from parents, coaches, and fans (Lord, 2000). In addition, dramatic anecdotes further illustrate the problem. For example, on July 5, 2000, the father of a 10-year-old boy fatally beat another hockey player's father over a disagreement about body checking. A week earlier, a disgruntled parent coach in Florida broke the jaw of a 13-year-old umpire; and in 1999 in Virginia, a mother slapped a 14-year-old official when she disagreed with a call (Butterfield, 2000). Many have used the term *sports rage* (offensive behavior, both verbal and physical, that results from unfavorable sport outcomes) to describe a host of instances that have included both verbal and physical assault on players, coaches, or officials. But perhaps the best definition comes from Heinzmann (2002), who described it as "any physical attack upon another person such as striking, wounding, or otherwise touching in an offensive manner, or any malicious verbal abuse or sustained harassment which threatens subsequent violence or bodily harm" (p. 67).

Heckling players is not a new phenomenon in many sporting events. For example, the student section at Duke University basketball games is well known for its collaborative effort to influence opponent free-throw shooting. Professional athletes have also become quite accustomed to profanity and verbal abuse from their fans, but there are still times when even these athletes fail to stay within the boundaries of the fan–spectator relationship. The inappropriate levels of aggression, competitiveness, and overinvolvement appear related to the ways in which it has become culturally and communicatively normative to do sport. These practices appear to have spilled over into youth settings not simply through wider discourses and influences but as coaches, parents, and fans communicatively enact their own sporting ambitions and identities in highly competitive and aggressive ways.

Most important to our discussion is the rise of vulgar behavior on the part of parents that commonly occurs at events designed for 4- to 5-year-old participants. More moderate forms of sports rage have occurred as parents' unsportsmanlike conduct has become more aggressive. Resent data suggests that 15% of parents or spectators will embarrass their children at a sporting event (Vandenabeele, 2004), and Lord (2000) notes that an informal survey conducted by the Minnesota Amateur Sports Commission found that 45% of sport participants had experienced being yelled at by adults, called names, or insulted during competitive events. Seventeen percent had even reported instances of physical abuse (hitting or slapping), with a handful of the athletes surveyed even reporting that they preferred that their parents not attend their events or practices. Much of this behavior has been linked to the fact that sports attrition rates are on the rise, with most youth participants dropping out by age 13, leading many organized sports associations to require all parents to either complete sportsmanship training or sign a code of conduct statement before their children can participate. Family communication scholars argue that the family is an important socializing agent for children, and the way children view their athletic experience is dependent on the way their parents communicate to them about the importance of sports and what occurs while participating.

SPORT SOCIALIZATION

Each society, culture, or subculture has an innate need to train its members for the roles and norms necessary for its survival. This socialization process involves a society's ability to transfer its norms, practices, routines, traditions, and general knowledge to its next generation. Sport has been viewed as a legitimate source for this socialization process. Roberts, Treasure, and Hall (1994) argue that, "in play, games, and sport, children are brought into contact with social order and the values inherent in society, and are provided a context within which desirable social behaviors are developed" (p. 631).

Grounded in a family socialization model (Mead, 1934), the sport socialization movement argues that learning would occur from two important sources: (1) through athletes' exposure to the sport (e.g., the actual enactment of sport, interacting with other athletes, following rules and procedures developed for the sport); and (2) the reinforcement that is received from others (e.g., role models, peers, parents, coaches) while engaged in those sporting activities. Much of the sport socialization literature stems from research that views interaction with others as an effective method for internalizing appropriate and expected behavior.

Sport involvement at a young age is mostly unidirectional as parents make the initial/primary decision to enroll the child, and proper motivation on the part of the parent will produce the best likelihood for athletic success and continued performance. Parents with an active interest in sports are more likely to expose their children to sports at an early age and allow sports to become an important part of the family's leisure time (Baxter-Jones & Maffulli, 2003). For example, consider the level of success Andre Agassi would have experienced if his father had not introduced him to tennis at an early age. The same could be said for our previous examples, begging the question "Where would Eli and Payton Manning be without Archie?" or "Where would Serena and Venus Williams be without Richard?"

Parents are likely to encourage sports participation because of the perceived benefits they anticipate their child will receive, as well as personal benefits that come as by-products to their participation (Wiersma & Fifer, 2008). These *parental benefits* include aspects such as seeing the child's enjoyment, skill improvement, and success. They also experience a sense of community as they interact with other parents. Practice becomes an outlet allowing parents to interact with other like-minded adults as well as serve on organizing boards that further perpetuate the cycle of sport competition. *Child benefits* include the potential for participating in a competitive environment that allows one to experience winning and losing in addition to learning valuable lessons about sportsmanship, teamwork, and handling adversity. Teammates over time become close friends, even overlapping

Tiger and Earl Woods at youth golf clinic

boundaries beyond the field, court, and/or mat as they integrate into things such as family rituals, birthday parties, social gatherings, and even holiday activities. Many parents noted their child benefits because sport also serves as an important alternative to nonphysical activities, most notably videogames. Brustad (1988) argues that an athlete can experience a number of emotions toward the sports he or she competes in, and these emotions facilitate motives such as affiliation, achievement, release, power, and independence (see Table 9.1).

Yet sports only offer the potential for creating a context where positive developmental characteristics are fostered; the benefits noted above are often contradicted by a variety of challenges for both parents and children. *Parental challenges* include the considerable expense required for competing at high levels (traveling clubs, camps, training materials). The time commitment is also significant, which potentially detracts from other forms of family time, causing parents to make difficult choices between competition, other leisure activities, or even academics. *Child challenges* include finding a balance between being a child and an adult as the seriousness of sports has increased. Parents also note the growing emphasis toward sports that detracts from academic commitments that could have otherwise been fulfilled. Mostly they note the intensity that comes from coaches and other parents. Although such by-products of the youth sporting environment have resulted in a number of unintended consequences from this shift to a sport culture in our society, many parents find themselves encouraging sports participation because of the important family-based socialization function it serves. As more family time and resources are devoted toward

Table 9.1 Young Athlete Motives for Sports Participation

Athlete Motive	Description
Affiliation	The potential to establish an association with a particular team or sport and be a part of something bigger than themselves.
Achievement	The ability to obtain success in sports and work toward a level of excellence or skill acquisition.
Release	An avenue for expending energy or aggressive behavior.
Power	The perceived sense of clout obtained outside the sport or the ability to exert authority over teammates.
Independence	The liberty to perform in an environment free from anxiety and pressure.

sports, there is an increased opportunity for parent–child interaction that serves as feedback (both support and pressure) to encourage/discourage ongoing participation.

PARENT–CHILD SPORTS INTERACTION

Parents not only encourage young athletes, but they also assist to interpret their child's experiences, which are then used to shape perceptions about abilities, establish expectations, and foster a valence structure about the sport itself (LaVoi & Stellino, 2008). Parents have an opportunity to provide support or pressure through their verbal or nonverbal behavior on the side-lines or in private family settings. When assessing technique for encouraging sports participation, Roberts and colleagues (1994) found parents most commonly emphasize goal reaching, followed by pointing out the child's personal improvement or growth, importance of trying, and providing rewards for hard work and overcoming difficulties. These findings also indicate that children perceive two conceptually different types of parental involvement, one that represents *parental facilitation* (paying fees, purchasing equipment, providing transportation, attending games) of the children's activity participation and one that suggests *parental control* by imposing performance standards.

Mother teaching daughter basketball fundamentals

Encouragement in the form of *parental support* consists of behaviors or comments that athletes perceive to foster athletic participation, with evidence to suggest that supportive parents (noninterfering with a focus on effort rather than winning) utilized more open communication and encouraged children to develop at their own pace. When feedback is provided in a positive light, the support perceived by athletes can increase their enjoyment, perceived sport importance, increased involvement in a range of sports, and general self-esteem.

Parental influence can also produce detrimental results when *parental pressure* involves messages that continually focus on success and foster improbable and impossible expectations of a child. Ego building involves instances where parents' natural instinct is to wish for their children's success in their respective sport, often producing a curvilinear relationship with a child's stress and parental involvement. When examining the negative repercussions of parental involvement, messages that continually focus on success and performance-based outcomes establish an expectation in children that winning is the only relevant sports outcome. Parental pressure has been related to athletes' fear of failure, guilt, anxiety stress, and dropout rates and is inversely related to athlete enjoyment. Parents have an opportunity to provide support or pressure through their verbal or nonverbal behavior in private family settings and as spectators at sporting events.

Case Study: Elena Says Enough

There are times when the gift of athletic talent can be a curse for young athletes as parents develop long-term expectations for their child at an early age. Such was the case for Elena Delle Donne, former 6'4" guard for Ursuline Academy in Wilmington, Delaware. At age 15, Elena was featured in a profile on ESPN depicting her as the LeBron James of women's basketball. Her athletic abilities on the basketball court were so outstanding that she was heavily recruited by almost every major Division I basketball team in the country. During the ESPN profile, she talked about her love for the sport, and her parents reinforced the fact that they seldom had to push her to compete. To them, the basketball court they erected at their home, the multitude of summer camps, and the hours of training that were endured every day were all Elena's idea.

During her senior year, Elena verbally committed to play for legendary Connecticut Huskies coach Geno Auriemma, even leaving home after graduation to get a head start on her collegiate career by moving to campus to take part in summer school and begin workouts with the team. However, 2 days later, Elena returned home and informed her teammates and Auriemma that she intended to give up her basketball career. In follow-up interviews, Elena confessed to the fact that she had lost the passion for the game of basketball at the age of 13 and that she was "living a lie." Many questioned her intentions, feeling that she was attempting to be released from her commitment to Connecticut. Her coach, teammates, the media, and even her family questioned how someone at the top of her sport could not be committed to playing. The ability to play in college or even as a professional is a privilege that should not be squandered, they said, because so many dream of this opportunity to only have it crushed because they lack the necessary skills.

Parental pressure is an underlying issue that many young athletes are forced to deal with, even talented athletes. For Elena, the subliminal pressure that her parents placed on her to compete caused her to reject the lack of passion she was experiencing for basketball. When this occurs, it is only a matter of time before an athlete finds a way to change his or her course. Some fake injuries, lash out, or in Elena's case, simply walk away. This isn't to say that she has completely lost her love for sports. At the start of her freshman year, she transferred to the University of Delaware, where she is now a member of the women's volleyball team and where expectations have not yet been set for her to perform at the highest level.

1. How is it that Elena's parents were unable to see that she had lost the passion to play basketball?

2. What about our society makes it so hard for people to accept that a talented athlete would not want to compete?

Private Family Settings

The type of parental pressure or support an athlete receives will often depend on the level of involvement the family has in sports. For example, parents with moderate levels of involvement create the ideal sporting experience because they are able to find a balance between the competitive and enjoyment objectives from sport participation. When parents demonstrate low involvement, the athlete is likely to experience heightened uncertainty, which can be an anxiety-provoking experience. It is difficult for a young athlete to develop a commitment to a sport when parents demonstrate limited interest (i.e., "I can drop you off at the game, and then I'll pick you up afterwards"). Stress is likely to emerge when highly involved parents exert pressure on their children and occurs when athletes reflect upon comments about their performance or fear of letting the parent down.

Turman (2007) conducted interviews with parents of young athletes to explore the factors that necessitated a talk with the child about the nature of their sports participation in the private family setting. Four prominent themes were identified, beginning with *playing time,* which included instances where parents confronted their child's frustration about playing time by interpreting the situation from the coaches' perspective. Such positive encouragement was found to help focus athlete attention on many of the factors the athlete controlled, including working to do his or her best and using the time on the bench to learn from teammates. Parents also emphasized athlete behavior that extended beyond the athletic ability of the child, suggesting that making contributions to the team and having the right attitude were the biggest determining factors for deciding playing time.

Sport politics was the second most common topic of talk focusing on factors outside the control of the child's athletic ability and resting on the subjective decision making of the coach. A wide range of issues were addressed by parents, including the perception that coaches showed considerable favoritism to their own child or older athletes and athletes that attended camps or extra practices, as well as overreliance on star athletes. When such behaviors were perceived, parents reported a need to talk about the politics of sports with their children. In these instances, parents still reminded athletes that they must work harder to overcome these hurdles. *Negative coaching behaviors* are actions where parents questioned the coaches' objectivity and ethical practices with their child or the team. In these instances, parents learned about coaches' behavior through their child's first-hand account of practice and locker room behavior, requiring them to explain to their child(ren) how coaches' behavior was inappropriate. When faced with coaches that displayed behaviors that fell within this classification, parents used the private family setting as a place to interpret the coaches' behavior for the child.

Sport competitiveness was the final topic of talk and included instances where parents perceived sports had become too competitive by placing an overemphasis on winning. A majority of these utterances focused on the role of parents and sports organizations, which either pushed kids or established policies that eliminated athlete enjoyment. These parents perceived that winning was promoted to be more important than learning to play the sport and that overbearing parents inadvertently discouraged their own desire to have their children participate. As a result, parents indicated a need to address this topic with their children as a way to encourage continued participation by deemphasizing such inappropriate behavior.

Sideline Interaction

Sport spectators, and parents in particular, feel an innate need to provide public disclosures at sporting events, yet this type of interaction highlights the harmful nature of such parental comments and behaviors. Bigelow (2005) noted that 45% of sport fans felt that parent sideline behavior was a legitimate problem, while 46% felt it was the most significant problem facing youth sport programs. How a child reacts to the sport environment will be a direct reflection of what

Table 9.2 Types of Sport Talk in the Family Setting

Family Sport Talk	Definition	Example
Playing Time	Conversations about the extent that an athlete is obtaining adequate participation levels.	"If you don't see an increase in playing time then maybe you need to reconsider going out for swimming next year."
Sport Politics	Discussion about the decision-making practices employed by the coach to determine participation levels or player positions.	"It always seems that your coach puts in his own daughter at the end of the game even though the seniors should be getting an opportunity to play."
Negative Coaching Behavior	Interaction to discuss or question the coaching practices or behavior used to guide a team.	"I don't think it is useful for your coach to discipline the entire team because of what one of your teammates did."
Sport Competitiveness	Conversation about the heightened levels of competitiveness generated from sport participation.	"I accept that winning is important, but are there ways to still be competitive and make the experience enjoyable for the kids?"

he/she observes from parents/coaches. Much of this occurs through modeling as children develop the positive (congratulating players, supportive comments) and negative sport behaviors (failing to shake hands, questioning officials) by observing parents and coaches in this environment. Positive spectator behaviors have been found to be a strong predictor of player positive sportsmanship, just as negative behavior on behalf of the spectator predicts negative behavior from athletes. Interestingly enough, negative coach behavior does not appear to influence negative modeling by players, suggesting the ". . . perception might exist that one of the coaches' roles is to argue with referees so when they do, players are less likely to notice. When parents, however, argue with referees, it is more noticeable because it is outside the expected role of the spectator" (Arthur-Banning et al., 2008, p. 13).

The feedback young athletes receive from parents in the stands has been categorized into three general types (positive, negative, and neutral). Observations at a variety of basketball, soccer, and baseball games indicate that 51% of the parents' comments were positive, followed by negative (32%) and neutral (16%) comments (Blom & Drane, 2009). *Positive comments* include statements that reinforce or support athlete performance and include encouraging comments like "nice play," "go Kevin," or

Father coaching son's youth football team

"good work." *Negative comments* represent statements made toward their own team or athletes that attempt to correct or scold behavior such as "Don't take that shot," "You need to put in more effort," or "Did you even show up to play?" *Neutral comments* include important remarks that reinforce coaching strategies or features of the sport such as "Keep your eye on the time" or "Talk with your teammates."

A Matter of Ethics: Parental Passion

Parents are expected to provide support for their children in sports, regardless of the outcome on the court or field. However, many recent cases reveal that parental involvement in youth sports often interferes with the play on the field or the child's emotional satisfaction off of it. Parents have embarrassed themselves or their children (or both) frequently enough that the stereotypical character portrayed by Will Farrell referenced at the outset of this chapter may feel more like truth than fiction.

In 2007, Dion Pendleton, Sr., was banned from attending his son's football games at North High School in Evansville, Indiana. Pendleton had allegedly argued with the team's football coach and later criticized a referee during a game. As reported by the *Evansville Courier & Press,* Pendleton admitted to a confrontation with the football coach but insisted his comments to the referee were no different than those made by other parents. Meanwhile, officials of the local school district declined to comment.

The details of this particular case are somewhat vague, which is perhaps why it is worthy of our consideration. In other words, it leaves us to wonder exactly what Mr. Pendleton did or didn't do or say and, more importantly, invites us to consider what behavior *would* warrant his exclusion.

1. How much parental involvement is too much?

2. Should parents be allowed to question a coach's decision?

3. Should they yell at game officials or opposing players from the stands?

4. How do *you* feel when you hear your parents' voices at a game?

There is the possibility that ". . . receiving multiple cues from several adults, children may be confused and distracted. If athletes receive this information while focusing on performing a new skill . . . their level of frustration and confusion may be multiplied" (Blom & Drane, 2009, p. 12). For instance, parents who offer their child erroneous appraisals of their athletic ability are often thought to create a level of self-esteem dissonance (Mach, 1994). This self-esteem dissonance (the need to seek similarity between an individual's self-judgment and that of significant others) makes it difficult for young athletes to determine which messages are genuine. Unfortunately, a strong positive relationship has been observed between the judgments parents provide and an athlete's perceived physical ability (after controlling for actual ability), whereby parent messages about athletic ability have the capacity to override environmental cues that may come from the coach (McCullagh, Matzkanin, Shaw, & Maldando, 1993). When young athletes rely solely on the reinforcement provided by parents, they are likely to have psychological development issues.

SEX DIFFERENCE IN PARENTAL INFLUENCE

Early research in the area of sport socialization affirms that a variety of factors determine how parents will decide to influence their child's sports involvement. Often parents encourage children to participate for a number of reasons (e.g., values of physical activity, discipline, etc.), and differences have been found that are reflective of both the parent's and child's sex. Communication research argues that children are often socialized into either masculine or feminine communication cultures through their participation in a variety of sex-segregated games and sports as they mature. Wood (1996) argued that "games socialize children into understandings of how, when, and why to talk" (p. 150). As a result, specific communication behaviors are learned early in a child's life and are influential in determining how children communicate throughout their lifespan. This is important to note when considering that such masculine and feminine communication cultures appear to be a function of the parental support that young athletes receive to participate in various athletic activities. For instance, research in the early 1980s has shown that fathers had the most influence over the behavior of male children, while mothers were more likely to serve the same function for girls. Traditionally, research on family sport socialization supported the notion that parental pressure and support were provided by the male parent, yet trends in youth sports involvement suggest equal levels of support from male and female parents regardless of the athletes' sex.

In Chapter 5, we discussed the role that Title IX has had for balancing the role of male and female participation, and it appears realistic that parental approaches to encouraging this participation would evolve and increase the likelihood that female parents may begin to perform a central role in their child's sports participation. Blom and Drane (2009) observed no difference in the disposition of mother and father comments at sporting events, yet there were more positive comments at girls' events and more neutral comments at boys' events. Stein, Raedcke, and Glenn (1999) also found that fathers were more likely to produce feelings of stress for both male and female athletes, and Leff and Hoyle (1995) found that male athletes viewed their fathers using more forms of pressure when compared to their mothers, while female athletes in their investigation perceived similar amounts of pressure from both parents. This transformation over the past 20 to 30 years suggests a number of possible implications for the way masculine and feminine communication styles are likely to form in future generations.

CONCLUSION

The parent–child relationship can be influenced dramatically when sport enters into the family equation. As we have noted throughout this chapter, sport is a continually evolving phenomenon that appears to be making parent–child interaction increasingly complex. The transition from a game to a sport culture has further facilitated things such as sport rage, the emphasis toward greater sport socialization, and discourse in the public and private settings. This also bridges the boundary between parents and coaches, with alarming consequences. Although our focus in this chapter has been to emphasize the potential consequences of increased parental participation, we would be performing a disservice if we didn't end this chapter by also demonstrating the role that sports can have for fostering positive parent and family relationships. For example, our society is ripe with examples of parents like Dick Hoyt, whose son Rick was born with significant brain damage after complications during birth left him unable to control the use of his limbs. Despite these difficulties, Rick became an avid sports fan who eventually asked his father to help him participate in a charity run for a high school classmate who had become paralyzed. Dick responded by pushing his son in the 5-mile run, and the event was such a life-changing experience for the two that Dick began to enter them both in more races, ultimately qualifying for the Boston Marathon in 1984. As if that was not enough, they soon took on the challenge of competing in a variety of triathlons, where Dick pulled/pushed his son in a small dingy/cart during the swimming, bicycling, and running portions of the event. To date they have participated in more than 200 triathlons and competed in more than 20 Boston Marathons. This example is one of a thousand different stories that reinforce the importance that sport can have in the parent–child relationship as sport becomes a central context/environment where parents interact with their children. As sport and family continue to intersect in meaningful ways, the evolution of this important interpersonal relationship will also continue.

REFERENCES

Arthur-Banning, S., Wells, M. S., Baker, B. L., & Hegreness, R. (2008). Parents behaving badly? The relationship between the sportsmanship behaviors of adults and athletes in youth basketball games. *Journal of Sport Behavior, 32,* 3–18.

Baxter-Jones, A. D., & Maffulli, N. (2003). Parental influence on sport participation in elite young athletes. *Journal of Sports Medicine and Physical Fitness, 43*(2), 250–255.

Bigelow, B. (2005). Youth sports survey results. Retrieved April 6, 2009, from http://www.bobbigelow.com/documents/.

Blom, L. C., & Drane, D. (2009). Parents' sideline comments: Exploring the reality of a growing issue. *Online Journal of Sport Psychology, 10*(3).

Brustad, R. J. (1988). Affective outcomes in competitive youth sport: The influence of intrapersonal and socialization factors. *Journal of Sport & Exercise Psychology, 10,* 307–321.

Butterfield, F. (2000, July 11). A fatality, parental violence and youth sports. *The New York Times,* A14.

Heinzmann, G. S. (2002, March). Parental violence in youth sports: Facts, myths and videotapes. *Park & Recreation, 37,* 66–73.

Hirschhorn, K. H., & Loughead, T. O. (2000). Parental impact on youth participation in sport: The physical educator's role. *Journal of Physical Education, Recreation & Dance, 71*(9), 26–29.

Jellineck, M., & Durant, S. (2004). Parents and sports: Too much of a good thing? *Contemporary Pediatrics, 21*(9), 17–20.

Kassing, J., Billings, A. C., Brown, R., Halone, K. K., Harrison, K., Krizek, B., Mean, L. J., & Turman, P. D. (2004). Enacting, (re)producing, consuming, and organizing sport: Communication in the community of sport. *Communication Yearbook, 28,* 373–409.

Lavoi, N. M., & Stellino, M. B. (2008). The relation between perceived parent-created sport climate and competitive male youth hockey players' good and poor sport behavior. *Journal of Psychology, 142,* 471–496.

Leff, S. S., & Hoyle, R. H. (1995). Young athletes' perceptions of parental support and pressure. *Journal of Youth & Adolescence, 24,* 187–203.

Lord, M. (2000, May 15). When cheers turn into jeers. *U.S. News & World Report, 128,* 52.

Mach, F. (1994). Defusing parent–coach dissidence. *Scholastic Coach, 63*(10), 5–6.

McCullagh, P., Matzkanin, K. T., Shaw, S. D., & Maldonado, M. (1993). Motivation for participation in physical activity: A comparison of parent–child perceived competencies and participation motives. *Pediatric Exercise Science, 5,* 224–233.

Mead, G. H. (1934). *Mind, self and society.* Chicago: University of Chicago Press.

Roberts, G. C., Treasure, D. C., & Hall, H. K. (1994). Parental goal orientations and beliefs about the competitive sports experience of their child. *Journal of Social Psychology, 24,* 631–645.

Stein, G. L., Raedeke, T. D., & Glenn, S. D. (1999). Children's perceptions of parent sport involvement. It's not how much but to what degree that's important. *Journal of Sport Behavior, 22,* 591–601.

Turman, P. (2007). Parental sport involvement: Parental influence to encourage young athlete continued sport participation. *Journal of Family Communication, 7,* 151–175.

Vandenabeele, R. (2004, August). Save our sportsmanship. *Coach & Athletic Director,* p. 72.

Wiersma, L. D., & Fifer, A. M. (2008). The schedule has been tough but we think it's worth it: The joys, challenges and recommendations of you sport parents. *Journal of Leisure Research, 40*(4), 505–530.

Wood, J. T. (1996). She says/he says: Communication, caring, and conflict in heterosexual relationships. In Julia T. Wood (Ed.), *Gendered Relationships* (pp. 149–162). Mountain View, CA: Mayfield.

SUGGESTED ADDITIONAL READING

Anderson, J. C., Funk, J. B., Elliott, R., & Smith, P. H. (2003). Parental support and pressure and children's extracurricular activities: Relationships with amount of involvement and affective experience of participation. *Journal of Applied Developmental Psychology, 24,* 241–258.

Engh, F. (2002). *Why Johnny hates sports: Why organized youth sports are failing our children and what we can do about it.* Garden City Park, NY: Square One.

Kidman, L., McKenzie, A., & McKenzie, B. (1999). The nature and target of parents' comments during youth sport competition. *Journal of Sport Behavior, 22,* 54–68.

Reilley, R. (2005, July 20). Strongest dad in the world. *Sports Illustrated, 102*(25), p. 88.

Shields, D. L., Bredemier, B. L., LaVoi, N. M., Power, F. C. (2005). The sport behavior of youth, parents, and coaches: The good, the bad, and the ugly. *Journal of Research in Character Education, 3*(1), 43–59.

CHAPTER **10**

Player–Coach Relationships in Sports

Many people assume that possessing athletic ability translates well into possessing critical coaching skills. Yet there is much more to coaching than athletic ability. The capacities to shape team goals, enhance athletic skill, and relate to players are essential attributes that can escape even the most talented athletes who seek to transition into the instructional side of sports once their competitive cycles have ended. We can point you to a number of highly successful coaches who have never been able to compete at the highest levels of their sports. For instance, Todd Haley, head coach of the Kansas City Chiefs, never played football (not even in high school) before he emerged through the coaching ranks to lead an NFL team. Even though he had limited success as a head coach, there are also numerous examples of talented athletes who failed to make successful transitions into coaching (i.e., Isaiah Thomas, Michael Irving, etc.). Such examples are fairly common in sports as less tangible characteristics often mark the difference between a skilled technician and a successful coach. The ability to communicate effectively is essential, marking the difference between successful and unsuccessful coaching. Jowett (2009) recently noted that ". . . while an athlete may have a chance in sport by going it alone, the athlete and the coach in partnership have more and better chances of success" (p. 34).

Sport success can be tied to a number of factors: athletic talent, team financial resources, fan support, luck, and so on. Regardless of the impact these factors have in determining success or failure in sports, the coach can be a central catalyst in this equation; as a result, coaches often receive the praise or blame for athletes' or teams' accomplishments. The way our society conceptualizes leadership places a significant emphasis on the coach to manage athletes (at all levels) to perform at optimal levels. This is never more evident than when we consider the importance of the coach in bonding a collection of individual athletes in team-based sports. For example, try to identify one highly recognizable coach for an individual sport. Name the coach for Olympic champion Michael Phelps, Ladies Professional Golf Association champion Annika Sorenstam, Women's Tennis Association champion Steffi Graf, or seven-time Tour De France winner Lance Armstrong. Do the names Bob Bowman, Henri Reis, Heine Gunthard, or Chris Carmichael sound familiar? If we provided you these names, you might be able to link one of these athletes to his or her coach. What if we were to ask you to identify the coach for the Pittsburgh Steelers during the 1970s, current NCAA women's basketball coach for the Tennessee Volunteers, the U.S. hockey team during the 1980 Olympics, or the Los Angeles Lakers? Even if you couldn't name them off the top of your head, it is likely that you have heard of Chuck Noll, Pat Summit, Herb Brooks, or even Phil Jackson.

Our tendency to attribute team success to the coach has its benefits for coaches who are fortunate to work with highly skilled athletes, but the desire

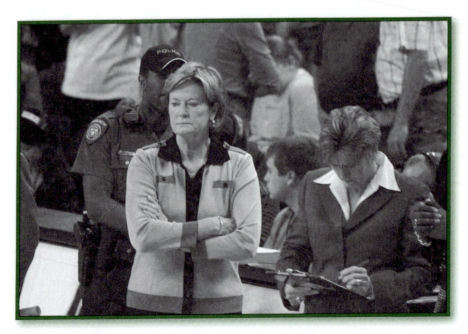

Pat Summit

to blame coaches for poor team performance can be a hidden pitfall of the sport landscape that coaches often fail to overcome. Because the coach–athlete relationship is challenged by the fact that winning is such an important outcome in sports, we begin this chapter by exploring the influence such expectations have on the need for coaches to win at all levels. In Chapter 9, we discussed the important role that parents play in fostering sports participation, and we extend this discussion in this chapter by briefly uncovering the parent–coach relationship as an ever-evolving feature of how sport is enacted. The remainder of the chapter shifts to the important role that communication serves in the coach–athlete relationship as we explore the range of styles that coaches draw upon as they interact with their athletes to prepare them for competition. Here we emphasize how the positive coaching movement has produced surprising results for coaches who embrace an athlete-oriented approach when seeking the appropriate balance between positive and negative comments to increase performance and general orientation toward competition. When this orientation is transferred into competitive context, the interaction that coaches have with players has been found to produce positive results. When these statements or messages are examined within the context of competitive interaction, there are a variety of opportunities to motivate, foster team cohesion, and provide a broader perspective for the importance of sport beyond the athletic context. For you to gain a deeper appreciation for the communication-based complexities that coaches face as they develop relationships with their athletes, we include discussions of (a) sport outcomes and coaching; (b) parent–coach relationships in sports; (c) leadership orientations; (d) positive coaching; and (e) communication contexts. We begin by examining the pressure coaches have to win.

SPORT OUTCOMES AND COACHING

Vince Lombardi is often criticized for suggesting that "winning isn't everything, it's the only thing." While many coaches might be unwilling to acknowledge the fact publicly, the outcome for every contest does matter. Many youth sports leagues have even established policies that restrict keeping score to limit the emphasis on winning. Yet this doesn't keep athletes as young as 4 years of age from tallying the score in their heads or even restrict parents from making comments about the team's performance. It's quite common to hear these same 4-year-olds talking about "If we would have been keeping score, we would have won!" after their games. Scoreboards, "most valuable player" titles, and team/player rankings were created for this purpose, as we are predisposed to consider our achievements in relation to those around us. Ask high school coaches if winning matters when they arrive home after a loss to a collection of "For Sale" signs in their lawn. Pressure to achieve from supporters and boosters is higher than ever. As a result, school boards, athletic directors, and team owners are under considerable pressure to fire coaches who can't achieve as expected. In Major League Baseball, each year it isn't uncommon for two or three managers to be fired within the first month of the season after failing to meet fan or owner expectations. Mondays during the NFL season have often been referred to as "Black Monday" because so many firings occur after losses on Sunday.

Operationally, coaches serve two important roles for their teams (teacher and game manager), which equally contribute to a team's ability to win. At all levels of play, these competing roles have the ability to force coaches to make decisions about what's best for the team versus what's best for the athlete. Roberts (1984) argued that sport offers a "forum" in which athletes learn a great number of skills, including "responsibility, conformity, subordination of the self to the greater good. . . . effort, persistence, and delay of gratification" (p. 251). However, coaches are constantly confronted with the "win at any cost" mentality in sports that requires them to do more than simply educate athletes. We are taught at a young age to win, and winning at all costs becomes an ethical issue that coaches and athletes alike are expected to overcome. It seems that even when coaches violate rules, this practice can be validated if done to maintain competitiveness. Bart Starr, NFL Hall of Fame quarterback and former coach of the Green Bay Packers, was reprimanded by the league early in his coaching career for violating NFL recruiting policies. In his apology to Packer fans, he noted that he was only doing what was expected to ensure a competitive advantage for the team, causing Kruse (1981) to observe that in sport rhetoric, the very ethic of sport suggests it's a coach's duty to bend the rules if it aids in his/her team's ability to win. Players and coaches in all sports often joke that "if you ain't cheating, you ain't trying."

This mounting pressure to win increasingly impacts the coach–athlete relationship as coaches are required to make decisions that are less about athlete development (character, skill, etc.). Even in developmental leagues, coaches are accused of playing to win versus playing to learn, and parents have added to the complexity of this issue, as our section on sport rage in the previous chapter attests. The rare exception might be coaches for minor league baseball teams who are less concerned about wins and losses than they are about the development of their potential major league talent. Because sports have become more specialized, coaches are now granted even more exposure to their athletes at levels never before seen. This year-round access has the potential for coaches to understand the styles that are most appropriate for fulfilling both features of the coach–athlete relationship (development and winning). Making this even more difficult is the fact that as the avenues for competitive sports have grown, so has the general athletic ability of young athletes. However, just because young athletes can perform feats traditionally set for adults doesn't mean they are both cognitively and emotionally ready to cope with the pressures that coaches might put on them for their effort. Cote's (1999) research on Olympic athletes found that it was not until at least 10 years of age that participation becomes important for an athlete to be competitive at the international level. This suggests that a coach who is making developmental-based decisions for athletes at young ages is unlikely to assist in the long-term performance for these players. This further supports the notion that athletes' win and loss rates at an early age are irrelevant beyond the psychological awareness that young athletes might have. In spite of his statement about winning early in his career, Lombardi was later quoted as saying, "I wish to hell I'd never said that damned thing (that winning is everything). What really counts is the effort (having a goal). That sure as hell doesn't mean for people to crush human values and morality" (Masin, 2007, p. 5). Despite Lombardi's retraction, parents continue to make the coach–athlete relationship difficult because of the overreliance on winning. Face it: More people remember Lombardi's first assertion than his second one.

Case Study: Winning Isn't the Only Thing After All

In the first section of this chapter, we explored the "win at all cost" model represented in sport today, but there are stories that emerge every so often that demonstrate how coaches and athletes can still embrace the honorable side of competition. Such was the case in 2008 when the Central Washington University Wildcats softball team played host to Western Oregon University. Before the start of their doubleheader, Western Oregon was one game ahead of Central Washington in the standings for the Great Northwest Athletic Conference race. After losing the first matchup, Central Washington needed to win the second game to ensure that their playoff hopes remained intact. When Sara Tucholsky stepped up to the plate in the second inning for what could be her final at-bat as a college athlete, she performed a feat that she had never achieved in her four years of collegiate ball. A .153 hitter on the year, Tucholsky hit a three-run home run and began sprinting toward first base. In her excitement, she strode to first base as she looked up to watch the ball clear the center field fence, causing her to miss the bag and tear her anterior cruciate ligament in her right knee.

(Continued)

(Continued)

She was able to crawl back to first base, but because rules specify that a player must be able to advance around the bases unassisted from teammates, Tucholsky was at risk of having a substitute runner replace her at first causing her home run to be replaced.

As the head coach and umpire considered the team's options, Mallory Holtman, the first baseman for the Western Oregon team, offered to have her teammates carry Tucholsky around the bases for the score. The rules specified that a player must be unassisted by teammates to advance, but there appeared to be no such stipulation when it came to the opposing team assisting an injured player. Holtman recruited her shortstop teammate Liz Wallace to assist her, and together they picked up Tucholsky and advanced her around the diamond, pausing at each base to ensure that she was able to touch the bag as specified in the rules. After the game, Holtman was quoted as saying, "In the end, it is not about winning and losing so much . . . It was about this girl. She hit it over the fence and was in pain and she deserved a home run." Western Oregon went on to win the game 4–2 and eliminated Central Washington from playoff contention, but both teams learned a valuable lesson about the integrity that sport can produce. Acts of sportsmanship like this are often overshadowed by more unsavory acts by coaches and players. For example, at the conclusion of the final track event that cost his team the conference title, a head coach recently approached the officials, noting that the athlete had been wearing a friendship bracelet violating established rules prohibiting jewelry. The athlete was disqualified and team points were stripped, causing the team to lose its conference title.

1. How difficult would it be for you to perform a similar act for an opponent?

2. Take yourself out of the context of a softball team. Would any of your coaches have allowed you to perform such an act if it meant the possibility of losing?

3. What do the actions of these players say about the coach–athlete relationship?

PARENT–COACH RELATIONSHIPS IN SPORTS

In Chapter 9, we spent considerable time providing an overview of the parent–child relationship in sports, demonstrating the significant role that parents play in encouraging sports participation. This relationship also carries over into the coach–athlete relationship as sports participation often necessitates the need for parent–coach interaction, making the coaches' jobs increasingly difficult. Many coaches have observed that parents serve as primary obstacles in their attempt to coach young athletes. Mach (1994) noted that "misunderstandings between the coach and the parent later lead to clashes of opinion between the parent and the child and then between the coach and the child" (p. 5). Coaching clichés such as "The best coaching jobs are in orphanages because there are no parents there," or "If it isn't one thing it's a mother" add credence to the fact that coaches struggle with the interaction they have with parents. The competing notions of "everyone should be allowed to play" and "win at all costs" provide opportunities for conflict between parents and coaches. For example, in 1999, Rodney Carrol, a volunteer youth baseball coach in Brunswick, Ohio, was sued by the father of one of his players after the team went 0–15. The parent complained that the ineffective coaching cost his son a chance to participate in a tournament in Florida. A mother in Canada sued the coach of her 14-year-old's hockey team for the cost of league registration, camps, and mental anguish after her son was benched in what she considered to be a crucial game. The fact that more than 1,300 lawsuits had been filed between 1997 and 2002, ranging in violations such as game strategies and starting status to instructional approaches, further exemplifies the difficult environment that coaches at all levels are expected to navigate. Despite a coach's attempt to establish rigid boundaries for communicating with parents, playing status appears to be a unique factor that necessitates the need for parents to establish direct and indirect contact with coaches.

Kirk and MacPhail (2003) found that coaches believe a significant number of parents were *"antagonists"* who overemphasized the skills of their children and demanded that much of the coach's time and effort be devoted to their children. Assessment of parent types classified parental positioning into several categories. *"Nonattenders"* were likely to drop off children at practice or games but never stayed to watch. *"Spectators"* were parents that attended all practices but took no part in helping with practice or the management of the team. The *"helpers"* were described as parents who contributed time and effort to assist the coach. These parents typically begin as "spectators" who transitioned into assisting after their children had been properly introduced to the sport. Their final parent classification was the *"committed member,"* who assisted the coaches, maintained contact with other parents, and helped manage the sports organization. Turman, Zimmerman, and Dobesh (2009) extended this research to explore the techniques parents used to develop relationships with their child's coach and what necessitated the need for those relationships. The lowest-level relationship was classified as the *spectators* and included parents who maximized their distance from the coach but made conscious efforts to ensure the coach recognized their presence and level of support. These parents attended a number of practice sessions and supported their child's athletic involvement by attending all games, volunteering to provide team meals, or providing snacks or refreshments. The second level was classified as the *enthusiasts,* representing those parents who made a point to offer insight or encouragement to the coach but also made a conscious effort to establish only a surface-level relationship. Their interaction focused mainly on the accomplishments or actions of the team as a whole and excluded recognition of individual children's accomplishments. One key distinction between the enthusiast and the spectator relationship was the motive behind the interaction with the coach. Enthusiast parents appeared to use these opportunities to demonstrate their level of knowledge about the particular sport as a way to establish a level of status or influence over coaching decisions. These parents worked to demonstrate a high level of interest and subject knowledge in the sport beyond what a spectator would attempt. The third level relationship is characterized as the *fanatic,* consisting of parents who perceived permeable boundaries between themselves and the coach. These parents were willing to address issues and topics directly, either face-to-face or over the phone. This interaction was seldom described in a negative manner by parents and was more common in smaller communities where parents and coaches often associated away from the sport. When this occurred, parents often used external interests as a logical excuse for talking about sports.

A Matter of Ethics: Just Following Orders?

For many young players, the authority of a coach is not to be questioned. Children are particularly likely to trust their coaches and believe that their decisions are in the best interest of everyone on the team. Thus, players are often willing to carry out any coach's order, even if it is unethical.

Some youth sports employ rules that mandate all team members have the opportunity to play during a game, a policy that can heighten the tension between competition and education. In 2005, Little League coach Mark Downs Jr. allegedly gave a 9-year-old player on his team $25 to intentionally throw a ball at an 8-year-old teammate. The 8-year-old was autistic, which limited his ability to play. Downs was prosecuted for aggravated assault, corruption of minors, and reckless endangerment. Prosecutors said he paid the 9-year-old because he didn't want the other boy to play in a playoff game. Downs was found guilty and sentenced to a prison term of 1 to 6 years.

Few would dispute that having a child intentionally throw at another is unethical. But this case perhaps raises other questions as well.

1. To what extent should youth sports mandate that every child gets to play?

2. Are youth sports really about education, competition, or both?

3. How should youth sports choose their teams' coaches?

4. What is the role of parents?

5. As for the outcome of the case, is a sentence of up to 6 years appropriate for this incident?

Coaches are faced with a number of challenges as they establish boundaries that negotiate the extent of the interaction they need to have with external stakeholders in the sport experience. As they attempt to orient more directly toward the internal consistencies, coaches are faced with a number of choices as they select the appropriate style/orientation for best leading their athletes.

LEADERSHIP ORIENTATIONS

To start this section, we offer you a glimpse at two competing coaching styles from coaches in the NFL. In 2005, Mike Tice was in his second year as the head coach for the Minnesota Vikings, successfully leading his team to a 4–0 start. At the time, the media touted him as being a players' coach who could get the most out of athletes by communicating with them at their level. It was believed that Tice, as a former player, best understood what made athletes tick, and he developed a fun and democratic environment that appeared to help his players achieve their utmost potential on the field. Tom Coughlin, the new coach for the New York Giants, was a study in contrast. He was viewed as a strict disciplinarian who had unique rules that frustrated his veteran players. He asked players to attend team meetings and then fined them for being on time rather than 15 minutes early. The veteran players on the team were vocal and outspoken to the media about how his "old-school" regimen was hindering their ability to bond as a team. This appeared to play out on the field as the team went 2–2 to start the season. One might wonder which of these two competing coaching styles is more likely to produce a successful team in the NFL. Based on what we have provided above, which do you believe is more likely to have produced success throughout the remainder of the season? We will hold the answer to that question until the end of this section.

Coach–athlete relationships are fostered differently among athletes based on the style(s) the coach decides to employ. The Multidimensional Leadership Theory (MLT) proposed by Chelladurai and Saleh (1978) operationalizes effective sport leadership by examining the way coaches understand member characteristics (e.g., the athlete's need for achievement or affiliation in the sport), situational characteristics (e.g., size of the team, amount of formal structure involved in the sport, task) and required leader behavior. To examine how coaches utilized these three variables in determining appropriate behaviors, a five-dimensional representation of leadership strategies in athletics has been proposed. These dimensions include (a) *autocratic behaviors,* or the extent to which coaches create a separation among athletes by establishing their position and authority over the team; (b) *democratic behaviors* utilized by coaches to foster participation by the athletes when making decisions related to the sport; (c) *social support* to satisfy interpersonal needs of the athletes; (d) displays of *positive feedback* to motivate athletes and demonstrate appreciation; and (e) *training and instruction* to foster the development of athletes' skill and knowledge aimed at improving performance in the sport (see Table 10.1).

MLT is premised on an assumption that a coach must be cognizant of the leadership preferences of his or her athletes, as well as understanding their maturity level, to adjust the leadership style that is most appropriate for the time. Overall, a number of team and athlete characteristics have been found to influence preferences for coaching styles, with collegiate and professional athletes preferring more autocratic behaviors, youth and high school athletes preferring training and instruction, and athletes with limited performance expectations having a stronger preference for positive feedback. Others have concluded that teams with high cohesion were likely to perceive their coaches as using relatively elevated levels of training and instruction.

When collapsing four of the five styles (democratic, training and instruction, social support, and positive feedback) into one general prosocial style, studies have found that this type of behavior is positively associated with athletes' affective learning toward sports (Turman & Schrodt, 2004). Contrary to prosocial behaviors enacted by coaches, an autocratic leadership style (e.g., antisocial or custodial behaviors enacted by coaches) is inversely correlated with athletes' affective learning, suggesting that coaches who rely solely on autocratic leadership behaviors may find their athletes demonstrating less appreciation for the sport, their teammates,

Table 10.1 Multidimensional Leadership Behaviors Used by Coaches

Leadership Types	Definition	Example
Autocratic	Direct and controlling approach where the coach has the final decision-making authority for the team.	"If you want to make this team then you will do what I ask without question."
Democratic	Egalitarian approach where the coach encourages athletes to be involved in the decision-making process for the team.	"For this last play, do you think it will work best if we give Jennifer a chance to make the last shot?"
Social Support	Encouraging approach that allows the coach to demonstrate a level of caring for athletes.	"I'm proud of what you have accomplished even if we weren't able to win this game."
Positive Feedback	Providing constructive statements that help to provide positive reinforcement for what occurs during practice and competition.	"Keep up the good work and it will pay off at the end of the season."
Training and Instruction	Feedback that focuses on athlete and team skill development.	"Kicking the ball toward the center of the field at this point in time will set up the clear shot for your teammates."

and most importantly, their coach. Even when accounting for success, it has been found that autocratic leadership in the presence of moderate to high levels of positive feedback may actually increase an athletes' developmental learning, whereas the sole use of autocratic leadership behaviors may lead to a decline. This tends to support "traditional," anecdotal notions that effective coaching is inherently a form of "tough love." In other words, coaches can enact autocratic leadership as long as athletes know that their coaches have

Brenda Frese

their best interests in mind and can occasionally communicate some form of positive feedback. At the very least, coaches who rely solely on the use of autocratic leadership may find that the deleterious effects of such behavior greatly outweigh athletes' need for positive feedback (consider the Mike Leach incident at Texas Tech that led to his removal as the head football coach in 2009).

Interview: Brenda Frese, Head Women's Basketball Coach, University of Maryland

Q: How have roles/responsibilities of a coach changed since you began coaching?

A: There are a few areas in which I think the responsibilities of a head coach have really evolved. In recruiting, it's now essential that the head coach be directly involved on a regular basis and not delegate to assistants. Recruits and their support groups expect a relationship with the head coach. Fortunately, I've always been a very hands-on head coach and really want to get to know the young people I'm possibly bringing into our program. Another area is the Internet. It can be used to inform and promote, but it is also something that coaches have to monitor to make sure their players aren't sharing any photos or information that can generate a negative response. Our players are in the public eye and really can't live the "normal college life." The Internet has also unleashed a bevy of anonymous experts who are free to publish their opinions on everything from basketball to basket weaving. That can be good, but it has also led to a lot of misinformation.

Q: What has proven to be the most effective means of motivating your players?

A: Being positive and building up the self-esteem of my players has been, by far, the most effective method for me. I want them to believe they can accomplish anything, whether in basketball or life. Nobody goes out on the court intending to fail, so I don't usually see the benefit in making them feel even worse.

Q: To what degree do you feel your job includes surrogate parenting?

A: There's definitely a parenting aspect. Sometimes a player will feel more comfortable talking to their coach than their actual parent. I've always had an open door for my players and they know they can talk to me about anything. We also see players from dysfunctional family backgrounds, and they really need someone to provide guidance and stability.

Q: **What aspects of coaching tend to be universally true regardless of gender or the sport being played?**

A: Regardless of gender or sport, you're going to find coaches who are equally passionate and just as competitive. You're also going to find coaches that seek a way to connect with their athletes and motivate them.

Q: **Do your communication strategies with your players change in different on- and off-court environments?**

A: I would say that my communication with my players is conducted in a consistent manner, whether on or off the court. That being said, the heat of the game is a very unique setting in which both players and coaches often see their intensity levels rise.

Q: **What is the biggest change you have enacted in your coaching communication strategies in the years you have coached?**

A: Some of our communication strategies have actually been legislated by the NCAA. We used to be able to text message recruits; now that's illegal. I also try to have periods where they are not on their phones or Sidekicks, because young people want to do so much of their communicating through electronic devices that they talk to each other less. It's important to foster the face-to-face conversation. It's the best way to get to know and understand each other.

This brings us back to the example of the two coaches we presented to you at the start of this section. Although Mike Tice had been able to lead his team to a 4–0 start during his second season, the team was soon plagued by a public relations nightmare after approximately 40% of the team was involved in a boat cruise incident involving exotic dancers during their bye week. The team finished the season with a 6–10 record and soon traded or released a number of star players who were identified by team officials as having disciplinary problems. Despite the fact that these were professional athletes, their maturity level still required a coaching style that demanded respect for the authority of the coach. Tice was soon fired after another unsuccessful season in 2005. Tom Coughlin's team finished roughly the same, ending the season with a 5–11 record, but players grew accustomed to his autocratic style as they soon determined that Coughlin withheld praise until player performance warranted it. Since that time, Coughlin has led the Giants to multiple postseason berths, as well as winning the 2008 Super Bowl. Although it is difficult to attribute the outcomes for these events solely to the coaching styles employed by these two coaches, the heightened need for positive feedback from coaches is one of the central premises set forth by those involved in a new approach to coaching referred to as the positive coaching movement.

POSITIVE COACHING

In the opening section of this chapter, we discussed the constant tension that coaches face because of the importance our society places on winning. Recognizing this tension, a group of coaches from varying sports throughout the United States has joined together to form the *Positive Coaching Alliance.* The mission of this organization is to engage coaches to encourage athletes to enjoy sports as a positive character-building experience. This movement has been geared toward youth sport organizations, but the efforts of this organization carry over into both the collegiate and professional levels. Phil Jackson, head coach of the Los Angeles Lakers and coach of 10 NBA championship teams, has been an avid supporter of the program since its inception in 1998. He affirms that his coaching philosophy centers around the ability to use positive feedback with his players by ensuring that approximately 75% of his comments to players focus on positive rather than negative statements/messages.

When coaches draw upon punitive actions to influence their athletes, they invite stress; yet positive feedback and reinforcement strategies have been found to have a greater impact on athletes' optimal performance, satisfaction levels, enjoyment, and self-esteem. Jowett (2007) notes that the most appropriate way to view the coach–athlete relationship is through four interrelated constructs that include closeness, commitment, complementarity, and co-orientation. *Closeness* includes the affective ties that form between a player and coach as an aspect such as a sense of liking and respect develops. *Commitment* emerges in this relationship when a cognitive attachment is created and the athletes begin to sense a long- rather than short-term orientation toward the coach. *Complementarity* occurs as the athlete and coach begin to communicate from a perspective of cooperation and affiliation. Lastly, *co-orientation* represents athletes' and coaches' abilities to understand the duality of their relationship by recognizing a division between mutual friendships while also existing in a relationship that reflects superior–subordinate behaviors. Each of these dimensions has been found to positively influence the depth of a coach–athlete relationship.

Coaches' positive orientation toward players also has an impact on the self-fulfilling prophecies for their players. A self-fulfilling prophecy occurs in sports when coaches view athletes differently (based on gender, ability, level of enthusiasm) and provide differential treatment. Soloman, DiMorco, Ohlson, and Reece (1998) state, "When coaches' perceptions of an athlete are consistently communicated and understood by the athlete they can impact the athlete's future performance and psychological growth in a positive or negative manner" (p. 445). Athletes with limited performance expectations are said to receive more technical instruction from their coaches, while those with high expectations are reinforced or encouraged at greater levels. As a result, these low-expectancy athletes are likely to view their experi-

Phil Jackson

ence more negatively when compared to high-achieving athletes. *High-expectancy* athletes have been shown to prefer more instruction and positive feedback, encouragement, and positive reinforcement. *Low-expectancy* athletes are asked fewer questions by their coaches and receive fewer skill practice opportunities, fewer constructive comments, and higher levels of criticism. A cyclical effect is likely to occur in these situations. Coaches interact in a more negative fashion, which then causes the low-expectancy athlete to withdraw and decrease motivation. This is then recognized by the coach, who then provides feedback that can then cause athletes to completely withdraw.

Positive coaching or support-based communication aids in reducing uncertainty that athletes might be experiencing with their sport. When uncertainty is eliminated, the relationships have been found to be less ambiguous, complex, and unpredictable. Naylor (2007) noted,

> The role of teacher is to educate, nurture, and empower athletes providing opportunities for personal growth and development. These are objectives that are easily accomplished in practice, yet decisions and behaviors of coaches during competitive situations are often at odds with educational ideals. (p. 32)

In the section that follows, we attempt to explore this dichotomy within the context of coach–athlete interaction during competitive situations.

COMMUNICATION CONTEXTS

The coach–athlete relationship can occur in a variety of contexts, giving coaches a range of options for communicating with players. For instance, coaches are no longer limited by the confines of the athletic season, as many sports have become year-round activities for youth, high school, collegiate, and professional athletes. In many instances, coaches attempt to begin building this relationship before an athlete has even joined the team. For example, text messaging has become such a powerful tool employed by college coaches in their recruiting efforts that the NCAA has recently established limits on when these messages can be sent to players. Kelvin Sampson (head basketball coach at Indiana University) was even fired for violating these text messaging policies.

When placed within the window of the traditional season, coaches are most likely to communicate with players during practice or competitive events. Performance feedback is an important feature of any instructional process whereby coaches are afforded the opportunity to provide an assessment of athletes' overall performance. As the positive coaching movement might attest, the messages coaches select to frame their feedback can directly influence the attributions athletes make about their athletic experience. For example, a coach's decision to place the blame on the team's star athlete after a loss is quite different from one who might choose to encourage the player who missed the final shot that marked the end of the season. The coach may also place the blame on him- or herself or even make a point to build up players who have been struggling by using the pregame speech to challenge them to perform beyond their means. Gallmeier (1987) followed a professional hockey team throughout the season and noted that the coach relied upon the pregame speech to "psych up" players, especially in situations where the coach didn't have access to the players throughout the day. Players exposed to these speeches were found to have higher levels of self-efficacy and larger margins of victory. Not only are athlete outcomes influenced, they self-report that the pregame speech is an important function that the coach fulfills for the team, with most athletes noting a strong desire for an emotional response from their coach.

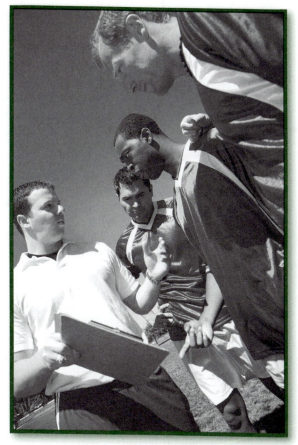

Soccer coach explaining strategy

The messages coaches select can be powerful predictors for how athletes view their athletic experiences, and most individuals are predisposed to interpret behaviors, actions, and events that occur around them in connection with their causes. People have an innate need to find an explanation for why an event occurred, which allows us to better control our surroundings; when one is unable to understand the reason why, the world is rendered unpredictable. The messages that coaches employ during these competitive situations have also been found to produce feelings of regret as athletes are called upon to reflect upon what could have or should have happened. *Regret* is defined as a complex emotion causing individuals to make judgments about events they take part in, and they have the ability to feel regretful not only about their participation in past experiences but also about how decisions concerning future events are made.

The need to use messages that connect antecedents and outcomes is likely to increase as individuals or groups are faced with winning and losing situations. For instance, Turman (2005) identified six types of regret messages used by coaches during their pregame, halftime, and postgame speeches. The most predominant was *accountability regret,* which represented coaches' need to assign blame or praise following their team's first-half performance. By focusing their players' attention on factors that reduced the team's ability to win, coaches were able to implicitly demonstrate that if these antecedents were addressed by the team, a more positive outcome would result at the end of the contest ("If we just would have gone for it on fourth down, we could have won the game"). *Individual performance regret* messages were used to help magnify the potential self-regret felt by athletes after a poor performance/outcome. A majority of these messages occurred during the coaches' pregame comments to the team and included a combination of counterfactual antecedents (e.g., "If you play hard") and upward counterfactual outcomes (e.g., "You will feel satisfied"). Thirdly, *collective failure regret* signified messages that demonstrated how athlete performance was potentially linked to the disappointment of their teammates or coach ("If you don't give 100% on every play, you will be letting this team down"). *Social significance regret* was derived from the coaches' efforts to construct the game as socially significant for their players. For instance, as the season began to draw to a close, a number of coaches began to call attention to the fact that athletes in their senior year were drawing closer to their final game or direct their athletes' attention toward the significance of the upcoming event for both the team and their school ("Letting them come in here and push you around isn't something our fans will accept"). Fifth, coaches relied on r*egret reduction* primarily during the postgame interaction; it characterized coaches' attempts to reduce the potential regret felt by athletes after a loss ("If we hadn't tried for that long pass, we still would have lost the game"). Finally, as the season drew to a close, a number of coaches relied on regret messages that described the *future regret* players would experience as a result of a team loss. It appeared that coaches used this foreshadowing of events and the potential emotional response athletes would feel afterward to identify antecedents that athletes could employ to control their future outcome ("Lose this game and you'll take it to the grave").

Turman (2007) further explored the impact of regret on a variety of athlete outcomes and found that success and status determine the extent to which athletes will perceive increases in coach performance and future regret messages. Hastie (1999) explored coach–athlete interaction during time-outs, observing a positive relationship with athlete performance for the team calling the time-out. He noted that messages fell within three categories, including (a) *technical statements*—messages that correct the behaviors of players both positively and negatively; (b) *tactical statements*—proactive or reactive statements that use a combination of questions or focus on consequences; and (c) *psychological statements*—general encouragement or reasoning statements that attempt to draw attention or focus athletes. The messages or statements employed in each of these contexts (pregame, time-outs, halftime, and postgame interaction) provide a brief glimpse into the nature of the coach–athlete relationship during competitive situations (see Table 10.2).

Table 10.2 Coach Regret Message Types Employed During Competitive Situations

Message Type	Definition	Example
Accountability Regret	Statements that emphasize the factors that contributed to a team's unsuccessful performance.	"When you fail to pass the puck around to your teammates, it's difficult to score points."
Individual Performance Regret	Messages that place specific blame on an individual occurrence or event that signaled a team's loss.	"If we just would have tried for a two-point conversion, we wouldn't have lost in overtime."
Collective Failure Regret	Statements geared toward reinforcing the need for the team to work together to ensure success.	"Despite losing Jackie to an ankle injury, we can all pull together in the second half to win."
Social Significance Regret	Messages that reinforce the broader impact of sport beyond just the outcome for the event.	"The people of this town are expecting you to win this game, so don't hold back anything tonight."
Regret Reduction	Statements that are used by the coach to reduce the feelings of regret that players might be experiencing after a contest.	"I know that winning is important, but I would hope that you have learned from this experience and can use it to get better as we move forward as a team."
Future Regret	Emphasis on the significance of the team's outcome as an approach to help reinforce a team's desire to win.	"When you get to a championship game, either you give it everything you have or it will haunt you for the rest of your life."

CONCLUSION

In this chapter, we have introduced you to a number of factors that directly influence the coach–athlete relationship. As one considers the tension that coaches face as they make decisions about winning versus the developmental needs of their players, a number of styles are likely to emerge. The rhetorical and communicative resources that a coach draws upon determine not only a team's success but also how athletes view and interpret their sport experience. Having a coach who emphasizes a positive orientation toward coaching could be important for young athletes who are seeking an enjoyable experience from their sport participation.

On the other hand, collegiate or professional athletes are more inclined to have coaches who draw upon the authority of their position to ensure the highest levels of success. This does not mean that coaches have to take a punitive approach to obtain the desired response from their athletes, as even professional coaches must understand the emotional turmoil that athletes can experience in the "just business" model for professional and collegiate athletics. Although he is often vilified by the media for his antics during games and harsh treatment of players, Bob Knight (former NCAA basketball coach who currently holds the all-time record for most career wins in NCAA men's basketball) is often described by his former players in affectionate terms. His autocratic behavior was a function of the competitive nature of NCAA basketball, but he also possessed skills for teaching the fundamentals of the sport while producing some of the highest player graduation rates in the nation. Vince Lombardi was viewed in a similar fashion by his players. Many describe him as a coach who was intent on winning but who could also connect with players on a personal level in one-on-one situations. Developing a suitable balance in one's communication style is what marks the difference between coaches who effectively foster positive relationships with their athletes and those who don't.

Bob Knight

REFERENCES

Chelladurai, P., & Saleh, S. D. (1978). Preferred leadership in sports. *Canadian Journal of Applied Sport Science, 3,* 85–92.

Cote, J. (1999). The influence of family in sports: A review. *International Journal of Sport Psychology, 21,* 328–354.

Gallmeier, C. P. (1987). Putting on the game face: The staging of emotions in professional hockey. *Sociology of Sport Journal, 4,* 347–362.

Hastie, P. A. (1999). An instrument for recording coaches' comments and instructions during time-outs. *Journal of Sport Behavior, 22,* 467–478.

Jowett, S. (2007). Interdependence analysis and the 3 + 1C's in the coach–athlete relationship. In S. Jowett & D. Larallce (Eds.), *Social psychology in sport* (pp. 15–27). Champaign, IL: Human Kinetics.

Jowett, S. (2009). Validating coach–athlete relationship measures with the nomological network. *Measurement in Physical Education and Exercise Science, 13,* 34–51.

Kirk, D., & MacPhail, A. (2003). Social positioning and the construction of a youth sports club. *International Review for the Sociology of Sport, 38,* 23–45.

Kruse, N. W. (1981). Apologia in team sport. *Quarterly Journal of Speech, 67,* 270–283.

Mach, F. (1994). Defusing parent–coach dissidence. *Scholastic Coach, 63*(10), 5–6.

Masin, H. L. (2007, September) Remember the "only thing"? *Coach & Athletic Director,* p. 5.

Naylor, A. H. (2007). The coach's dilemma: Balancing playing to win and player development. *Journal of Education, 187,* 31–48.

Roberts, G. C. (1984). Achievement motivation in children's sport. In J. G. Nicholls (Ed.), *Advances in motivation and achievement: Vol. 3* (pp. 251–281). Greenwich, CT: JAI Press.

Solomon, G. B., DiMarco, A. M., Ohlson, C. J., & Reece, S. D. (1998). Expectations and coaching experience: Is more better? *Journal of Sport Behavior, 21,* 444–455.

Turman, P. D. (2005). Coaches' use of anticipatory and counterfactual regret messages during competition. *Journal of Applied Communication Research, 33,* 116–138.

Turman, P. (2007). Coach regret messages: The influence of athlete sex, context, and performance on high school basketball coaches' use of regret messages during competition. *Communication Education, 56,* 333–353.

Turman, P., & Schrodt, P. (2004). Coaching as an instructional communication context: Relationships among coaches' leadership behaviors and athletes' affective learning. *Communication Research Reports, 21,* 130–143.

Turman, P., Zimmerman, A., & Dobesh, B. (2009). Parent-talk and sport participation: Interaction between parents, children, and coaches regarding level of play in sports. In T. Socha & G. Stamp (Eds.), *Interfacing outside of home: Parents and children communicating with society* (pp. 171-188). New York, NY: Lawrence Earlbaum.

SUGGESTED ADDITIONAL READING

Heath, S. B. (1991). "It's about winning!": The language of knowledge in baseball. In L. B. Resnick, J. M. Levine, & S. D. Teasley (Eds.), *Perspectives on socially shared cognition* (pp. 101–124). Washington, DC: American Psychological Association.

Kassing, J. W., & Infante, D. A. (1999). Aggressive communication in the coach–athlete relationship. *Communication Research Reports, 16,* 110–120.

Llewellyn, J. (2003). Coachtalk: Good reasons for winning and losing. In Robert S. Brown & Daniel O'Rourke (Eds.), *Case studies in sport communication.* Westport, CT: Praeger.

Turman, P. (2007). Coach regret messages: The influence of athlete sex, context, and performance on high school basketball coaches' use of regret messages during competition. *Communication Education, 56,* 333–353.

Wooden, J. (1997). *Wooden: A lifetime of observation and reflection on and off the court.* Chicago: Contemporary Books.

CHAPTER **11**

Small Groups/
Teams in Sport

Throughout this text we have emphasized the significant impact that sport can have for individuals at varying levels. Parents encourage sport participation because they view it as an important socializing agent, fans can feel transcendence through viewing or taking part in rituals central to sport spectatorship, and coaches help shape their players' mindsets by emphasizing the important life lessons that can surface through the preparation for competition. Each of these contexts has one element in common: They all occur in groups. Groups and teams play a foundational role not only in how sport is enacted but also in how our society consumes and learns from the sport experience. For example, more than half of today's children are involved in some type of organized group sport, suggesting that many will reach maturity after acquiring much of their understanding about the nature and structure of small-group interaction from sports and games. We all learn from our group experiences, and because many of these groups are composed primarily of sport-type groups, it seems relevant that much of what we learn about group practices, norms, roles, and how to communicate would take place within a sport context. Furthermore, as we gain a stronger appreciation for the impact sport participation might play on the development of various communication behaviors, a stronger emphasis could be placed on sport as an important informal learning context with societal implications.

With this background in mind, this chapter seeks to explore these issues by providing perspective on the influence of communication within the context of sport and games. Sport is overflowing with examples of teams filled

Sportsmanship in action at the conclusion of a youth soccer game

with talented individuals who have failed to achieve success in the face of inferior opponents, supporting the fact that team interaction is a critical factor in success. Sport teams can easily be distinguished based on the level of interdependence required by athletes during competition, a function that is mediated by communication. *Independent teams* include those where the culmination of individual effort contributes to a team's performance (i.e., wrestling, track and field, gymnastics, etc.), while *interdependent teams* require that athletes collaborate to ensure victory (i.e., football, baseball, hockey, etc.). We begin this chapter by examining the complex communication events that contribute to team cohesion levels. Although variables including team performance and athlete inputs/outputs have been found to strongly influence cohesion, team interaction and coaching behaviors/strategies also contribute to ensuring a team's winning potential. Also, as your experience might attest, there are a number of group processes unique to sports. Sport teams often introduce coaches and players to an important set of group processes (e.g., norm development, power, leadership emergence, etc.) that are central to framing the team experience. We explore each of these processes under a communication lens in an effort to highlight unique group functions that occur in sport teams. Finally, we conclude this chapter by demonstrating the role that sport and games have for developing the unique communication behaviors that distinguish masculine and feminine communication cultures. Such gender differences become quite pronounced and have the potential for influencing one's future group interaction. As we explore each of these major themes throughout this chapter, we anticipate that you will develop a broader appreciation for the direct and indirect ways that participation in sport teams affects your everyday experiences.

TEAM/GROUP COHESION

Maximizing effort to win is an essential feature of sport, but to achieve this goal, it is critical that individual team members be equally invested in ensuring team success. For this to occur, team members must experience a sense of connection, which has been assessed in terms of team cohesion levels. *Cohesion* is an important sport outcome defined as the sense of belonging or sense of morale individuals experience as a function of their team membership. There has been some speculation that success and cohesion can be used interchangeably, as 83% of studies indicated a positive relationship between cohesion and performance (Widmeyer, Carron, & Brawley, 1993). Scholarly work on cohesion

Huddle at a fastpitch softball game

suggests that team cohesion is mediated by two dimensions reflecting the *task* (e.g., desire to achieve the group's goals) and *social* functions (e.g., desire to develop and maintain relationships) fulfilled by the group.

Much of this cohesive environment has been influenced by a number of factors driven by communication. Such feelings have been described as "we-ness" because members are more likely to use the term *we* than *I* when referring to the team (hence, the saying that there is no *I* in *team*). Drawing attention to one's individual performance in team sports can be viewed as a detriment to the cohesive environment fans are likely to expect. For example, the NCAA implemented strict rules that prohibit football players from on-field celebrations that draw attention to the individual rather than the team. Significant backlash is also likely to occur when athletes present the impression they are not playing to peak potential. During the 2004 NFL season, Randy Moss was heavily criticized for statements he made suggesting he didn't give 100% every play, especially in situations when he didn't expect to receive the ball. Despite his potential as a future Hall of Fame receiver, he was subsequently traded early in his career because of his on- and off-field behaviors that management perceived to be detrimental to the team. A similar situation occurred during the 2002 MLB season as Pittsburgh Pirate Derek Bell indicated he would be going into "Operation Shutdown" during training camp when he found out he was being asked to compete for a starting position. Research has even shown that the presence of *social loafing* behaviors (the extent team effort and performance do not meet the combination of individual abilities and potential) mediates team cohesion in sports (Hoigaard, Tofteland, & Ommundsen, 2006). They found that cohesive groups were less likely to experience social loafing, resulting in heightened team performance levels.

Interview: William Wanger, Senior Vice President of Research and Programming, FOX Sports

Q: **What are your official responsibilities in your role at FOX Sports?**

A: I run the programming and research department for the FOX Sports Television Group that is responsible for the program scheduling, strategic research analysis, and consumer research for FOX Sports, FOX Sports.com, and our cable sports channels, such as Speed and FOX Soccer Channel. Our departmental goal is to raise ratings and increase revenue for FOX Sports. We interact with every area of FOX Sports, including sales, corporate communications, marketing, production, operations, and finance.

Q: **Within the organizational structure, what formal groups exist? To what degree must they interact with each other?**

A: FOX Sports is organized in departments that work very closely with each other. Daily interaction among departments is particularly important for a television production unit that relies on multiple disciplines to get an event or show produced and on the air. For example, for a sport like the NFL, the programming group must decide which game each affiliate station will receive; the production group must assign announcers to each game based on those assignments; games must be marketed; field operations must have the proper equipment at each remote site; graphics must be created; commercials need to be sold; story lines and coverage need to be publicized; the game production crews must prepare for each game; and operations must ensure the game airs properly. On Sunday night, the research group must record all the information that happened during the day in terms of timings so Nielsen can produce an accurate television rating. Finally, finance will see how the rating, commercial revenue, and expenses compare to budget plans.

Q: **How does FOX Sports ensure the delivery of a cohesive, consistent mediated sports product?**

A: Senior management of FOX sports determines the production philosophy for each sport and communicates it to the entire division during the production seminars and weekly meetings. From that point, each game production unit plans its production to fit under the overall FOX Sports philosophy.

Q: **How formal is the FOX Sports leadership/management structure?**

A: There is a very formal management structure at FOX Sports that includes the chairman and CEO of FOX Sports, a president, and several department heads that run the division. While there is a formal structure, FOX Sports has fewer people than most sports divisions at broadcast or cable networks, which leads to a nimble, bold, and innovative team.

Q: **One sport your network covers a lot is NASCAR—a sport that many falsely believe to be an individual sport rather than a team one. How does/can your telecast help alleviate this misconception?**

A: While it might not look like it, NASCAR is truly a team sport. The crew chief runs the team from the top to bottom, including engine builders, mechanics, spotters,

(Continued)

(Continued)

and pit crews. The team needs to function well together or the driver will not win races. To show the team aspect of the sport, FOX utilizes a team of pit reporters to interview crew chiefs on strategy and highlight pit crew performance. In addition, we have two former crew chiefs as part of the FOX race team who help to inject the team aspect of the sport.

Q: In terms of power, how much does prior experience and institutional memory factor into who has a voice in determining the choices that go into a telecast?

A: FOX Sports has the best and most experienced producers in the business, with the two executive producers, David Hill and Ed Goren, each having decades of production experience all around the world. Their experience has a tremendous impact on each telecast.

Coach's Impact on Cohesion

Teams at all levels of competition spend considerable time, energy, and resources to unravel factors that enhance team effectiveness, with much of this emphasis placed in the areas of cohesion. Because the team's cohesion level affects individual group member behavior, numerous scholars emphasize the important role of the coach in fostering cohesion to further enhance team performance (see Chapter 10). Research has even shown considerable need for cohesion among the members of the coaching staff (Martin, 2002). Recent investigations of coaching strategies suggest that positive relationships between coaches and athletes have the potential to positively influence team cohesion levels. For instance, Turman (2003) interviewed college athletes regarding the specific communication behaviors displayed by their coaches that deterred or promoted team cohesion. Two different behaviors were found to deter cohesion among athletes. Athletes described *inequity* as situations where coaches showed favoritism to a particular athlete or group within the team, utilization of poor communication skills, and/or bragging about the ability of other athletes. Favoritism included situations such as allowing individual athletes to do less work or miss team functions (i.e., meetings, events, practices) without reprimands. This is consistent with other research that has explored jealousy in sports, where categories such as scholarship funding and attention from the coach were found to be negatively correlated with team cohesion levels (Schelling-Kamphoff & Huddleston, 1999). The second theme included *embarrassment and ridicule,* reflecting behaviors such as yelling at athletes or benching them for poor performance. This type of behavior appeared to not only influence the athlete being reprimanded but also affect other players who witnessed the events.

Five behaviors/strategies were identified that have positive effects on promoting team cohesion. *Sarcasm and teasing* consisted of joking, mocking, and ridicule of athletes that allowed them to collectively laugh together. Athletes reported that forms of sarcasm drew them closer because coaches were able to show a nonsport side that worked to build relationships between players. *Motivational speeches* were influential because of the way they allowed athletes to interact as a team afterward while also stressing team over individual effort. Cohesion was further fostered when coaches focused on relinquishing personal agendas for the good of the team. When the team faced a *quality opponent,* the respect coaches afforded the opposition increased cohesion as players bonded at higher levels. When coaches described opponents with respect, athletes perceived increased cohesion after accepting that no opponent should be taken lightly. Some alluded to the connection and focus of their teammates during weeks they played higher-caliber opponents, as coaches often approached difficult games differently during pregame speeches. Matchups in international soccer competition between Real Madrid and FC Barcelona in Spain or the women's basketball teams at the University of Connecticut and University of Tennessee are just a few examples of instances where significant rivalries assist to bond players at higher levels. Focusing on the rivalry helped establish a clear "us" versus "them" quality threaded throughout a coach's behavior leading up to the contest. Coaches fostered *athlete-directed techniques* by encouraging teammates to develop their own connection, including spending time together off the field, lifting weights and studying together, or scheduling team picnics. Finally, athletes reported that the use of a *team prayer* during pregame and postgame interaction was a successful strategy because it emphasized that every team member must perform up to his or her maximum ability. Internal conflicts and tensions among athletes appeared to be eliminated, as the prayer would often bring the team together as a unit just prior to competition.

Case Study: More than Talent Required

Although athletic talent of individual team members can be a significant predictor for team success, there is support for the fact that teammates need to develop a strong social connection to help coordinate their efforts. High school, collegiate, and professional sports are filled with instances where teams with unlimited potential have failed to achieve their anticipated outcomes because the sense of "we-ness" has been lacking from the group. At the start of the 1999–2000 NBA season, the Los Angeles Lakers hired Phil Jackson, who had recently retired after coaching the Chicago Bulls to six NBA titles. With two of the league's most talented players (Kobe Bryant and Shaquille O'Neal), Jackson was considered to be a pivotal piece in the puzzle as he helped lead the team to three titles during his first three seasons. The following year they went 11–19 to start the season, ultimately recovering to finish with more than 50 wins. However, they were eventually eliminated from postseason play by the San Antonio Spurs at the conclusion of the 2003 season.

During the offseason, Jackson sought to further position the team to win his fourth championship with the Lakers. Management aggressively pursued a trade for Karl Malone from the Utah Jazz and Gary Payton from the Seattle SuperSonics. With a lineup that included Bryant, O'Neal, Malone, and Payton, many considered the Los Angeles Lakers team to be one of the most talented groups of players ever amassed on one team in NBA history. With four future Hall of Fame players taking the floor each night, the team appeared unstoppable on paper. However, the team faced early setbacks during the season resulting from a number of injuries to the starting lineup and tension between the team's two star players. Despite these difficulties, the Lakers ended the regular season with a .700 record and advanced into the 2004 NBA playoffs, where they were eventually eliminated in five games against the Detroit Pistons. Tension further escalated during the postseason between Bryant and O'Neal. Bryant even displayed considerable disagreement with Jackson's coaching style as he publicly criticized Jackson for employing a game strategy that did not fully utilize his talents. Jackson soon demanded that Bryant be traded. In response, the Lakers front office eventually sided with Bryant as they traded O'Neal and terminated their contract with Jackson. The Lakers failed to make the playoffs the next two seasons and were unable to return to championship form again until Jackson returned as the head coach for the 2007–2008 season.

1. To what factors would you attribute the team's inability to win a fourth championship with the talent it had amassed?

2. How might the presence of four superstar players inversely affect the team's ability to foster a cohesive environment conducive to winning?

3. Where might you fit Bormann's process of residues as a contributing factor in explaining the problems this team confronted?

Each of these coaching strategies works to establish team rituals that not only foster team cohesion but also institute important norms, roles, and processes that determine appropriate behavior on the team. As participation in teams is an essential feature of sport, sport participants are likely to be exposed to a combination of both rewarding and detrimental grouping processes. We explore each of these areas in the following section.

GROUP/TEAM PROCESSES IN SPORT

As we discussed in the opening paragraph, there is evidence to suggest that much of what individuals learn about group behavior, norms, and roles can be traced to their sport participation. This can produce both positive and negative outcomes for individuals' future behavior.

Group Norms

Group norms serve as a standard for how group members begin to understand how they are expected to behave as members of the team. These acceptable forms of behavior evolve over time and become powerful determinants for how team members are socialized. While sometimes related, *group roles* often emerge over time and represent the individual expectations attributed to group member behaviors. For instance, team captains are often assigned and expected to fulfill specific types of roles (i.e., "When there is a problem, Karen will call a team meeting"), while some can emerge from routine behaviors from a particular team member (i.e., "We always expect Chantel to be late for practice"). Although one would expect that acceptable norms are reinforced, scholars have exposed a range of norm behaviors (cheating, aggression, and rule violations) that violate the underlying tenets of competition. For example, officials in the NHL were evaluated to determine rule accuracy and correctness, yet it was found they were less concerned with these two officiating norms as they emphasized consistency and fairness during the game (Rains, 1984). For teams, a combination of competitive, practice, off-season, and social norms have been found to exist (Munroe, Estabrooks, Dennis, & Carron, 1999). *Competitive norms* included things such as the team's expected game preparedness and work ethic. Teammates are expected to be punctual and attend with a mindset that results in productivity from other players. *Practice norms* include many of the same game expectations yet did not tie directly to team productivity. Players were expected to work hard and be prepared and punctual. Lack of attendance was frowned upon by teammates, noting the direct perceived correlation between practices and team success during competition. During his time with the Philadelphia 76ers, Allen Iverson was heavily criticized by his coach, teammates, fans, and the media for routinely being late or absent from scheduled practice sessions. Many of you may have seen his famous 2002 postgame tirade where he criticized his coach and the media after he had been suspended for violating this important team norm. In the interview he noted, "We're sitting here, and I'm supposed to be the franchise player, and we're talking about practice." His response went on for 4 minutes and used the term "practice" 14 times. *Off-season norms* include behaviors such as keeping in contact with teammates and sharing workout strategies that are developed in the off-season. Players also expect others to maintain a healthy lifestyle that would not inversely affect the team while continuing to train and compete in the sport during the off-season. Finally, *social norms* represent the general atmosphere/climate teammates are expected to maintain, which include keeping others in high regard, avoiding physical conflicts, and remaining silent about internal matters of the team. Munroe and her colleagues concluded that "the development of group norms for social situations and during the off-season inevitably ensures that the interpersonal bonds within the team are characterized by stability, affective concern, and a sense of continuity" (p. 180). The findings depict favorable expectation for teammates, yet there are no guarantees that norm violation won't occur, especially when considering the fact that unproductive norms/rituals continue to exist in team sports.

Hazing in Sports

Hazing rituals are a common communicative norm (harassment, abuse, humiliation) that many consider to serve as important rites of passage for initiating new members into the group. As groups develop, there is a strong need for members to be socialized into the culture and history of the group, as members are commonly tested to determine their commitment to becoming a part of the team. Some even go as far as to suggest that hazing is an important team-building experience or even has a positive impact on team cohesion levels. When viewed as team member behavior toward new members, hazing can be a vicious tool for communicating power and team positioning. Hazing laws have been implemented in numerous states, with high schools and colleges imposing strict penalties on teams who still take part in this unproductive grouping experience. Often you will see media reports of incidents such as when a high school football player filed charges against his coach and school officials after senior players taped him to a goal post and then took turns kicking soccer balls at his head. There have also been more graphic examples, such as video footage that surfaced (Glenbrook North High School women's soccer team) showing teammates putting Tabasco sauce and vinegar in the eyes of freshmen players and covering them with fish guts, Spam, and pig intestines.

Despite the threat of stiff penalties, hazing continues to be a common occurrence that can depict an unconstructive feature of team sport participation. Despite this perception, it is difficult for many teams to curb this practice because of the customary recurring cycle of hazing; hazed underclassman take out their frustrations on other underclassmen when they later find themselves in leadership positions. At the professional level, media often portray trivial forms of hazing such as having male rookie players dress up as women, expecting them to carry equipment for veteran players, or requiring them to sing at team meals. For example, Larry English (the San Diego Chargers' first-round pick during the 2009 NFL draft) was forced to pick up a $15,000 dinner bill for returning players as an annual hazing ritual veteran players engage in. Well-intended bonding occurrences of hazing such as this are likely to be found each year during the start of most professional seasons. The *Sporting News* has also been known to ask a player from each team an embarrassing question at NFL training camps, which has been considered a mild form of hazing. However, it has been difficult to obtain accurate data on hazing at the high school and collegiate levels as only 12% of athletes report exposure to hazing (Hoover, 1999), yet more than 80% of these same athletes reported being involved in a range of specific hazing activities as a way of initiation. This suggests that athletes engage in hazing activities while also recognizing the negative perception that society has toward such activities in sport. Research connecting hazing to cohesion levels has been limited (Van Raalte, Cornelius, Linder, & Brewer, 2007), finding a strong negative correlation between hazing and task attraction. In this analysis, they distinguished between unacceptable and acceptable team-building behaviors (see Table 11.1).

Even though Raalte and her colleagues note a number of acceptable forms of team-building behaviors connected to hazing in team sports, hazing is generally frowned upon. Individual acceptance of such norms/rituals can be dependent on the individuals who occupy leadership positions on the team and the way they prefer to establish their bases of power.

Leadership Emergence and Power

Leadership is one of the most widely studied phenomena, and the impact that formal leaders have on teams was explored in Chapter 10 as we discussed the coach–athlete relationship. Athletes and teammates can also serve as an important source of formal (i.e., team captain assigned/selected by the coach) and informal leadership (emerge as an inspirational figure for the team). Some sports, like hockey, actually have team captains wear a "C" on their uniform to signify this *formal leader* assignment. Team captains on a football team are asked to represent the team during the coin toss or

Table 11.1 Unacceptable and Acceptable Team-building Behaviors Linked to Hazing in Sports

Team Building Types	Description
Unacceptable	
Passive Victim of Abuse	Instances where players have been kidnapped by fellow teammates, abandoned in isolated areas, tied up or taped without permission, or berated for non-sport-related behaviors.
Coerced Self-Abuse or Degradation	Forcing teammates to drink unknown substances or engaging in drinking contests. Also includes food and water deprivation or using rookies as personal servants.
Coerced Abuse of Others	Requiring teammates to harass other players or non-team members, destroy personal property, or engage in acts of vandalism or theft.
Acceptable	
Skill Development and Assessment	Requiring teammates to participate in nonmandatory preseason or early workouts or practices that might include physical exertion or tests of endurance unrelated to sport performance.
Coerced Deviant Behavior	Requiring teammates to engage in tattooing, piercing, or branding. Can also include public displays of embarrassing clothing and/or simulated sex acts.
Team Socialization	Involve teammates in public performances that include skits, singing, dressing up, or team roast.
Required Positive Behavior	Established team policies requiring grade point averages, study sessions, community service, or other behaviors that produce favorable public exposure.

communicate with officials when deciding to accept/decline penalties during the course of the game. *Informal leaders* assume a different set of behind-the-scenes roles for the team, which may include relationship building, fostering cohesion, or resolving team unrest during times of conflict. They are likely to emerge in situations where task behaviors are necessary to enhance team norms and functioning (Dupuis, Bloom, & Loughead, 2006).

Formal and informal leadership is important to consider in this section because group communication processes are essential to determining how leaders emerge in sport teams. Think about how you attempt to assess your place in the groups you encounter (decision-making group, intramural team, or professional sport, etc.). It is not uncommon for you to assess others in relation to yourself by comparing strengths and faults. Through this process, you are able to determine who wishes to be a bystander on the team (determined to be a support player) and who seeks legitimate leadership positions. Those who fail to give 100% to the team or who are deemed to have limited contributions are quickly eliminated from consideration. You are then left with those whose contributions are of most interest to the team.

Bormann (1996) refers to this process as a method of residues, whereby we seek to eliminate individuals from contention until we are left with those we are most willing to consider. Burtis and Turman (2009) describe this as an informal and ". . . interaction-based negotiation. It is usually not done in a particularly cruel or overt manner (except when children chose teams during recess). We just start paying more attention to people whose potential for giving direction we place closer to the center of our palate of choices" (p. 108). On sport teams, there are particular factors that seem to lend themselves to this emergence process. The most talented players (e.g., Michelle Akers, Cheryl Miller, etc.), certain positions (goalie, point guard, etc.), or even veteran players are likely to remain standing after this process of residue has transpired. The extent to which teammates engage in interpersonal interaction in team sports appears to increase perceived leadership capacity. People who play central positions on a softball team that require *significant interactive tasks* (catcher and infielders) are more likely to emerge as informal/formal team leaders when compared to those in *low-interacting positions* (pitchers and outfielders). Grusky (1963) found that individuals in these positions in baseball are more likely to assume manager positions after their playing careers have ended. This has been less likely to occur in sports where low interaction or consistency exists (e.g., hockey, soccer, etc.).

A Matter of Ethics: Tragedy in Waco

College coaches have been involved in numerous controversies in recent years, ranging from Iowa State's Larry Eustachy being photographed while drinking at a party with University of Missouri undergraduates to the University of Alabama's Mike Price's alleged tryst with a Florida stripper. Perhaps most tragically, in 2003, Baylor University basketball coach Dave Bliss attempted to discredit a former player who had been murdered by a teammate by concocting a story that the player was a drug dealer. The scheme was designed to cover up improper tuition payments that Bliss had made on behalf of two players at Baylor. When the story was made public, Bliss was quickly ousted and the university, which prides itself on its religious affiliation, faced a public relations nightmare.

(Continued)

(Continued)

The story became public, at least in part, because Baylor assistant coach Abar Rouse had audiotaped conversations with Bliss that included details of the cover-up. Rouse, who felt that Bliss's actions undermined the Christian mission of the university, reported the information to the National Collegiate Athletic Association (NCAA). For many, therefore, Rouse was seen as fulfilling his ethical obligations as a coach and a man of deep religious faith.

Yet the college basketball community treated Rouse differently. Rather than viewing him as an ethical standard bearer, his fellow coaches instead saw him as someone who broke an unwritten rule that mandates loyalty to team under all circumstances. Even Mike Krzyzewski, the highly esteemed coach at Duke University, emphasized the need for coaches to submit to an "all for one, one for all" mentality. "If one of my assistants would tape every one of my conversations with me not knowing," he said, "there's no way he would be on my staff." Other coaches appeared to agree with this sentiment, given that Rouse still has no position as an assistant basketball coach.

This case highlights the tensions that exist between individual and team principles. Although sports often cultivate a positive conception of teamwork, they also can impose a sense of loyalty that asks individuals to compromise their own integrity.

1. What are the implications of Rouse's case for our understanding of teamwork?

2. Was it appropriate for him to tape his conversations with Bliss? What other options could he have pursued?

3. Do you think it is fair that the college basketball community has, in effect, exiled Rouse from the game?

As this process of residues unfolds, teams begin to operate under established bases of power inherent in the coach, captain, or informal positions. Bases of power (coercive, reward, legitimate, referent, and expert) can be traced to important communication attempts with team members (French & Raven, 1959). *Coercive* power is dependent upon a player's belief that leaders will follow through with punishments. *Reward* power exists in the form of positive feedback from leaders such as acknowledging achievements or offering words of praise. *Legitimate* power is more closely associated with formal leadership positions, warranting compliance due to the nature of the coaching position. This legitimate power can be distributed across assistant coaches who make playing status decisions or apply pressure on behalf of the coach. Informal leadership positions often rely on *referent* power, which is the capacity to garner compliance from others based on their desire to form/maintain positive relationships. Coaches have the ability to rely upon referent power for rookie players who have a strong desire to identify and satisfy their coaches. At the start of each NFL season, HBO follows a different team in the program *Hard Knocks,* which depicts players on the bubble for making the team whose primary concern is making a favorable impression on the coaching staff. Finally, *expert* power is derived from athletes' ability to perceive the competence of individuals in formal leadership positions. Lacking a clear understanding for the sport, previous success, or skill will be detriments to one's ability to gain compliance from team members using this power base. Possessing a combination of referent and expert power is likely to stand out both internally and externally for the team. Group processes collectively work to determine how individuals reflect upon their team experiences. However, these processes are not relegated to sport participants, as fans/spectators also take part in important grouping practices that further establish their sport identities (see Table 11.2).

Table 11.2 Power Bases Employed in Small-group Sports

Power Type	Description	Example
Coercive	Use of punishments by a team leader to obtain compliance from other team members.	"If you don't start passing the ball around then I'm going to ask the coach to pull you from the game."
Reward	Providing resources (positive encouragement, playing time, etc.) to encourage compliance in achieving team outcomes.	"It's unselfish play from players like Sandra that have helped us to be the team that we are."
Legitimate	Relying upon one's formal position to ensure compliance from players or teammates.	"As the team captain, I feel it's necessary that we stay after practice and run to improve our conditioning."
Referent	Using player or teammate desire for a strong relationship to gain compliance.	"If you expect me to respect you as a player, then you need to be willing to put in the additional effort that is necessary."
Expert	Drawing upon one's skill or knowledge to emphasize why compliance is necessary.	"Having coached five conference championships, I know that the best way to approach this season is to run extensively during practices each day."

Social Identity and Sport

Consider how you might respond to the question "Who are you?" To answer this question, it wouldn't be uncommon for you to respond by making the connection you have to group or team affiliations, many of which are sport related ("I'm a Minnesota Lynx fan," or "I was a member of a high school state championship team"). In Chapter 8, we established the significance of performing identity in sport, as one's social identity is profoundly linked to the social groups and networks he/she aligns with, and one's personal identity is further advanced by maintaining membership in a highly valued social group. For example, if you find yourself in an environment where you are the sole supporter for your favorite team, you are likely to experience a decline in your social identity. A Dallas Cowboys fan transplanted to Philadelphia or a Boston Red Sox fan who is the only one cheering for his/her team in a bar filled with New York Yankees fans is likely to experience a significant decline in social identity because the familiar group network is no longer valued or recognized. Wann (2006) recently noted that

> By identifying with a local sport team, an individual becomes attached to a larger social group. These associations to other fans form the basis for a valuable connection to society at large and serve as a buffer to loneliness, isolation, and so forth. (p. 80)

Herbie Husker

Research findings here suggest that team identification with a local team has a positive relationship with individual physiological health, more so than an individual's identification with distant teams.

The above line of thought has a legitimate connection to social identity theory, which suggests that individuals relate to others in relation to their social groups rather than as independent/isolated individuals. To maintain a positive self-image, we are predisposed to make our group affiliations based on the potential impact such affiliations might have on enhancing that image to others. There is evidence to suggest that such affiliations have a significant positive impact on one's psychological well-being (Wann, Keenan, & Page, 2009). In Chapter 3, we discussed how bandwagon fans have waning interest in a particular sport franchises until an affiliation has the potential to produce a positive impact. For example, few people may be

Lance Armstrong

likely to follow cycling, but the sport grew in popularity in the United States as Lance Armstrong achieved considerable success. If this is the case, then what would explain why individuals continue to support teams or sports with limited potential for producing positive social identity connections? Most likely, these individuals consider their commitment to their team as a more meaningful aspect of their self-concept ("My support has never waned even though the Cubs haven't won a World Series for more than a century"). Players may change, but the team is the bond, leading to Jerry Seinfeld's observation that we're really just cheering for the jersey.

Four primary behaviors have been identified from group affiliation unique to teams (Jones, 2000). *In-group favoritism* includes preferential treatment given to members simply due to their association with the team. The belief appears to exist that only members possess positive behaviors or qualities due to the sense of team homogeneity that is fostered. For example, Nebraska Cornhusker fans have often considered themselves to be some of the most gracious fans in all of collegiate sports. They promote this assumption among themselves, ultimately forgetting that in times of considerable success, it is easier to be gracious to an opposing team after a win. However, as their football program has struggled in recent years, this perception as a feature of their in-group favoritism has begun to wane. *Out-group derogation* occurs by assigning positive traits to group members and undesirable traits to individuals in the out-group. This often results in hostility to the out-group, which then provokes a reaction that is used to help reinforce these negative perceptions. This out-group derogation has been found to occur in two different forms: direct and general group affiliations. Members feel a strong connection to their team, in addition to the league/conference/sport they participate in. Los Angeles Sparks fans are generally likely to experience derogation toward teams in their own conference (the WNBA Western Conference). However, they will also experience similar out-group derogation when considering fans that do not follow women's basketball. The perceived benefits individuals feel they obtained from their team affiliation reflect *unrealistic optimism* as fans with a greater connection to the team are more likely to experience a state of euphoria toward their team. Here fans are likely to promote an internal belief that success is always achievable despite the odds. Finally, fans noted a *sense of voice* that identification provides as they are able to overshadow unsuccessful performances by emphasizing athletic qualities the team possesses despite a loss. "The team may lose, but that is only because they play the game fairly." External factors are likely to emerge here as the source of poor performance (player injury, bad call by an official, etc.), and the ability to articulate such concerns and demonstrate support for the team after a loss are important parts of being a fan.

These four categories identified in Jones's work depict the in-group orientation that is likely to occur based on one's membership/affiliation with sport teams. Although this particular type of orientation can be rather centralized (i.e., boxing fans are different than those who watch mixed martial arts), sport does have the potential for influencing larger cultural orientations. For instance, Deborah Tannen (1990), an established gender scholar at Georgetown University, noted that males bond because of a common sport language. This common language allows males to form a unique social network that promotes social bonding. Find yourself in the company of males with no identifiable similarities and the discussion most likely will turn to sports. Females, she contends, have no such common language, which might explain why it is not uncommon to find courses or seminars that provide women exposure to sport as a means of fitting into a sport culture. In the final section of this chapter, we explore how sport and games have the potential for establishing such cultures and also for contributing to the way we develop one of two orientations toward communication.

SPORT AND COMMUNICATION CULTURES

Communication research argues that at an early age, children become socialized into either masculine or feminine communication cultures (Maltz & Borker, 1982; Wood, 1996) through their participation in a variety of sex-segregated games and sports as they mature. Wood (1996) argued that "games socialize children into understanding how, when, and why to talk" (p. 150). As a result, specific communication behaviors are learned early, becoming influential in determining how children communicate throughout the course of their lives. Specifically, when examining the communicative influence of games, Maltz and Borker (1982) argue that games are influential in dividing individuals into a gender communication culture (masculine or feminine). They indicate that because children's games tended to be sex segregated during adolescence, boys (who play kill the carrier, tag, war, etc.) and girls (who play house, school, library, etc.) learn different appreciations for when, why, and with whom they should interact.

These differences can be distinguished in six unique ways, including the facts that (1) girls more often play indoors, (2) boys tend to play in larger groups, (3) boys' groups tend to include a wider age range of participants, (4) girls play in predominantly male games more often than vice versa, (5) boys more often play competitive games, and (6) girls' games tend to last a shorter period of time than boys' games. These differences lead boys and girls to rely on their social networks to learn their communication skills. Messner (1990) indicated that "the earliest studies of masculine identity suggested that boys were seen essentially as 'blank slates' who came to their athletic experiences to be socialized into 'male roles'" (p. 417). Boys are encouraged to participate in the outside environment and are seldom reprimanded for torn clothes, skinned knees, and dirty hands because this is considered a part of a masculine growth process. If girls participate in these same activities, it may be tolerated, but they are often classified or stereotyped because of their masculine qualities.

Wood (1996) uses the arguments set forth by these authors to suggest that those exposed to a masculine communication culture are more likely to use communication to achieve instrumental goals, assert individual status and authority, and ensure their status by using communication to establish individual positioning and power. Boys learn at an early age that exerting one's authority is a valued communication skill, and those deemed in highest regard during games include those with the greatest skill or knowledge of the game itself. The rules are clearly established, and the only changes to those rules can occur during situations where slight interpretations are available. Those who know the rules the best or use their communication skills to work around the rules can easily establish their status among the participants.

Those involved in a feminine communication culture are

Children playing tag

more likely to become skilled at using communication to "build connections with others," "include others," and "cooperate, respond, show interest, and support others" (Wood, 1996, pp. 152–153). Many of the sex- segregated games girls are exposed to have general tenets that assist in establishing the ground rules for play. As a result, each time a new game begins, they are required to communicate effectively and establish the rules for play that will be amenable to all those involved. Many of these games involve small groups (sometimes just two or three players), requiring the development of relation-ship-building skills that are essential for ensuring that the game continues. Establishing power, authority, or status is a part of these games, but there is an underlying understanding that there must be a balance; "You can't always be the teacher, the librarian, or the mom every time we play." When players feel slighted, they are more likely to leave, and the game ends as a result. To ensure this doesn't occur, one must manage relationships effectively to ensure the longevity of the game. Group-based games are intended to pro-vide children with enjoyment and skill development, yet indirectly they serve as activities that assist in building important communication skills. Ultimately, these skills developed at play in these groups transcend into the formation of masculine and feminine communication styles used in adult-hood to listen, manage conversations, and resolve conflict.

CONCLUSION

Because of the pervasiveness of sport, it is likely that your participation in activities surrounding sport and games will have a lasting impact on the way you communicate in group, organizational, and interpersonal contexts. With this in mind, we developed this chapter to expose you to the unique communication events that exist within team sports to demonstrate how group interaction in this context can influence numerous elements of our day-to-day activities. The sense of connection you have with group mem-bers can be traced back to team experiences, and it is understandable that you would expect other group activities to facilitate similar levels of cohe-sion. Just as coaches can manage cohesion levels, it is understandable to assume that leaders can positively/negatively impact your desire to achieve similar objectives with those around you. The same is true when consider-ing the grouping processes that occur in team sports. Although sport teams can provide unique grouping experiences, the basic tenets sur-rounding norm development, socialization, leadership emergence, or social identity are reflected in a majority of the groups you come into contact with. Even something as detrimental as hazing is likely to occur in more cordial groups as members engage in acceptable team-building exercises that are an important socialization phase for group development. Lastly, we explored the impact of sex-segregated games that have been found to play an integral role in the development of our communication orientations. A greater appreciation for sport can be achieved as you consider how your participation in sport teams or group-based games shapes communicative approaches outside the sport context.

REFERENCES

Bormann, E. (1996). *Small group communication: Theory and practice.* Edina, MN: Burgess Publishing.

Burtis, J. O., & Turman, P. D. (2009). *Leadership communication as citizenship.* Los Angeles: Sage.

Dupuis, M., Bloom, G. A., & Loughead, T. M. (2006). Team captains' perceptions of athlete leadership. *Journal of Sport Behavior, 29,* 60–78.

French, J. R., & Raven, B. (1959). The bases of social power. In D. Cartwright (Ed.), *Studies in social power* (pp. 150–167). Ann Arbor: University of Michigan Press.

Grusky, O. (1963). The effects of formal structure on managerial recruitment: A study of baseball organization. *Sociometry, 26,* 345–353.

Hoigaard, R., Tofteland, I., & Ommundsen, Y. (2006). The effect of team cohesion on social loafing in relay teams. *International Journal of Applied Sports Sciences, 19,* 59–73.

Hoover, N. C. (1999). *National survey of sports teams.* Alfred, NY: Alfred University. Retrieved November 10, 2009, from http://www.alfred.edu/sports_hazing/.

Jones, I. (2000). A model of serious leisure identification: The case of football fandom. *Leisure Studies, 19,* 283–298.

Maltz, D. N., & Borker, R. (1982). A cultural approach to male–female miscommunication. In J. J. Gumpertz (Ed.), *Language and social identity* (pp. 196–216). Cambridge: Cambridge University Press.

Martin, K. A. (2002). Development and validation of the coaching staff cohesion scale. *Measurement in Physical Education and Exercise Science, 6,* 23–42.

Messner, M. (1990). Boyhood, organized sports, and the construction of masculinities. *Journal of Contemporary Ethnography, 18,* 416–444.

Munroe, K., Estabrooks, P., Dennis, P., & Carron, A. (1999). A phenomenological analysis of group norms in sport teams. *The Sport Psychologist, 13,* 171–182.

Rains, P. (1984). The production of fairness: Officiating in the National Hockey League. *Sociology of Sport Journal, 1,* 150–162.

Schelling-Kamphoff, C., & Huddleston, S. (1999). *Jealousy in collegiate track and field athletes.* Proceedings of the Association for the Advancement of Applied Sport Psychology annual convention, Banff, Alberta, Canada.

Tannen, D. (1990). *You just don't understand: Women and men in conversation.* New York: Ballantine.

Turman, P. (2003). Coaches and cohesion: The impact of coaching techniques on team cohesion in the small group sport setting. *Journal of Sport Behavior, 26*(1), 86–104.

Van Raalte, J. L., Cornelius, A. E., Linder, D., E., & Brewer, B. W. (2007). The relationship between hazing and team cohesion. *Journal of Sport Behavior, 30,* 491–507.

Wann, D. L. (2006). Examining the potential causal relationship between sport team identification and psychological well-being. *Journal of Sport Behavior, 29,* 79–95.

Wann, D. L., Keenan, B., & Page, L. (2009). Testing the team identification-social psychology health model: Examining non-marquee sports, seasonal differences, and multiple teams. *Journal of Sport Behavior, 32,* 112–124.

Widmeyer, W. N., Carron, A. V., & Brawley, L. R. (1993). Group cohesion in sport and exercise. In R. N. Singer, M. Murphey, & L. K. Tennant (Eds.), *Handbook of research on sport psychology* (pp. 672–692). New York: Macmillan.

Wood, J. T. (1996). She says/he says: Communication, caring, and conflict in heterosexual relationships. In Julia T. Wood (Ed.), *Gendered Relationships* (pp. 149–162). Mountain View, CA: Mayfield Publishing Company.

SUGGESTED ADDITIONAL READING

Chelladurai, P., & Kuga, D. J. (1996). Teaching and coaching: Group and task differences. *Quest, 48,* 470–485.

Lever, J. (1976). Sex differences in the games children play. *Social Problems, 23,* 478–483.

Swain, S. (1989). Covert intimacy: Closeness in men's friendships. In B. J. Risman & P. Schwartz (Eds.), *Gender and intimate relationships* (pp. 71–86). Belmont, CA: Wadsworth.

Turman, P. (2008). Coaches' immediacy behaviors as predictors of athletes' perceptions of satisfaction and team cohesion. *Western Journal of Communication, 72,* 162–179.

Waldron, J. J., & Kowaiski, C. L. (2009). Crossing the line: Rites of passage, team aspects, and ambiguity of hazing. *Research Quarterly for Exercise & Sport, 80,* 291–300.

CHAPTER 12

Crisis Communication in Sports Organizations

At any given time, individuals within sport organizations can find themselves confronting a pending crisis that requires some form of response to help shape the reaction for those outside the organization. For example, in 1999, John Rocker, a relief pitcher for the Atlanta Braves, placed himself in a situation in which he was obligated to provide a public accounting of his behavior. During the 1999 National League playoffs, he landed in the national sports spotlight after spitting at the opposing team's fans and giving them the finger. Later that winter, Rocker conducted an interview with *Sports Illustrated* in which he made a number of derogatory statements targeting African Americans and homosexuals. After noticeable public outcry from his teammates and the public, Rocker was forced to attend sensitivity training and was suspended from the game of baseball for several months.

Similarly, after the player strike in 1994, Major League Baseball (MLB) was facing considerable public backlash because of increased ticket prices and player salaries. Confronted by a considerable decline in fan support, the league made a dramatic rebound in 1998 as Mark McGwire and Sammy Sosa squared off to break Roger Maris's long-standing home run record. Fan interest, attendance, and television coverage of these two players helped to revitalize baseball. However, after being accused of steroid use by a former teammate, McGwire was called to testify in 2005 during a special congressional hearing on steroid use in baseball. Ultimately, he tarnished his image as he refused to answer direct questions about his alleged steroid use, noting, "I'm not here to talk about the past. I'm here to be positive about this subject."

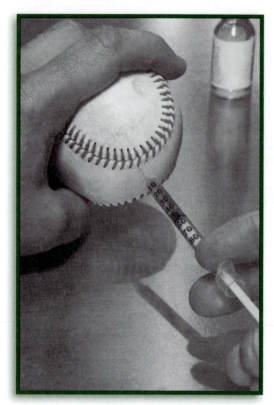

Baseball in the steroid era

Soon afterward, Sammy Sosa was linked to steroid use and McGwire confessed to using steroids throughout his career, causing fans and MLB to deal with issues regarding the record-setting season posted by these two players and eventually many others (i.e., Alex Rodriguez, Manny Ramirez, etc.).

These two examples reflect only a small handful of situations in sport that occur almost on a daily basis for players, coaches, owners, fans, organizations, and even leagues who are likely to face looming crises that can have an adverse effect on public perception. A crisis can result from a number of competitive situations (i.e., cheating, fighting, brawls, etc.) off-field occurrences (i.e., scandal, assault, player abuse, etc.), or reflections about sports (i.e., racial overtones, gender bias, press-conference outbursts, etc.) that require one to respond to the occurrence. Crisis in sport has a profound ability to require organizations to manage information in response to the fans'/spectators' need to make sense of what has transpired. As a crisis unfolds, individuals are confronted with a range of options for framing and responding that can be influential in shaping public opinion. Much of this involves communication processes that occur within the frameworks for (1) sensemaking and information management, (2) image repair and apologia, and (3) antapologia. We begin here by first exploring the role of communication in the sensemaking process. In this section, we highlight the major elements involved in sensemaking as it relates to fan dichotomies for winning and also the important influence that information management can have for shaping spectator reactions. The second major section in this chapter provides insight into the response to sport crises in two different forms. The first reflects individual responses to events in the form of an apology (or what communication scholars describe as *apologia*) to facilitate image repair. After a public event, the resulting outcry often requires that individuals apologize for their part in the event, which can take a number of forms, and sport apologia has its own set of nuances that influence fan/spectator acceptance. As we discussed in Chapter 3, the growth of new media has had a significant influence not only on the way that fans consume sport but also on how they are able to contribute to that consumption. In the final section, we explore how this portal (i.e., talk radio, fan blogs, editorial comments, etc.) has further shaped *antapologia* (the response to an apology) as a greater number of fans are now afforded an opportunity to publicly react to perceived sport crises.

SENSEMAKING AND INFORMATION MANAGEMENT

Sensemaking and information management can be viewed through a variety of lenses and serve important functions for the need to further communicate about sport crises. The first reflects the way in which we are programmed to accept sport outcomes, while the other is represented in the way that the media are able to frame our interpretation of the sporting events. While we explore this issue in greater depth in other chapters in this text, we provide a brief discussion here to emphasize the implication it has for shaping public opinion.

Sport participants and consumers constantly face a win/loss dichotomy in which ties are considered to be lose–lose situations for all involved (an internal crisis or tension). Torres and McLaughlin (2003) noted that as a society, we find it difficult to see resolution in events that end in a tie, as most sports require a winner be declared. Sport organizations have responded to such internal dichotomies for fans by employing the shootout in hockey and trading goal shots in soccer. High school and collegiate football provide each team an opportunity to score from the 25-yard line (even imposing that teams must attempt a two-point conversation in situations where a third overtime is required). Ties require all involved to engage in an internal sensemaking experience that is difficult to resolve when the dichotomy of sport necessitates the need for a winner and loser to be identified. For example, during the 1984 Orange Bowl, University of Nebraska football coach Tom Osborne decided to go for a two-point conversion to win rather than end the game in a tie. After failing to convert, Nebraska lost the game—costing Osborne his first national championship. When asked to explain his play calling during the postgame interview, Osborne noted that "I don't think you go for a tie in that case. You try to win the game."

Sport organizations are continually faced with managing the perceived crisis that emerges for fans as they attempt to fill a void left after a tie goes unresolved. Even in situations where winning isn't the ultimate goal, we expect a winner to emerge. Youth sport leagues establish rules to emphasize the developmental nature of the sport, yet that doesn't keep players, coaches, and parents from pronouncing a winner or loser at the end of a contest. The need for a definitive winner took center stage during the 2002 MLB All-Star Game, when Bud Selig (MLB Commissioner) decided to call the game after it went into extra innings and both teams were down to the final pitcher rotation. Public outcry was so significant that the following season, MLB established that the winner of the All-Star Game would secure home-field advantage during the World Series for the team that emerged from the conference championship. Torres and McLaughlin (2003) argue that the distinction for fans may be influenced by the fact that they are either outcome or resolution seekers in their orientation toward sport. *Outcome seekers* are attracted to the basic elements of sport but are primarily motivated by the need to establish a clear winner or loser. *Resolution seekers* are more likely to view contests as a central point where athletic promise or superiority can be displayed over the quest for excellence. Consider for a moment where you might fall on this continuum. When you support your team, are you more concerned about ensuring their victory or hoping to see a good game/contest? If the latter is more accurate, then you would be a resolution seeker, and the conclusion of a contest that ends in a tie might be the ideal sports outcome. The question that then arises for those that might fall under this classification is whether they are true sport fans. Reflect on our definition of sport in Chapter 1 when noting Bell's (1987) definition, which states, "Sport is a repeatable, regulated physical contest producing a clear winner" (p. 2).

Connected to our internal disposition to making sense of sporting events in relation to the achievable outcome is the fact that the media can be influential in shaping our impressions of what occurs during the contest itself. This information-management process is reflected in the work of Billings (2008) regarding coverage of the Olympic Games, which relies heavily on back-story montages that assist in setting the stage for viewers as they watch what is believed to be live coverage of the events. This staging was also affirmed by Mullen and Mazzocco (2000) in their assessment of the methods used by television producers to portray head coaches during the Super Bowl. In an attempt to create a more compelling viewing experience, producers were found to use advances in technology between the 1969 and 1997 broadcasts to alter reality for the home viewer, whereby "they, in effect attempt to create a story with mythical qualities complete with plot, protagonist, antagonists, climax, and denouement" (p. 358). The coach was portrayed as a corporate leader, exemplifying both hero and villain roles at any given point during the game. When sport organizations and media outlets manage the flow of information and sport outcomes in these ways, consumer expectations are shaped, requiring responses when internal and external violations occur. Despite the fact that such occurrences have become common features for the way sport is produced and consumed, there are numerous instances when organizations/franchises, athletes, and coaches are required to engage in individual image repair after unanticipated events. This image-repair process involves a well-established line of research known as *apologia,* which we explore further in the following section.

A Matter of Ethics: Commissioner Salary Caps

Other than the election of Barack Obama as president, the dominant news story in the United States in late 2008 and early 2009 was the nation's economy. A severe recession, sparked by risky practices in the home lending industry and a subsequent collapse of the stock market, placed the U.S. economy in its worst shape in a generation, with some arguing that it was the worst economic crisis since the Great Depression (1929–1941). In this context, many Americans and media outlets focused sharply on expenses and spending habits that appeared irresponsible or selfish.

Sport was not immune to this crisis. Indeed, when baseball fans learned in early 2009 that MLB Commissioner Bud Selig earned an annual salary of more than $18 million, some reacted with outrage. Fans were already disillusioned by the high salaries given to players, and it seemed that perhaps this was simply more evidence of the national pastime's greedy proclivities. In such difficult economic times, many wondered, how could the commissioner accept such a large salary (some of which came in the form of a bonus)?

Meanwhile, perhaps recognizing the public relations struggles that plagued Selig, NFL Commissioner Roger Goodell announced that he would freeze his salary and cut his total compensation between 20% and 25%. In the words of a league spokesperson, "The commissioner believes it will take a collective sacrifice of everyone to get through this difficult economic environment." Although his salary remained at $11 million, Goodell positioned himself as someone sensitive to fans' growing concerns about the financial state of sport.

1. When a broad crisis afflicts the nation, to what extent are those involved in sports expected to respond?

2. Was it improper for Selig to earn as much money as he did?

3. Was Goodell acting *more ethically*, or was he exploiting a public relations opportunity?

4. Should we view commissioner salaries as benchmarks of fiscal responsibility? What about league profits? Player salaries?

Image Repair and Apologia

Research on public apology related to image has generated two important bodies of literature—apologia and image repair. Communication scholars have defined *apologia* as discourse that focuses on the "self-defense" needed to combat external personal attacks on one's character (Ware & Linkugel, 1973). The actual theory of *image restoration* is based on the assumption that maintaining a positive face is a primary communication goal (Benoit, 1995). Image itself is threatened when an act is perceived as reprehensible by a relevant audience. However, the most prominent extension to *apologia* stems from Benoit's (1995) work on image repair. Benoit sought to create a more complete theory of accounts, apologies, and image repair strategies. He argues that human beings inevitably face situations of real or alleged wrongdoing and these situations are recurring and damaging to reputations. Consequently, when one's actions are considered "reprehensible" to a "salient audience," that individual's image is damaged and must be repaired.

Benoit and McHale (1999) contend that "rhetors have five general options for self-defense: denial, evade responsibility, reduce offensiveness, corrective action, and mortification" (p. 267), yet much of the research on apologia has been rooted in political discourse. As you might recognize, sport figures routinely find themselves in the spotlight as they are required to engage in a similar practice of image repair employed by public officials. Kruse (1981) recognized this feature about sport and was one of the first to explore apologia in this context. She suggests that much like political discourse, an underlying ethic of team sports (the team is greater than any individual members) warrants that sport participants embrace apologia differently. Within this general ethic of team sport, Kruse contends that the interests of the team must be placed above one's own ego or individual accomplishments. This assumption rests upon a number of basic tenets, suggesting that one never (a) criticizes the game or sport while serving as a participant or ex-participant, (b) accepts defeat until the contest has concluded, and (c) takes part in activities or events (internally or externally to the sport) that can inversely affect the team's performance. In her examination of sport apologia, Kruse (1981) identified a number of situations requiring apology on the part of the athletes and successful strategies that resolved ethical violations, including (a) suggesting that the team would be unaffected by the ethical violation, (b) shifting responsibility to the sport organization, (c) stressing a desire to be a team player, and/or (d) placing the blame on the emotion of the situation.

Kruse also conceded that there are specific situations in sport that do not warrant an apology after a violation, as she noted that fans expect coaches and players to work within the framework of the rules to win games. "Consequently, sport personalities who cheat are unlikely to be called upon by the fans to make public apologies, even though the media and other teams' followers might label their conduct 'im-moral'" (p. 279). You might recall the incident that unfolded during the 2007 NFL season when Bill Belichick (head coach of the New England Patriots) was accused by a former assistant coach of videotaping defensive signals during the game. Although Belichick faced considerable fines by the NFL, there was substantial backlash from coaches and the media against the former assistant for airing what many considered to be inside information about coaching practices. As this example attests, the need for image repair is likely to occur in a number of situations occurring at both the organizational and individual levels. We explore the unique circumstances that surround the image-repair function for sport organizations, athletes, and coaches when faced with anticipated and unanticipated crises in sport (Harris, 1990).

Organizational Image Repair

Sport organizations at all levels can face considerable need to engage in image repair after events outside their control can shake public confidence. There are numerous examples of sport crises that have been handled effectively, and while organizations are often faced with unanticipated events, the response to those events can be influential in determining public reaction. To handle such events effectively, it is important for organizations to take control of the situation and report facts in a consistent manner.

Over the past century, MLB has faced events including the Black Sox scandal during the 1918 World Series, a player strike in 1994 that eventually cancelled the World Series, and a betting scandal involving a one-time future Hall of Famer Pete Rose during the 1987 season. Until recently, Rose refused to admit that he had bet on baseball, and his apology (primarily for not telling the truth rather than for betting) almost 20 years later

Pete Rose

failed to adequately resolve what he had done in the eyes of many critics. The MLB response to the situation represented an indisputable need to demonstrate to the public that the integrity of the game was indeed intact, so much so that they imposed a lifetime ban on Pete Rose for his involvement in gambling. Baseball Commissioner A. Bartlett Giamatti focused his decision to ban Rose on the issue of integrity, noting that "one of the game's greatest players has engaged in a variety of acts which have stained the game, and he must now live with the consequences of those acts . . . Let it also be clear that no individual is superior to the game" (as cited in McDorman, 2003, p. 5). To eliminate the public impression that the "fix is in," such harsh consequences have been implemented in a number of sports. More recently, the NBA faced a similar situation in 2008 after Tim Donaghy (a long-time official) pleaded guilty to betting on games in which he officiated and made calls affecting the point spread in those games. After an FBI investigation led to Donaghy's arrest, it was uncovered that he had been betting on games since the 2005 season and had strong ties to organized crime. NBA commissioner David Stern took control of the story when it initially broke, emphasizing terms like "betrayal" and "trust" as he assured fans that an internal investigation would demonstrate that this was an isolated incident.

Even more peripheral sports can often find themselves confronting events that can be detrimental to their ongoing vitality. During the 2002 Winter Olympics in Salt Lake City, Utah, two Canadian skaters (Jamie Sale and David Pelletier) received the silver medal for their performance behind a Russian skating pair during the mixed pairs competition. Shortly after the awards ceremony, the International Olympic Committee was confronted with serious allegations of vote tampering. Ottavio Cinquanta's (head of the International Skating Union) initial statement to the public about the event indicated there was no evidence of wrongdoing and promised an internal review. Eventually, it was uncovered that a French judge had been pressured into altering her vote in exchange for a vote for a French pair in the ice dancing competition to be held the next day. The judge's score was thrown out, resulting in a tie, the awarding of two sets of gold medals, and a lifetime ban for the judge. Speculation surrounded the future of ice skating as an Olympic sport as the Olympic Committee considered downsizing skating events.

Although many would contend that sport currently walks a fine line with entertainment, the clear divide for fans is the uncertainty surrounding the outcome. These examples depict organizations faced with scandals that target the integrity of sport, as fans and spectators begin to question whether contest outcomes are fixed. Analysis of each of these organizational crises presents two different reactions to the events that necessitated image repair. While baseball may continue to experience unrest regarding the lifetime ban placed on Pete Rose, the commissioner's response at the time has been recognized by many as a necessary reaction to deter public perception surrounding the legitimacy behind baseball's outcome. Cinquanta's attempt to bury the impropriety that occurred in the mixed pairs event cast further doubt surrounding a sport that employs judges that can suffer the fallibility of human bias. When image repair is required for athletes, they are faced with a set of challenges that are unique to the choices an organization is asked to confront.

Interview: Ian McCaw, Athletic Director, Baylor University

Q: **You became Athletic Director at arguably the most difficult point in the history of Baylor athletics.** *A men's basketball player has been murdered at the hand of another player, a coach had been found to solicit fabricated testimony, and recruiting violations abounded.* **What did you regard as "Day One" priorities?**

A: The most striking observation that I made initially was that staff morale was incredibly low. Our coaches and staff felt violated by what took place. Moreover, the constant media coverage of the scandal and seemingly daily revelations about additional issues took a toll on their confidence in their employer and, in some cases, self-esteem. Subsequently, we began the healing process with our various constituencies, including our alumni and friends. At the same time, we needed to work with the investigative team and to establish a system of checks and balances to ensure that measures were put in place to avoid similar problems in the future.

Q: **How did you combine your aims to fix immediate institutional problems with those you were facing in terms of media and public relations fallout?**

A: We acted on the institutional issues first because my main concern was ensuring that our coaching, administrative, and support staff were functioning and focused on achieving success and advancing our program. Once we felt that we had stabilized the department, we began to meet with the media in an effort to re-establish our credibility, explaining how our program would operate moving forward. We set up face-to-face meetings with key media outlets where we openly and honestly answered all of their questions (no matter how difficult they were). This was a critical part of re-establishing trust. The media was willing to give the new administration a fresh start and, in most cases, were very supportive.

(Continued)

(Continued)

Q: You decided to recertify your entire department with the NCAA. What were the benefits or drawbacks to these decisions?

A: Baylor had imposed several penalties before I arrived; the Committee on Infractions imposed several additional penalties after the case was heard. There is no question that this case was one of the most serious in NCAA history, making the sanctions among the most severe ever levied. When Baylor's turn for NCAA certification arrived, we had an opportunity for a fresh start in many ways. During the self-study process, Baylor was certified and recognized by the NCAA as one of only two institutions in the history of the certification program to have no issues raised. This was an important step in restoring the credibility of the athletics program, both internally and externally.

Q: Your basketball program was placed on probation for a very long time—through the summer of 2010. How does one balance the need to acknowledge the severity of the previous problems with people who currently may feel they are being punished for transgressions committed by people who have long since left Baylor?

A: This is one of the most frustrating aspects of dealing with an NCAA case. The individuals most responsible for the scandal were no longer employed at Baylor when sanctions were imposed. In turn, the harsh sanctions levied severely impacted coaches, staff, student-athletes, alumni, and fans who truly were innocent. It has been suggested that more of the penalties in these cases need to follow the guilty individuals as opposed to remaining with an institution. While Baylor had an opportunity to appeal the sanctions, it chose not to given the serious nature of the transgressions that took place.

Q: What would be your best piece of advice for any sports organization undergoing a crisis situation?

A: Put in place measures to best avoid a crisis situation from occurring. Also, I strongly encourage athletics directors to work with campus administration to develop a crisis management plan. Through our experience, Baylor learned the importance of having a solid compliance program with experienced staff, proper procedures, effective monitoring, and a comprehensive rules education program. If a crisis develops, the best response is to act with integrity, transparency, and accept responsibility for any shortcomings that contributed to the crisis.

Athlete Image Repair

The Pete Rose example discussed in the previous section would appear to fit nicely in this portion of the chapter; however, we would like to focus our attention here on image repair that positively employs the basic tenets of apologia. One such case is tennis legend Billie Jean King's comments surrounding her disclosure of an extramarital, lesbian affair with her secretary. After the story broke, King made her official apology in three different settings, which included a press conference, an appearance on a television news program, and an interview in *People* magazine. During each of these interviews, King successfully *bolstered* (attempting to connect the accuser with something positive) herself by having her husband at her side. Nelson (1984) noted that "they entered the news conference holding hands, and during the press meeting the tennis star occasionally rested her head on her husband's shoulder. Following the conference, the two kissed in front of the camera" (p. 93). Using this strategy, along with defense by her tennis peers, Nelson concluded that when an individual or supporters of the individual use *transcendence* (joining something to a larger context) as a strategy, it is possible to shift the situation into another context viewed favorably by the audience. In King's case, this was privacy and personal autonomy, and essential to this strategy was consistency in the presentation by King, her peers, and the media after the apology was performed (see Table 12.1 for a complete list of resolution strategies).

In a more recent situation, Los Angeles Lakers guard Kobe Bryant was accused in 2003 of sexual assault against a front desk employee at a Colorado resort. During a press conference, Bryant (seated next to his wife) refuted the allegations, stating that "nothing that happened June 30th was against the will of the woman who now falsely accuses me. I made the mistake of adultery. I have to answer to my wife and my God for my actions that night . . ." Rogers (2003) argues that Bryant's public apology encompassed elements of denial, differentiation, and mortification, taking on what Ware and Linkugel (1973) describe as an absolutive stance. When faced with an attack on one's image, the only response is to vehemently deny the allegations. The case was ultimately dropped after the accuser refused to testify at the trial, but Bryant's squeaky-clean image was tarnished as his endorsement contracts with a number of major companies were terminated. A similar stance was taken by Tiger Woods after a crash outside his Florida home in 2009 led to his formal apology for having multiple affairs that had lasted more than 2 years.

Table 12.1 Verbal Self-defense Resolution Strategies Employed During Apologia

Resolution Type	Description	Example
Denial	An attempt by the perpetrator to change the meaning or connotation of the act being questioned.	Kobe Bryant arguing that he is guilty of infidelity and a violation of the sanctity of his marriage but not rape.
Bolstering	An attempt to link the perpetrator or the act itself with something positive.	Billy Jean King sitting with her husband during interviews after she was accused of having a lesbian relationship.
Differentiation	An attempt made by the perpetrator to disconnect the event from the larger context.	Pete Rose suggesting that when he bet on baseball, it was solely about gambling and had nothing to do with his role as a manager.
Transcendence	An attempt made by the perpetrator to connect the event to a larger context.	Michael Vick suggesting that his involvement in a dog-fighting ring was linked to his cultural upbringing and background as a youth.

This initial incident caused considerable backlash for Woods, who was dropped by a number of endorsers despite never having been formally charged with a crime.

Another case occurred in the aftermath of the events leading up to the 1994 Olympic Games after speculation mounted regarding Tonya Harding's involvement in the attack on U.S. teammate Nancy Kerrigan. During an interview with CBS reporter Connie Chung, Harding attempted to deny the allegation that she had helped plan an attack on Kerrigan at a practice facility in Detroit. Although Harding's husband was the actual perpetrator, she relied heavily upon the technique of bolstering by suggesting that she had been abused by her ex-husband, insisting she worked hard for a chance at the gold medal, and expressing concern and sorrow for the attack. She also employed denial strategies by rejecting the accusations that she had been involved and claimed she had no prior knowledge regarding her ex-husband's involvement in the attack. She repeatedly attacked those committing the assault in an attempt to restore her image. Benoit and Hanczor (1994) concluded that Harding's use of bolstering, denial, and attacking the accuser were "clearly appropriate" because the past had shown them to be effective in situations where an individual has been "accused of heinous acts" (p. 425).

While King's and Bryant's images after their crises have been restored, many have failed to forgive Harding for the events that transpired prior to the 1994 Olympic Games. Why do you think this might be the case? What appears to be different about these situations that necessitated the need for a formal public apology? Many considered this to be a unique situation in sport because of the fact that no Olympic athlete prior to this event had been accused of attempting to injure a teammate. Kruse (1981) contended that one of the essential principles guiding the ethic of sport is that one's behavior does not have a detrimental impact on the team's performance. Had Kerrigan gone on to win the gold medal, public opinion for Harding might be considerably different. As athletes are required to embrace the underlying ethic of sport, coaches are faced with a unique set of challenges influenced by both the need for apologia and rebuilding their teams in the wake of crisis.

Coach Image Repair

As our section on sport organizations might attest, organizations are required to respond to allegations of wrongdoing and often enforce strict penalties to ensure that unanticipated events are not likely to occur again. While this might account for the necessary organizational response for player behavior, coaches have been found to be just as likely to engage in acts that necessitate apology. For example, in 2005, long-time Temple basketball coach John Chaney was forced to apologize after postgame comments where he acknowledged that he had purposely inserted a bench-warmer into a game against St. Joseph University to commit hard fouls against a player he referred to as a "goon." Chaney was suspended for the remainder of the season due largely to the fact that a St. Joseph's player suffered a season-ending injury. After numerous incidents (choking a player, throwing a chair onto the court, and berating university officials) as the head coach at Indiana University, Bob Knight was terminated as the head men's basketball coach after violating a no-tolerance policy implemented by the president.

Both of these examples represent instances that mark the departure of a high-profile coach. Yet, in the wake of their departure, new personnel (namely coaches and their staff) are often left with the daunting task of moving the team/organization forward in light of the series of events. For example, during the late 1990s, the University of Minnesota men's basketball program was heavily sanctioned by the NCAA for numerous violations of academic fraud by the head coach, his staff, and university academic counselors. After the corruption was exposed and new coaching staff was hired, they were then required to go about dealing with the stiff NCAA penalties that ensued resulting in four primary consequences (Kihl & Richardson, 2009). First, *sanctions* placed considerable restrictions on the coaching staff to fulfill their responsibilities in the areas of recruitment. Using the uncertainty surrounding the extent of the sanctions, other institutions worked to create an attitude of paranoia as a way to draw away the institution's recruits. The heightened media speculation also required coaches to deal with the sensationalism that occurred, having negative connotations for the players that remained from the previous administration. Coaches were forced to manage as they dealt with the postscandal period, which basically stripped the program of its national prominence. They noted recruits are most interested in playing for a team that ". . . has national television exposure, consistently competes in the NCAA tournament, and is a successful major program" (p. 287). Without the potential for these three elements, it became difficult to draw recruits into the program.

Stakeholder separation was the second issue that emerged as long-term stakeholders (players, boosters, academic community, administration, etc.) began to slowly disconnect from the program. Players that remained after the scandal found it difficult to connect with the new coaching staff, while shame and embarrassment were common themes displayed by the broader campus community. Even the coaching staff from other sports felt a need to isolate themselves from the men's basketball program, resulting from fear that public perception would be connected to all University of Minnesota athletics. The two final themes included the coaching staff's need to manage *reform policies* and *multiple roles*. The first here included the climate of suspicion that appeared to remain after the sanctions were imposed. Faculty and administrators felt a need to be more involved in the day-to-day administration of the athletic department and the men's team more specifically. The coaching staff was also required to wear numerous hats beyond traditional coaching responsibilities, as they were frequently required to respond to academic fraud and public scrutiny. In the end, each of these concerns suggests that "suffering is the core category that derives from the consequences and harmful outcomes related to academic corruption" (Kihl & Richardson, 2009, p. 300). What Kihl and Richardson describe here represents the way in which teams are asked to respond to the aftermath of unintended events. Just as a governing body has the potential to impose formal sanctions as they did with the Minnesota basketball team, there are a number of ways in which informal sanctions can be presented. As institutions have become more concerned about the potential impact that official NCAA sanctions might have on a program, they have become more likely to impose their own sanctions in the hope of getting to resolution earlier. Such was the case for the Duke lacrosse team after allegations surfaced that members had raped an exotic dancer. Duke University responded by cancelling the season and firing the head coach before an official investigation was completed. Furthermore, the three accused athletes were eventually cleared.

SPORT ANTAPOLOGIA

As the above section suggests, defense of one's behavior to the media and fans represents an important feature of sport consumption within today's society. However, advancing forms of mediated technology have allowed fans a greater public platform on which they can dispel their reactions to what occurs in sport organizations. In Chapter 3, we discussed the significance that sport blogs have for allowing fans an opportunity to add their

Signs during the Duke lacrosse scandal

perspective to the dialogue of events that surround sport. A more traditional form of this environment has been sport talk radio, which continues to gain in popularity. Such programs

> [O]pen a public space where the ideas and attitudes of ordinary people seem to matter, enabling the fans and broadcasters to share dramatic interpretations about the relationship between sport and society, whether or not these interpretations correspond to reality. (Zagacki & Grano, 2005, p. 46)

In their review of sport talk radio in Baton Rouge, Louisiana (home of the LSU Tiger football team), Zagacki and Grano demonstrated that this medium was influential in helping fans cope with perceived crises that surrounded team losses. Losses for many of these fans were perceived as a personal attack that resulted from the internal identity crises that stemmed from the strong sense of identification they had with their team. Sport talk radio provides these fans an opportunity to vocalize their frustration and overcome the eminent internal crisis they are experiencing.

One other unique feature of sport is the fact that athletes and coaches are often asked to provide commentary/reaction immediately after competition. Coaches take part in postgame interviews as they leave the field, athletes are confronted by media in the locker room, and sport organizations have increasingly mandated that coaches and players take part in press conferences to feed the sport fans' need for information. For losing coaches and players, this enhanced exposure also increases the need to engage in self-defense disclosure. Such self-defense discourse involves what Ryan (1982) described as the speech set of *kategoria* and *apologia* (attack and defense), whereby any critical focus on the apology should also examine the attack preceding it. Athletes', coaches', owners', and organizations' behavior clearly necessitated the need to defend their actions, especially when such behaviors had the potential for dramatically impacting long-term image. However, focusing exclusively on the *apologia* itself ignores a third component, which Stein (2006) referred to as *antapologia* (response to *apologia*). *Antapologia* is an important feature of the apologetic situation because the rhetor may choose to construct the initial image repair based on what he/she perceives to be the likely response by the offended person(s). When the discourse addresses the account of the act, it constitutes an instance of *antapologia*.

Turman, Stein, and Barton (2008) evaluated the Zinedine Zidane head-butt incident during the 2006 World Cup championship game in which

Zidane physically assaulted an opponent after he allegedly made a derogatory slur toward his sister. After the incident, Zidane made a formal response to the public, which many argued failed to adequately apologize for his behavior. Turman and company (2008) assessed blog responses from fans to the apology, noting five antapologia situations. First, the apologia represented *character flaws of the accused* as fans argued that a nonapology for one's actions is reflective of poor character, suggesting that the lack of apology became a greater reason for revoking Zidane's status as a role model than his actual on-field behavior. Other fans appeared to *attribute motives* to the apologia, and in this case fans called into question the overall sincerity of Zidane's *apologia*. Here fans identified potential motives behind the discourse, which included implications that Zidane's words were provided to him by other people and that the media may have played a role in allowing Zidane to account for his behavior more easily. Other fans argued that the *apologia is incomplete,* suggesting that the response was deficient because he only expressed regret and therefore did not offer a full mortifica-

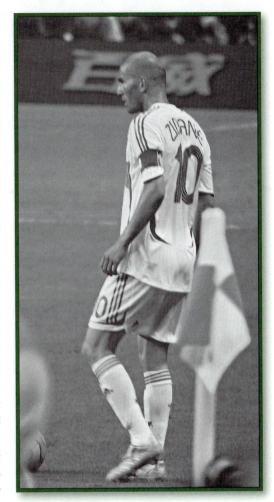

French soccer player Zinedine Zidane

tion for his behavior. Fans are able to recognize the distinction between apologizing (or even regretting) harmful behavior and feeling sorry that consequences result from the act. The apologia was also perceived to be *untrue and dismissed,* as fans argued that portions of the apology were patently false, lacking in credibility, or devoid of evidentiary support. Here, the fans dismissed the idea that Materazzi, the victim, may have insulted Zidane during the course of the entire match, arguing that Materazzi did not have sufficient time within the video clip to provoke Zidane with three offensive remarks.

Case Study: Headbutt Heard Round the World

Inappropriate behavior by coaches, players, owners, and even fans can occur during sporting events, and in most situations, sport organizations levy fines to limit their frequency. Our willingness to forgive such acts often hinges on the outcome for the team/individual. As Kruse (1981) noted, sport participants are always confronted with the challenge of demonstrating that their behavior does not inversely affect the outcome. When the athletes perform on a larger stage, the greater the need to apologize for inappropriate behavior when it is perceived to impact the contest's outcome. With viewership topping 30 billion for the 3-week event, no other sport in the world draws as much attention on a global level as the FIFA World Cup tournament that occurs every 4 years. The 2006 championship match, in which France and Italy squared off, was marked by a headbutt to the chest of Italian center Marco Materazzi by World Cup outstanding player Zinedine Zidane during the closing minutes of the contest. The resulting penalty was deemed to be instrumental in allowing Italy to overtake a superior French team to win the World Cup in a 5–3 sudden-death shootout. Afterwards, Zidane refused to apologize for his actions, alleging that Materazzi provoked him by insulting both his mother and sister. Many fans continued to criticize Zidane's on-field behavior, but debate ensued as a result of the justifications he made during his apology.

As you might conclude, Zidane's on-field behavior clearly necessitated the need to defend his actions, especially when considering that weeks before the World Cup began, Zidane officially announced his retirement from soccer at the conclusion of the tournament. Many felt that his actions during this final game scarred his otherwise illustrious career. The media were influential in fueling the controversy, and public response to the apology continued to demonstrate a lack of support for the justification provided. After the World Cup incident, no official response was made by Materazzi, as he had little to say about the event. However, the media frenzy created conditions that necessitated a formal explanation from Zidane. As this defense was not forthcoming, much of the discourse that emerged after the event included fan criticism of the apology along with an equal number of fans acting as surrogates for Zidane as they offered their own defense of the apology. The fans were not directly impacted by the events that transpired on the soccer field, but they felt connected to the situation because of their emotional involvement in both the sport and the 2006 tournament.

1. Are there times when the justification for an athlete's on-field behavior negates the need to apologize for the event?

2. How much do you believe the outcome of the game influenced fan reaction to Zidane's on-field behavior?

3. As you might read a story that covers a formal apology from athletes, how likely are you to read the comments posted by other fans? Do these comments have an impact on shaping your perceptions of the events that unfolded?

Although several *antapologia* strategies offered criticism in response to the *apologia,* many of them functioned to defend the *apologia.* During the World Cup incident, fans took on the role of surrogate apologizers in an effort to strengthen Zidane's defense. The strategy used by fans in defense of Zidane's *apologia* is similar to the image-repair strategy of *bolstering,* where they attempt to offset the damage done to the player's image through the harmful act by emphasizing his positive characteristics. Fans counteracted the negative effects of the headbutt by emphasizing other aspects of Zidane's character.

The potential for antapologia does not rest solely on those participating in sports, but it can have an impact for those providing commentary for the events as they unfold. For example, in 2003 Rush Limbaugh commented during a segment on ESPN's *Game Day* that Philadelphia Eagle quarterback Donovan McNabb received considerable praise only because of society's desire to see a black athlete succeed at the position. Considerable backlash ensued, and despite his apology for the statement, Limbaugh was subsequently released. Howard Cosell's departure from *Monday Night Football* came shortly after he used the term *monkey* to describe a black player's performance on the field—something that resonated in Don Imus's comments about Rutgers University's women's basketball team when he referred to them as "nappy-headed hos" and "rough girls." In 2007, when the criticism for these comments began to mount, Imus set up a meeting to personally apologize for his comments about the Scarlet Knights. After a lengthy private discussion, the team accepted his apology, yet they contended that the comments themselves were not the most egregious act they incurred during the situation. Ultimately, the comments overshadowed the fact that the team had made it to the national championship game when Essence Carson (junior guard on the team) commented after the meeting with Imus, stating, "Where were these major networks when we were making history [on the court] for a prestigious university?" (Kinkhabwala, 2007, p. 18). In each of these situations, the act of apologizing was overshadowed by response from the black community negating the follow-up from these individuals in accounting for their statements.

CONCLUSION

Throughout this chapter, we have presented you with the scope of activities surrounding crisis in sport. We defined crisis as the combination of intended and unintended events that necessitates a response on the part of athletes, coaches, commentators, or organizations/franchises to either account for the behaviors or further respond to consumer concerns that might arise. We hope that our discussion here provides you with a greater appreciation for the intricate dance that ensues when these events unfold. They can be as routine as the daily press conference where coaches and athletes are asked to account for their on-field performance or decision making. They also occur on a grander stage, as was the case for Michael Vick, who was forced into making a formal apology after his conviction for cruelty to animals stemming from the promotion of dog fighting. In his apology rests the need to not only apologize for his actions but also establish a foundation for his eventual return to the NFL after he completed his prison sentence. His signing with the Philadelphia Eagles after the 18-month sentence might signal that he was successful in generating forgiveness in the minds of NFL fans or owners. As opportunities for consuming sports continue to expand, it is likely that sport consumers and participants

Michael Vick

will be faced with a need for internal sensemaking as well as instances of crisis that require ongoing image repair.

REFERENCES

Bell, J. B. (1987). *To play the game: An analysis of sports.* New Brunswick, NJ: Transaction Press.

Benoit, W. L. (1995). *Accounts, excuses and apologies: A theory of image restoration strategies.* Albany: State University of New York Press.

Benoit, W. L., & Hanczor, R. S. (1994). The Tonya Harding controversy: An analysis of image restoration strategies. *Communication Quarterly, 42,* 416–433.

Benoit, W. L., & McHale, J. (1999). "Just the facts, ma'am": Starr's image repair discourse viewed in 20/20. *Communication Quarterly, 47,* 265–280.

Billings, A. C. (2008). *Olympic media: Inside the biggest show on television.* London: Routledge.

Harris, C. (1990). Caught in a crisis. *College Athletic Management, 2*(6), 30–34.

Kihl, L., & Richardson, T. (2009). "Fixing the mess": A grounded theory of a men's basketball coaching staff's suffering as a result of academic corruption. *Journal of Sport Management, 23,* 278–304.

Kinkhabwala, A. (2007, April 23). The righteous Scarlet Knights. *Sports Illustrated, 106*(17), 16–18.

Kruse, N. W. (1981). *Apologia* in team sport. *Quarterly Journal of Speech, 67,* 270–283.

McDorman, T. (2003). The rhetorical resurgence of Pete Rose: A second chance apologia. In Robert S. Brown & Daniel O'Rourke (Eds.), *Case studies in sport communication.* Westport, CT: Praeger.

Mullen, L. J., & Mazzocco, D. W. (2000). Coaches, drama, and technology: Mediation of Super Bowl broadcasts from 1969 to 1997. *Critical Studies in Media Communication, 17,* 347–363.

Nelson, J. (1984). The defense of Billie Jean King. *Western Journal of Communication, 48,* 92–102.

Rogers, R. P. (2003). *Adultery, sexual assault, and the management of sports imagery: Kobe Bryant and image repair.* Paper presented at the annual meeting of the National Communication Association, Miami Beach, FL.

Ryan, H. R. (1982). Kategoria and apologia: On their rhetorical criticism as a speech set. *Quarterly Journal of Speech, 68,* 256–261.

Stein, K. A. (2006). *Apologia, antapologia* and the 1960 Soviet U-2 Spy Plane Incident. *Communication Studies, 59,* 19–34.

Torres, C. R., & McLaughlin, D. W. (2003). "Indigestion?" An apology for ties. *Journal of the Philosophy of Sport, 30,* 144–158.

Turman, P., Stein, K., & Barton, M. (2008). Understanding the voice of the fan: *Apologia, antapologia,* and the 2006 World Cup controversy. In L. W. Hugenberg, P. Haridakis, & A. Earnheart (Eds.), *Sports mania: Essays on fandom and the media in the 21st century* (pp. 86–102). Jefferson, NC: McFarland.

Ware, B. L., & Linkugel, W. A. (1973). They spoke in defense of themselves: On the generic criticism of apologia. *Quarterly Journal of Speech, 50,* 273–283.

Zagacki, K. S., & Grano, D. (2005). Radio sports talk and the fantasies of sport. *Critical Studies in Media Communication, 22,* 45–63.

SUGGESTED ADDITIONAL READING

Boyd, J. (2000). Selling home: Corporate stadium names and the destruction of commemoration. *Journal of Applied Communication Research, 28,* 330–346.

Hopwood, M. K. (2005). Applying the public relations function to the business of sport. *International Journal of Sports Marketing & Sponsorship, 1,* 174–188.

Miller, J. B. (1999). "Indians," "Braves," and "Redskins": A performative struggle for control of an image. *Quarterly Journal of Speech, 85,* 188–202.

Sanderson, J. (2008). "How do you prove a negative?" Roger Clemens's image-repair strategies in response to the Mitchell Report. *International Journal of Sport Communication, 1,* 246–262.

Scraton, P. (2004). Death on the terraces: The contexts and injustices of the 1989 Hillsborough disaster. *Soccer & Society, 5,* 183–200.

CHAPTER 13

The Commodification of Sport

College football is among the most popular and profitable sports in the United States. It draws large television audiences, produces millions of dollars in revenue, and generates considerable enthusiasm on college and university campuses across the country. In spite of its presence, however, some have voiced concern that treating college football as a commercial enterprise threatens the core values of higher educa-

Money, football, and America

tion. In the words of one observer, college football "has become a business, carried on too often by professionals, supported by levies on the public, bringing in vast gate receipts, demoralizing student ethics, and confusing the ideals of sport, manliness, and decency" (quoted in Smith, 1988, p. 214). While these words may sound like those of a contemporary critic, they actually came from the historian Frederick Jackson Turner in 1906. If college football was a commercial enterprise in the early 20th century, how do you suppose Turner would react to developments in the 21st century, such as the Southeastern Conference's $2.2 billion television contract with ESPN? Indeed, in more recent years, critics have echoed Turner's lament, paying particular attention to the ways that money and sponsorship have negatively affected college and university educational missions (McAllister, 1998, 2010; Sperber, 2001). In light of multimillion-dollar salaries for coaches, numerous high-profile scandals involving illegal recruiting, debate about whether players should be paid, long-term contracts that dictate television programming decisions, constant talk about athletic conference expansion, and endless cross-promotions between networks and sponsors, it is easy to see why some fear that college football has become excessively commercial.

Case Study: Unintended By-product of Commodification

On November 23, 2009, Northeastern University announced that it would terminate its football program after almost three quarters of a decade of competition. Less than 2 weeks later, the Board of Trustees at Hofstra University made a similar announcement regarding the future of its football program. Although it is not uncommon for colleges and universities to eliminate sport teams, football has often been viewed as "sacred" on most campuses, with only a small handful of institutions choosing to make such a move over the past century. Those that have eliminated these programs have often done so in response to meeting Title IX compliance and, more recently, to address considerable shortfalls in endowments brought on by the recession. While funding was an issue at these two institutions, the primary driver appeared to be an unwillingness to invest the millions of dollars that would be needed to improve the team to meet the school's ambitions.

Prior to the 2009 season, Northeastern University had experienced five straight losing seasons, similar to four losing seasons at Hofstra. Game attendance was also a contributing factor as neither institution could generate enough alumni or student support. During Hofstra's final season, the average attendance was fewer than 500 supporters, far short of institutional expectations for a program with an annual budget of $4.6 million each year. You might ask yourself why the situation facing these two programs fit into a chapter on commodification. This is because high-profile conferences are able to generate considerable revenue for even those teams with a history of unsatisfactory performance. For example, as we noted earlier, the Southeastern Conference has a 15-year, $2.2 billion contract with ESPN, and the Big 12 is currently in the middle of a 10-year, $100 million contact with Fox Sports to telecast conference games. Even the program at Baylor University (which has traditionally been in the cellar for this conference for the past decade) receives a portion of these funds. This revenue then assists in offsetting the costs for maintaining the program. Hofstra (Colonial Athletic Association) and Northeastern (Northeast-10 Conference) both participate in peripheral conferences in the I-AA Football Championship Subdivision that see limited television exposure. When considering the growing cost for coaching salaries and the need for luxurious stadiums to attract talented athletes and fans, it becomes increasingly difficult for a university to invest in a program in the hope that it will become commercially viable in the future. Institutions at this level are more likely to explore other priorities. In Hofstra's case, the school has indicated intent to shift the funding to the development of academic programs and need-based scholarships.

1. How does the termination of football programs at institutions like Hofstra and Northwestern impact college football? Are there any consequences at all?

2. How do you expect the continued commodification of collegiate sports to influence programs that may struggle to maintain their economic viability?

3. Is there a long-term future for athletic competition outside the Division 1 level when one considers the growing costs for institutional participation?

Although the perceived threat to higher education's integrity makes college football an appropriate target for some criticism, it is far from the only sport that is subject to commercialization and commodification. After all, the industry of sport in the United States alone is valued by *Street & Smith's* at $213 billion (Pegoraro, Ayer, & O'Reilly, 2010). With such money at stake, it is inevitable that sport will be affected by multiple and, at times, competing commercial interests. Although there is much to be said about the relationship between sport and commercialism in strictly economic terms, our purpose here is to examine the communicative impact of this relationship. As Wenner (2010) points out, "Consumer culture infuses our sporting identities and explains much about how our communities are approached and how we think of, and talk amongst, ourselves" (p. 1).

Because commercial interests and consumption practices contribute to how sport functions communicatively, our aim in this chapter is to examine the significance of thinking of sport in terms of **commodification.** Commodification is a term derived from critical scholarly traditions, especially the work of the 19th-century German theorist Karl Marx. It refers to the process by which capitalism transforms objects from their natural purpose to objects that are "for sale." We are not suggesting in this chapter that all commercial activities in sport are *bad,* for the very nature of sport entails a mixture of marketing and consumption. Moreover, it is important to acknowledge that commercialism does not always or necessarily produce commodification, as some sporting products are explicitly designed to be sold (Moor, 2007). Nevertheless, the explosion of the sport industry in recent decades has produced various concerns about the consequences of an overly commercialized sport culture. The balance, so to speak, between commodification and other roles sport plays could be viewed as skewed, diminishing other potential noteworthy benefits of the enactment and consumption of sport. With this in mind, our attention in this chapter is on four dimensions of the commodification of sport: (a) the inter-dependent relationship of sport and media, which often depends on the production of "spectacle"; (b) the consequences of corporate interests in sport, especially through sponsorship and naming rights; (c) the effects of commodification on identity and the tendency to view cultural groups as objects of consumption; and (d) how overly commercial practices in sport have provoked a movement toward nostalgia.

THE SPORTS/MEDIA COMPLEX

It is nearly impossible to conceive of contemporary sport without the media. Yet it is almost equally the case that media industries in the United States look to sport as central to their success. So while sport depends on the media to be visible to large audiences, the media relies on sport to generate sales and advertising revenue (McChesney, 1989). As an illustration, consider the merging of interests that led to the addition of the Anaheim Mighty Ducks franchise to the National Hockey League (NHL). In 1992, Disney released the film *The Mighty Ducks,* a story about a troubled lawyer who finds redemption when he is ordered to coach a youth hockey team. The film, which frequently has been compared to 1976's *The Bad News Bears,* did reasonably well at the box office and was especially popular with young audiences. Also in 1992, Disney paid the NHL $50 million for the rights to a new franchise based in southern California. They called the team the Anaheim Mighty Ducks, which represented a new milestone in movie marketing tie-ins. Not everyone approved of a name that defined a franchise in such stark commercial terms, but it was clear that both Disney and the NHL were eager to exploit the cross-promotional potential of their new relationship. That relationship developed further in 1993, when Disney purchased Capital Cities, the parent company of the American Broadcasting Company (ABC). Among ABC's holdings was the Entertainment and Sports Programming Network (ESPN), which Disney officials referred to as the "crown jewel" of their acquisition (Freeman, 2000, p. 232). Meanwhile, in 1992, ESPN had signed a new agreement with the NHL to broadcast games three nights a week. Thus, after 1993, the Walt Disney Company owned *both* the Anaheim Mighty Ducks *and* ESPN, the network that provided coverage of and commentary on the team's games. Although ESPN dropped hockey in 2004 and Disney sold the Mighty Ducks in 2005, for 12 seasons, sports fans might have wondered about the consequences of such synergy. Would ESPN commentators be fair in their observations of the Mighty Ducks? Would the NHL risk its television contract if it disciplined the franchise for some reason? Would revenues generated by ESPN's hockey broadcasts benefit the entire league, or would Anaheim receive disproportionate profits?

In the long run, Disney's investment in professional hockey was mostly a failure. Yet it is representative of the **synergy** that exists between sport and the media. As Wenner (2004) notes, synergy "is a vertical-integration strategy aimed at maximizing the ways that complementary holdings can strengthen each other through cross-promotion and marketing to make the corporate whole stronger than the sum of its parts" (p. 316). Because it has become so commonplace, the synergy between sport and media organizations has been the subject of communication scholarship that examines what is often called the "sports/media complex" (Jhally, 1984). Communication scholars who adopt this perspective express concern about the negative consequences of the sports/media complex, with particular attention to **accumulation** and **spectacle.**

Interview: Lawrence Wenner, Von der Ahe Professor of Communication and Ethics, Loyola Marymount University

Q: **What is the predominant impact of the overlap between capitalism and sport?**

A: The primary effect has been that the cultural place of sport has evolved in a certain direction. The logic of capitalism has come to dominate and naturalize the ways we think about and celebrate sport. Sport that does not readily advance corporate interests and attract desirable audiences is pushed to the margins; it has to meet the media test. Sport becomes transformed into a product with media-friendly attributes rather than an athletic activity. Tightly constructed narratives with limited themes feature a celebritized notion of the heroic. This is at the essence of what I have called "mediasport." Sport that succeeds here is necessarily changed; its success depends on its ability to undergird the promotional culture at the heart of media and marketing.

(Continued)

(Continued)

Q: **Many fans have the notion that sport used to be more "pure" and now is "corrupt." Do you agree?**

A: Certainly things have changed. Such feelings likely come from a nostalgic yearning for the "good old days"—putting on rose-colored glasses. There is ample evidence that earlier times in sport were more corruptible. Perhaps "times were simpler" or "sport more pure." More likely, things seemed that way because we were more naïve and there was less public scrutiny. While there are many shortcomings in today's sports journalism and sport organizations, their policing—when combined with a very leaky communication environment—makes corruption much more difficult. Fans have lost patience with athletes who are spoiled, criminal, or both, but I'm not sure this adds up to corruption.

Q: **What is the harm in commodifying sport through efforts such as selling stadium naming rights or marketing cross-promotions?**

A: These are similar but different issues. Both demonstrate the power of what I have called "sports dirt," which involves the power or logic of the (positive) associations we have with sports strategically appended to other products or services in the marketplace to make them more appealing. Thus, sports "grease the skids" to "seal the sell." I call this sports dirt in that it is matter out of place that doesn't quite belong where it has been repositioned. There is no inherent reason that using sports makes sense to sell a car or beer; using sports to do so is dirty. Marketers create illogical connections between our positive associations and something being sold. The same is true with cross-marketing efforts: We sell two otherwise unconnected things, say a franchised hamburger with a sports team or event. What does one have to do with the other? Nothing, and certainly nothing that has not been manufactured, but the power of sports, on average, helps the burger more than vice versa. The garnering of our goodwill is blinded in a way by our own positive associations with sport.

Q: **Tiger Woods is poised to become the first athlete to earn more than $1 billion in endorsements. Is his case an anomaly or a sign of things to come?**

A: Both. Few athletes will dominate their sport in the way he has. Woods has "out-Jordaned" Michael Jordan. Still, athletes that mate dominance in their sport with charisma that appeals to broad audiences will be few and far between. Such iconography is fragile. Tarnish can stain even a David Beckham or Lance Armstrong. Celebrity can turn to notoriety. Just ask Mark McGwire or Tonya Harding. Still, because the upside is so great, the search for the next Tiger Woods will continue.

> **Q: Is there an upward trajectory to the commodification of sport?**
>
> **A:** The hypercommercialization of sport is inevitable. Big-time sport has so drifted into another realm that it may have put itself at risk. There is a building anger with many things that define the commodification of sport. There will be some pushback by the sports consumer and increased interest for minor league and collegiate (and even high school) sport where some modicum of authenticity remains. There is much to dislike about today's overhyped world of sport. Something has to give here.

Jhally (1984) maintains that sport should be understood *primarily* as an institution of capitalism. Although most fans would acknowledge that the sport industry generates millions of dollars in revenue, they would be reluctant to reduce its meaning only to profits and losses (wins and losses, perhaps). Rather, sport is more commonly viewed as a form of entertainment or escape. In other interpretations, sport provides community and a sense of belonging. Even though sport can be these things, Jhally insists that sport exists to make money. Thus, decisions that are made between sports leagues and television networks, for example, can be understood as efforts to maximize profits at the expense of any other concerns. Jhally (1984) argues that this focus on accumulation of wealth becomes not a product but the organizing logic of the sports/media complex. As a result, the human interests of those involved become secondary to the material interests of those who run sport and media organizations.

Two brief examples can illustrate Jhally's contention. For example, did the New York Yankees need to spend nearly $1.5 billion to construct a new Yankee Stadium, which opened in 2009? Surely, the stadium is designed to generate revenue for the franchise through its corporate sponsorships, luxury boxes, and entertainment amenities. However, these extra features inevitably mean that ticket prices will be higher, resulting in decreased opportunities for average fans to attend games in person (Ritzer & Stillman, 2001). Indeed, Yankee Stadium is representative of new forms of stadium excess. While the average ticket cost in MLB is just under $27, it is nearly $73 for the New York Yankees, by far the highest in baseball (Brown, 2009, para. 2). Even more striking is that some seats—given the glamorous name of "Legends Boxes"—sold for as high as $2,500 (face value) when the new stadium opened in 2009. Along with the high prices of actual tickets come the rising costs of parking, concessions, and souvenirs. *Team Marketing Report* provides an annual Fan Cost Index, which estimates the average cost for a family of four to purchase tickets, parking, concessions, and souvenirs at a big league baseball game (Greenberg, 2010). As you can see in Table 13.1, even for the most affordable of teams, attending a live game is no small investment!

This is of all the more concern since economic changes now mean that 75% of American families cannot afford to attend a live professional sporting event (Thompson, 2009). Despite this sobering reality, high-cost arena construction projects are the norm, not the exception, in contemporary sport. Simply put, single-purpose facilities with elaborate entertainment options are appealing both to fans and municipal officials, who are excited by the spectacle of sport and the promise that modern arenas will boost local economies. Unfortunately, independent research consistently reveals that such promises are an illusion, as the primary economic benefits of new stadium construction go to local investors and team officials (Trumpbour, 2007). Meanwhile, the fans for whom these stadiums purportedly are built have fewer and fewer opportunities to experience and enjoy them.

Meanwhile, consider the controversy that has emerged regarding the use of performance-enhancing drugs in sport. For many observers, the primary reason that steroids use was widespread in Major League Baseball (MLB) was that each of the major interests involved—ownership, players, and media alike—refused to interrogate suspicious practices because the increased

Table 13.1   2010 Fan Cost Index for Major League Baseball

MLB Rank	Team	Average Ticket Cost	Fan Cost Index
1	Boston Red Sox	$52.32	$334.78
2	Chicago Cubs	$52.56	$329.74
3	New York Yankees	$51.83	$316.32
4	Chicago White Sox	$38.65	$249.60
5	Philadelphia Phillies	$32.99	$227.46
	MLB Average	**$26.74**	**$194.98**
26	Tampa Bay Rays	$19.75	$141.00
27	Los Angeles Angels	$18.93	$131.80
28	Pittsburgh Pirates	$15.39	$126.56
29	San Diego Padres	$15.15	$120.60
30	Arizona Diamondbacks	$14.31	$115.24

productivity allegedly linked to steroids was also producing large gains in revenue (Bryant, 2005). In the case of Yankee Stadium, the process of accumulation compromises the ability of many fans to identify with the team; in the case of steroids, it compromises the integrity of the sport. In both cases, something is lost when the commercial logic of sport is reduced *only* to making a profit.

New Cowboys Stadium

For Jhally and other critics, there is also a concern that the sports/media complex depends on the production of *spectacle*. As Kellner (1996) explains, "Spectacles are those phenomena of media culture that embody the society's basic values, serve to enculturate individuals into its way of life, and dramatize the society's conflicts and modes of conflict resolution" (p. 458). Events such as the Olympic Games or the Super Bowl can be understood as examples of the "ritualized spectacle" (Jhally, 1984, p. 53) that is produced by the sports/media complex. The problem with spectacle isn't necessarily the excess that seems to accompany such productions, although that might warrant criticism. Rather, it is that spectacles focus so persistently on elaborate productions and practices of consumption that audiences are conditioned to consume spectacular events passively. As a consequence, those who watch the Super Bowl, for example, may be more willing to accept problematic values embedded in the broadcast because they see them as components of the sport/media production.

Jhally (1989) makes this point in a discussion of political influences in the sports/media complex. As we discussed in Chapter 7, sport and politics are often intertwined. However, most fans are either unaware of or unconcerned with this relationship. One dimension of this, then, is the ubiquitous presence of the United States military in major sporting events. This is not a natural relationship; rather, it is one that has evolved over the years as sports media have attempted to capitalize on the *spectacular* nature of military imagery. As Jhally (1989) explains:

> Many major sports telecasts are saturated with militaristic values that start with the presentation of the colors, or the flying overhead of fighter airplanes as the "Star Spangled Banner" is sung. . . . The television presentation of these events is normally *highly* technically mediated, with elaborate camera angles, overlapping pictures of players, flags, and weapons, and careful use of juxtaposition and dissolves. The Super Bowl especially seems to be inextricably tied up with this militaristic ideology. (p. 84)

The point is not that the military should never be a component in a sports broadcast. Rather, it is that by making the military a constant and *normal* part of sports television, sports media discourage viewers from thinking critically about the political content that underlies the sporting events themselves. To do so, after all, would risk being un-American.

CORPORATE SPONSORSHIP

One of the most obvious signs of commercialism in contemporary sport is the nearly ubiquitous presence of corporate sponsors. Sponsorship is about more than companies purchasing space or time to advertise their products and services. Indeed, sponsorship now includes naming rights for stadiums, events, and even segments during broadcasts. Thus, no longer do viewers watch the Rose Bowl, they watch the "Rose Bowl Game presented by Vizio." Meanwhile, corporate names introduce segments from the Chevrolet Pregame to the Budweiser Hot Seat. Although a commercial presence has always been a part of sport, critics are concerned that the breadth of sponsorship has negative effects on sporting events and those who watch them. This is especially the case with respect to the frequency of advertising content and the rise of corporate names for stadiums.

McAllister (1998) argues that college bowl games have become a representative illustration of the spectacle that we discussed earlier in this chapter.

Yet he notes that the corporate sponsorship of these games, beginning in 1982 when the Tangerine Bowl was renamed the Florida Citrus Bowl, threatens the integrity of the sport. As he states, "The effects of this particular form of sponsored spectacle may serve to taint and devalue the essence of the event itself" (p. 366). Indeed, one would be hard-pressed to dispute that the subject of his analysis—the 1996 Tostitos Fiesta Bowl—was anything but one "giant commercial" for Tostitos chips (p. 368). While McAllister is worried that an overemphasis on commercialism threatens the amateur ethos of college sports, he also emphasizes that too much influence has been given to the sponsors to affect sports events and broadcasts. As an example, he notes a $7.9 million contract between Reebok and the University of Wisconsin which, had it been approved, would have prohibited any employee of the university from ever criticizing Reebok. More recently, only in a hypercommodified sport culture would the University of Central Florida lose a shoe contract with Adidas, as it did in 2009, because one of its players—the son of the legendary Michael Jordan—insisted on wearing Nike shoes.

Corporate sponsors clearly stand to benefit from such influence, and that influence continues to grow. In an updated study, McAllister (2010) notes that college football advertising revenue yields more than $450 million, while professional football generates more than $2 billion. As a result, through an analysis of the 2007 college football national championship game, he discovers that more than *80%* of the broadcast included some form of advertisement on screen. Consequently, he indicates at least six potential criticisms of this extensive presence:

1. Large college football programs benefit at the expense of small ones, while ticket prices limit accessibility to events.

2. Common promotion of products such as alcohol perpetuates dangerous behaviors.

3. Unethical corporate practices are left unexamined (thus tacitly accepted).

4. Commercials and actual content are increasingly blurred.

5. Athletic achievement itself is cheapened.

6. Encroachment of advertising into public arenas is legitimized.

The bottom line for McAllister is that "the continued acceptance and visibility of advertising activities in sports helps to normalize commercial intrusion not just in athletics, but in . . . other domains as well" (p. 18).

The influence of commercialism is not restricted, however, to sports broadcasts. Another means by which corporations advertise within sport is through the purchase of stadium naming rights. As the cost of stadium construction has exploded in the past 20 to 30 years, sports franchises have increasingly partnered with corporations who spend billions of dollars to name an arena. Although some ballparks and stadiums retain names that reference their location or affiliation—Dodgers Stadium in Los Angeles, for example—the majority of arenas have corporate sponsors. For example, imagine you live in or near Philadelphia and follow the four professional sports teams in that area. You would attend baseball games in *Citizens Bank* Park, football games in *Liberty Financial* Field, and basketball and hockey games in the *Wachovia* Center. Of course, this trend is not restricted to professional sports, as more and more college teams play their games in corporate-named arenas as well.

A Matter of Ethics: Spidey's Commercialist Web

Like all professional sports, baseball is, and always has been, a business. Therefore, Major League Baseball (MLB), as the chief proprietor of the national pastime, is invested not only in the game on the field but also in its ability to make money and develop promotional opportunities. By the late 20th century, these opportunities became increasingly linked to a strategy of synergy in which different entities engage in cross-promotions to mutually benefit from marketing their products and services (think about movie tie-ins with fast-food chains, for example).

In 2004, MLB announced an arrangement with Columbia Pictures, the production studio for *Spider-Man 2*. The new movie was expected to be a big box office hit that summer (and it was), so MLB officials saw it as an opportunity to draw attention to baseball. Thus, during three days in June, major league ballparks would feature advertisements for *Spider-Man 2* on first, second, and third bases. As one baseball executive put it, "*Spider-Man 2* Weekend is part of our continuing marketing efforts to appeal to younger fans in new and non-traditional ways." However, the promotion met with fierce criticism from those who felt that the integrity of the sport would be compromised through the overt commercialism of the advertisements. Consequently, MLB did not go ahead with its original plans.

Baseball has always been a commercial enterprise. However, many fans felt that the *Spider-Man 2* promotion would have crossed a line.

1. Do you agree that this promotion would have been excessive?

2. What, if any, would be the harm of having advertisements on the bases?

3. How much marketing and advertising are you willing to accept in order to watch or attend your favorite sports?

For some sports fans, stadium names are incidental. After all, does your experience at a San Francisco Giants game change if the ballpark is called AT&T Park instead of its previous names of Pacific Bell Park or SBC Park? Perhaps not, but communication scholars point out that the name of a stadium tells us something about the community in which it is located and it affects the identification between fans and franchises. As Boyd (2000) asserts, the name of a sports arena is important because it anchors "the building as a memory place and [makes] an identity statement about the city and the fans" (p. 331). Moreover, he suggests that people identify with sport and sports franchises because they connect them to one another in ways that other cultural forms cannot. The risk, therefore, is that if sport is reduced to "just another business," then its unique communicative aspects are diminished (p. 341). What is lost is the sense of history and tradition that sport so often provides. The corporate sponsorship of sports arenas thus contributes to the feelings of nostalgia that we will return to later in this chapter.

Identity for Sale

We should clarify that it is not only the events or arenas that are for sale in the sports/media complex. As Meân, Kassing, and Sanderson (2010) contend, "Sport comprises a site for commodification that is especially hard to resist due to its significance for identities and as a referent for meaning-making across a variety of interpretive communities" (p. 2). In other words, commodification in sport often functions to sell, if not actual people, *images* of people and cultures. As we discussed in Chapter 8, for example, those who object to the use of Native American mascots often do so on the grounds that such imagery presents Native American identity as a product to consume. Meanwhile, because high-profile athletes receive millions of dollars in endorsement money, they are often discouraged from acknowledging their race, gender, or class positions. Thus, it is important to examine the extent to which commercialism distracts us from substantive discussions of identity.

We discussed racial dynamics in sport in detail in Chapter 6. It is important to return to this topic because sport is one of the few arenas in which racial minorities achieve widespread exposure and praise. In particular, well-paid athletes of color are chastised if and when they suggest that race plays a role in the treatment they receive. The common conclusion is that no athlete can claim racism when he or she is making millions of dollars. Sportswriter William Rhoden (2006) uses this logic as a foil in his book *Forty Million Dollar Slaves,* a title that points to the inherent tensions experienced by many African American athletes. Consider the backlash directed at

Brendan Haywood in a Wizards "throwback" jersey

NFL quarterback Donovan McNabb, for example, when he told HBO's Bryant Gumbel that he believed black quarterbacks were held to different standards than white quarterbacks (something that decades of sport scholarship would support). When fans object to such observations, they demonstrate what Halone and Billings (2010) call "aversive racism" (p. 20), wherein dominant audiences reject the structures of racism even as they maintain negative views of individual minority athletes. Thus, the average basketball fan might decry racism at a social level but nevertheless lament that the National Basketball Association (NBA) is too strongly influenced by "hip-hop culture."

Even as the visibility of race is often hidden in individual instances, it is simultaneously promoted at the collective level in practices of consumption. Ironically, then, white sports fans might lament what they perceive as the detrimental influence of black culture even as they consume elements of that culture through products such as music and clothing. Perhaps no better example demonstrates this tendency than the explosion of "throwback jerseys" that were originally popularized in the hip-hop community and have since become highly desirable commodities for sports fans (Lane, 2007). The concern voiced by critics of these practices is that the identities, indeed the *bodies,* of racial minorities become objects of consumption. In a study of sports talk radio, Goldberg (1998) concludes that the practices of consumption that are so often tied to racial identity—rooting for a team, purchasing apparel, or imitating the behaviors of racial minorities—all but eliminate any serious discussions about race. Instead, the commodified athlete, especially the African American male, legitimizes "racist expression coded as race neutrality, racialized exclusions as color blindness, racist discrimination as market choices, as commodity preferences" (p. 220).

Goldberg (1998) also notes that sports radio "invariably represents men's interests" (p. 217). Thus, masculinity is also an important consideration when examining the commodification of sport. This point is made in Schuck's (2010) analysis of televised poker. Poker is not a "sport" in the conventional sense, yet Schuck argues that the equation of poker with sport positions it within dominant perspectives of masculinity. In particular, television

World Series of Poker winner Scotty Nguyen

broadcasts of poker promote masculine values of individual achievement and conquest, both of which are reinforced by commercials that routinely feature "masculine" goods like beer. While he notes that this relationship is not new, Schuck points out that by linking poker to familiar conceptions of masculinity, sport is a means by which dominant practices of consumption are reinforced. For poker to become a legitimate television event, then, men need to be featured in ways that adhere to dominant norms—that is, they should be aggressive, confident, individual, and successful. Most of all, they should purchase products that cultivate these traits, presumably all in the pursuit of beautiful women (Wenner & Jackson, 2009).

NOSTALGIA

In the wake of constant sports media coverage, new stadium construction, free agency, and rising ticket prices, it is not uncommon to hear sports fans long for the "good old days." The idea that sports were once more pure or that athletes simply played for the love of the game is common, especially among those of older generations. These feelings are typically understood as **nostalgia,** a word that translates to "homesickness." Nostalgia, then, expresses a desire to regain something that has been lost or to return to a place that is no longer accessible. There are numerous cultural, political, and social changes that have provoked nostalgia in recent decades, and the commodification of culture, including sport, is surely among those changes. As Sobchack (1997) suggests, dramatic changes produce a feeling that something has come to an "end," a feeling that places the "purity" of a collective identity at risk. In the United States, "nostalgia for a 'pure' American identity is also satisfied by sports" (p. 179).

Sobchack especially focuses her attention on baseball in movies, and she points to the theme of innocence that is characteristic of a film like *Field of Dreams* (1989). To emphasize the point, consider some of the baseball films you have seen that feature children. It is likely that you will recall films such as *Angels in the Outfield* (1994), *Little Big League* (1993), *Rookie of the Year* (1993), and *The Sandlot* (1993). Each of these stories uses children in one way or another to reconnect audiences with the "purity" of baseball. Notice, also, that they all were released at relatively the same time, a time when fans and media alike were increasingly cynical about athletes who they perceived to be arrogant, overpaid, and disconnected with fans. These Hollywood films happened also to overlap with some notable documentary features, including *When It Was a Game* (1991) and *Baseball* (1994).

Ken Burns's nine-part (updated with a tenth installment in 2010) documentary television series, *Baseball,* has received the majority of public

Field of Dreams

attention, but Aden (1995) looks to *When It Was a Game* to examine the uses of nostalgia. The documentary is an assemblage of home movies taken by major leaguers who played from 1934 to 1957. It features rare footage of some of baseball's greatest legends, including Joe DiMaggio, Jackie Robinson, and Ted Williams. The homemade quality gives the film a kind of authenticity that allows viewers to reconnect to a previous era. From a historical perspective, the movies are a fascinating glimpse into what many view as baseball's "golden age." Yet Aden explains how *When It Was a Game* returns viewers to a time and place that no longer exists. This is effective, he argues, because for many baseball fans who grew up in the 1930s, 1940s, and 1950s, economic and social changes have left them longing for something they can find comfort in, what Aden terms a "secure place of opposition" (p. 23). Although such a place may provide a temporary escape, he warns that it also fails to help people accommodate and adjust to change. In addition, nostalgia tends to present an overly romanticized vision of the past. In the case of *When It Was a Game,* for instance, Aden notes that the "good old days" celebrated in the documentary mostly occurred prior to baseball's integration and thus were marred by racist and classist sentiments.

Nostalgia is not only an effort to return to a time before commercial interests (allegedly) ruined the sports we love. Indeed, nostalgia has itself become a commodity, and a highly sought-after one at that. The throwback jerseys we referred to earlier in this chapter, for example, serve as a simple illustration of how memories of the past become the commercial products of the present. Given the proliferation of "retro" days at sporting events, there can be little doubt that franchises use these promotions as opportunities to sell more merchandise. At a larger level, a sport like baseball explicitly draws upon its history (and mythology) in ways that use nostalgia as a marketing ploy. As the title of Springwood's (1996) study of baseball nostalgia indicates, there are marketing opportunities from *Cooperstown to Dyersville.* Cooperstown, New York, is the site of the National Baseball Hall of Fame and Museum, while Dyersville, Iowa, preserves the actual field used in *Field of Dreams.* While both sites are certainly about baseball, they are also about using baseball as a commodity.

The consumption of baseball nostalgia is also prevalent in the "retro ballpark" trend of the 1990s and early 2000s. Beginning with Oriole Park at Camden Yards, which opened in Baltimore in 1992, major-league franchises increasingly drew upon architectural cues from the past when designing their ballparks of the present (and future). Most of these ballparks, such as those found in Cleveland, Arlington, Denver, Pittsburgh, and San Francisco, are located in urban centers and feature architecture heavy on brick and steel. Many of them provide spectacular venues for baseball, and throughout the

1990s they generated widespread enthusiasm and praise. In particular, they have been hailed as a return to an urban community that had been lost in the post–World War II years. As many critics have demonstrated, however, the construction of these facilities has provided only an illusion of community, as more often than not these projects are pursued to the benefit of wealthy outsiders at the expense of local residents. As Rosensweig (2005) maintains, these retro ballparks are more "urbanesque" than "urban," meaning that "they are carefully controlled, relatively homogenous environments, sometimes barely resembling the areas around the ball parks after which they are modeled and lacking much in common with the landscapes they replaced" (p. 130). In this way, baseball nostalgia promises an escape from the present or a return to the past, even though the very means of that experience—the retro ballpark—is a product of the highly commodified culture in which sport presently operates.

CONCLUSION

In this chapter, we have examined some of the more controversial issues associated with sport commercialism and commodification. The development of the sports/media complex, the production of spectacle, the consumption of identities, and the repackaging of nostalgia each reveal how deeply embedded commercial practices are within sport. Sport is, and nearly always has been, a money-making enterprise. Nevertheless, there are consequences to the extensive marketing, sponsorship, and product placements that are ubiquitous in sport. Rather than taking these practices for granted, it is important to consider whether the form or the degree of commodification is healthy. This does not suggest that money should not play a role in sport but that perhaps it should not be the only factor.

REFERENCES

Aden, R. C. (1995). Nostalgic communication as temporal escape: *When It Was a Game*'s re-construction of a baseball/work community. *Western Journal of Communication, 59,* 20–38.

Boyd, J. (2000). Selling home: Corporate stadium names and the destruction of commemoration. *Journal of Applied Communication Research, 28,* 330–346.

Brown, M. (2009). Average ticket price up 5.4 percent in MLB. *The Biz of Baseball.* Retrieved December 4, 2009, from http://www.bizofbaseball.com/index.php?option=com_content&view=article&id=3147:average-ticket-price-up-54-percent-in-mlb-yankeesmets-skew-total&catid=56:ticket-watch&Itemid=136.

Bryant, H. (2005). *Juicing the game: Drugs, power, and the fight for the soul of Major League Baseball.* New York: Viking.

Freeman, M. (2000). *ESPN: The uncensored history.* Lanham, MD: Taylor Trade.

Goldberg, D. T. (1998). Call and response: Sports, talk radio, and the death of democracy. *Journal of Sport & Social Issues, 22,* 212–223.

Greenberg, J. (2010, April 7). 2010 MLB FCI (update with Tigers and Angels changes). Team Marketing Report. Retrieved May 20, 2010, from http://www .teammarketing.com/blog/index.html?article_id=104.

Halone, K. K., & Billings, A. C. (2010). The temporal nature of racialized sport consumption. *American Behavioral Scientist 53,* 1645–1668.

Jhally, S. (1984). The spectacle of accumulation: Material and cultural factors in the evolution of the sports/media complex. *The Insurgent Sociologist, 12,* 41–57.

Jhally, S. (1989). Cultural studies and the sports/media complex. In L. A. Wenner (Ed.), *Media, sport, & society* (pp. 70–93). Newbury Park, CA: Sage.

Kellner, D. (1996). Sport, media culture, and race—some reflections on Michael Jordan. *Sociology of Sport Journal, 13,* 458–467.

Lane, J. (2007). *Under the boards: The cultural revolution in basketball.* Lincoln: University of Nebraska Press.

McAllister, M. P. (1998). College bowl sponsorship and the increased commercialization of amateur sports. *Critical Studies in Mass Communication, 15,* 357–381.

McAllister, M. P. (2010). Hypercommercialism, televisuality, and the changing nature of college sports sponsorship. *American Behavioral Scientist, 53,* 1476–1491.

McChesney, R. W. (1989). Media made sport: A history of sports coverage in the United States. In L. A. Wenner (Ed.), *Media, sport, and society* (pp. 49–67). Newbury Park, CA: Sage.

Meân, L., Kassing, J. W., & Sanderson, J. (2010). The making of an epic (American) hero fighting for justice: Commodification, consumption, and intertextuality in the Floyd Landis defense campaign. *American Behavioral Scientist, 53,* 1590–1609.

Moor, L. (2007). Sport and commodification: A reflection on key concepts. *Journal of Sport & Social Issues, 31,* 128–142.

Pegoraro, A., Ayer, S. M., & O'Reilly, N. J. (2010). Consumer consumption and advertising through sport. *American Behavioral Scientist, 53,* 1454–1475.

Rhoden, W. C. (2006). *Forty million slaves: The rise, fall, and redemption of the black athlete.* New York: Crown.

Ritzer, G., & Stillman, T. (2001). The postmodern ballpark as a leisure setting: Enchantment and simulated de-McDonaldization. *Leisure Sciences, 23,* 99–113.

Rosensweig, D. (2005). *Retro ball parks: Instant history, baseball, and the new American city.* Knoxville: University of Tennessee Press.

Schuck, R. I. (2010). The rhetorical lines on TV's poker face: Rhetorical constructions of poker as sport. *American Behavioral Scientist, 53,* 1610–1625.

Smith, R. (1988). *Sports and freedom: The rise of big-time college athletics.* New York: Oxford University Press.

Sobchack, V. (1997). Baseball in the post-American cinema, or life in the minor leagues. In A. Baker & T. Boyd (Eds.), *Out of bounds: Sports, media, and the politics of identity* (pp. 175–197). Bloomington: Indiana University Press.

Sperber, M. (2001). *Beer and circus: How big-time college sports is crippling undergraduate education.* New York: Holt.

Springwood, C. F. (1996). *Cooperstown to Dyersville: A geography of baseball nostalgia.* Boulder, CO: Westview Press.

Thompson, W. (2009). Yankee Stadium's Legends suite was sparsely populated at times this season—a sign of what greed does to loyalty. *Outside the Lines.* Retrieved December 4, 2009, from http://sports.espn.go.com/espn/eticket/story?page=091005yankeestickets.

Trumpbour, R. C. (2007). *The new cathedrals: Politics and media in the history of stadium construction.* Syracuse, NY: Syracuse University Press.

Wenner, L. A. (2004). Recovering (from) Janet Jackson's breast: Ethics and the nexus of media, sports, and management. *Journal of Sport Management, 18,* 315–334.

Wenner, L. A. (2010). Sport, communication, and the culture of consumption: On language and Identity. *American Behavioral Scientist, 53,* 1571–1573.

Wenner, L. A., & Jackson, S. J. (2009). Sport, beer, and gender in promotional culture: On the dynamics of a holy trinity. In L. A. Wenner & S. J. Jackson (Eds.), *Sport, beer, and gender: Promotional culture and contemporary social life* (pp. 1–34). New York: Peter Lang.

SUGGESTED ADDITIONAL READING

Aden, R. C. (1999). Integrating self and community as a means of finding homes: The shift from consumerism to altruism in *Field of Dreams.* In R. C. Aden, *Popular stories and promised lands: Fan cultures and symbolic pilgrimages* (pp. 219–249). Tuscaloosa: University of Alabama Press.

Butterworth, M. L., & Moskal, S. D. (2009). American football, flags, and "fun": The Bell Helicopter Armed Forces Bowl and the rhetorical production of militarism. *Communication, Culture & Critique, 2,* 411–433.

McAllister, M. P. (1999). Super Bowl advertising as commercial celebration. *Communication Review, 3,* 403–428.

Von Burg, R., & Johnson, P. E. (2009). Yearning for a past that never was: Baseball, steroids, and the American dream. *Critical Studies in Media Communication, 26,* 351–371.

Wenner, L. A. (1989). The Super Bowl pregame show: Cultural fantasies and political subtext. In L. A. Wenner (Ed.), *Media, sports, & society* (pp. 157–179). Newbury Park, CA: Sage.

CHAPTER 14

Fantasy Sports

Fantasy sports are one of the great dividers of modern sports fans: Some heavily committed sports fans mock the concept, not even understanding the basics, while others cannot imagine a world in which **fantasy sport** is not directly tied to the game at hand. What is without dispute is that the number of fantasy sport participants has reached critical mass (an estimated 27 million Americans now play annually; Fantasy Sports Trade Association, 2010) with $1.5 billion now being spent annually on fantasy sports (Klaassen, 2006), warranting a much closer examination of this relatively new phenomenon. Consider many of the aspects of the "game within a game" nature of fantasy. Much of what makes fantasy sport a draw for millions of Americans are the ties to communication—the interpersonal interactions with their friends, the media outlets that increasingly offer minutiae on player performance, the often bombastic rhetoric that is often included in e-mails related to the good or bad performance of fantasy sports teams. The advent of the fantasy sport era is not just a trend in sport, but one worthy of very close examination within communication and sport. This chapter will articulate fantasy sport (a) history, (b) rules and protocols, (c) motivations for play, (d) communities, (e) impact on many other aspects of the communication and sport field, and (f) future implications.

FANTASY SPORTS: A BRIEF HISTORY

Younger sports fans may have a difficult time comprehending a world before fantasy sports, but the evolution of the game has been relatively short, with its popularity particularly ascending since the 1990s. Harvard professor William Gamson is credited with creating the first form of fantasy sport (although he did not call it that) using professional baseball in 1960

(Schwartz, 2005). Several of his professor colleagues joined him in a fairly informal game in which each would score points based on how selected players performed in areas ranging from batting average to ERA. The first documented form of fantasy football arose 3 years later when four people connected to the Oakland Raiders organization developed a fantasy league called the Greater Oakland Professional Pigskin Prognosticators League (St. Amant, 2005). Based on the same concept as Gamson's (selecting players from different professional teams and assigning points to them based on their performance), the league gradually developed, although it was never patented or sold to the masses. The first player selected was George Blanda, undoubtedly because of his ability to score points as both the quarterback and place kicker for the Houston Oilers.

However, a major turning point in the evolution of fantasy sports occurred in 1979, when a group of New Yorkers, led by writer Daniel Okrent, developed a more sophisticated form of fantasy baseball called **rotisserie** (based on where the group often met to eat, New York restaurant La Rotisserie Francaise). Ironically, it was the stoppage of baseball (the long strike of 1981) that hastened the growth of rotisserie baseball as journalists wrote about previously niche stories because of the dearth of things to cover during the stoppage. They found fantasy sport to be of interest in an offbeat sort of way.

Fantasy sport, usually played online

For years, rotisserie resided largely in two forms (baseball and football) and was relegated mostly to fans who loved statistics and did not mind the time it necessitated to mine them from the local newspapers to determine fantasy winners. Participating in fantasy sport in the 1980s was a burdensome task, but the Internet dramatically altered that in the 1990s (see Felps, 2000, for an extended explanation). Suddenly, many more people who loved sports but did not previously play fantasy sports because of the legwork required opted to join online fantasy leagues because of the ease of statistical acquisition and league upkeep. Some leagues cost a modest amount of money while others were free and, as of the early 2010s, this format has largely stayed the same with just the bells and whistles changing. People can now purchase online draft kits, receive injury updates, and follow virtually every aspect of a player's life both on and off the playing field. As is true with many other facets of society, players get what they pay for, as more money invested provides things such as real-time updates of scores and fantasy guru advice. As a result of the information age, many more forms of fantasy participation are now available including basketball, golf, hockey, cricket, and auto racing. There are even nonsporting forms of fantasy leagues, ranging from Fantasy Congress (where people draft House and Senate members and score points based on their actions) and the Hollywood Stock Exchange (in which players are handed millions in imaginary money to invest in upcoming film projects based on how they think they will perform at the box office). The concept in all forms of fantasy leagues is roughly the same: Take events that are already occurring naturally within society and find a way to reconstruct the people acting in the events to predict and perform new assimilated meanings to the existing actions.

RULES AND PROTOCOLS

Leagues are formed in all sizes and formats, but they can be subdivided into face-to-face and online leagues. Either type typically requires the participation of 10 to 12 people (although this can vary), but the format changes the interaction and overarching structures substantially. Nearly all face-to-face leagues involve family, friends, or coworkers—people who already live in a fairly close proximity to one another. Officemates now follow fantasy football wins and losses in a similar manner to the March Madness NCAA basketball tournament bracket predictions. In these leagues, camaraderie is emphasized as people frequently join for ritualistic bonding and interaction just as much as the competition and focus on sport. The casual sport fan is more likely to participate in this type of league because of the people involved than for the potential for fantasy dominance.

Conversely, online leagues often include some of these same participants but are more likely to exist within looser friendship structures: geographically dispersed high school or college friends, loose contacts made in the business world, and the like. However, a large number of leagues exist online among total strangers. Often these leagues are formed for those who may not know of a dozen people with common interests in fantasy sport, those who do not desire the interpersonal or group functions that arise with other forms of fantasy sport, or those who wish to test their skills against the general population.

Once a league is formed and a draft date is set, many fantasy sports owners choose from a wide array of media materials designed to give them a leg up on the competition. Publications such as *Fantasy Football Index* and *Rotowire Fantasy Baseball Guide* dot the newsstands while organizations such as Yahoo!, Fanball, and ESPN offer online advice and columns promising insider information for enthusiasts. Some fantasy sport participants have been known to spend more than $100 per year on expert materials alone.

Draft day then arises, which can be as simple or as complex as those participating in the league wish it to be. Some online drafts merely involve the submission of a ranked list of players one wishes to draft, letting a computer program choose the players for each team based on these selections.

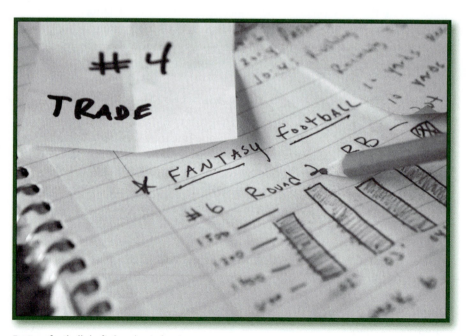

Fantasy football draft day cheat sheet

Other online drafts involve chat rooms, trades, and multihour designs. Face-to-face drafts, though, can be quite elaborate social events. Draft formats vary as well, but the most common involves mimicking the way most professional sports leagues hold their drafts, with teams possessing a numbered pick and then systematically selecting an athlete from a master list of available players. A popular variation on this system is the "snake" draft, where odd-numbered draft rounds are slated inversely in even numbered rounds. For example, in a 12-team draft, a team possessing the #1 pick would not have another pick until the draft "snaked" back to them at pick #24; a team with the #12 pick would also possess pick #13.

The other major form of fantasy draft format is the auction system. In this format, each team is granted a certain number of fantasy dollars with which it can purchase players for its team. A player is then opened for auction and the team that is the highest bidder receives him or her. For example, if a fantasy owner is allotted 300 fantasy dollars, the owner must determine if Alex Rodriguez is worth 50 of those dollars (which would leave only $250 left to complete the rest of their roster).

Scoring for fantasy sports varies from the rudimentary to the complex, usually depending on the degree of fanship and interest in the fantasy sports league at hand. For instance, a football league of casual interest may simply log yardage gained and points scored via touchdown, field goal, or point after touchdown; a league of avid interest may also score interceptions, fumbles, number of receptions, and other secondary statistics. Again, there are two major forms of scoring formats. The most prevalent in many types of leagues is the points format, in which statistics are assigned a point value (for example, one point for every 10 rushing yards) and teams select starting players who each accrue points based on these assignments. So, Matt Ryan's traditional sports statistics could look like:

Matt Ryan
Passing yards: 220
Touchdowns: 2
Interceptions: 1

But in fantasy football world they could look like:

Matt Ryan
Yardage (1 point per 30 yards passing) = 7
Touchdowns (6 points per TD throw) = 12
Interceptions (−2 points for each INT thrown) = −2
TOTAL: 17 fantasy points

These points are then totaled for all starters, teams play head-to-head matchups, and the team with the highest total wins.

The other format that is often popular most prevalently in fantasy baseball and basketball is category rankings. In this format, head-to-head games are not played; rather, overall statistics are compared to other teams in the league and teams receive points based on where they rank compared to the others. For instance, if there were a 10-team baseball league and one of the categories assigned was saves, here is how ranking points would be distributed (see Table 14.1).

In this example, one can see that placement matters more than final total. The distance between Team C and Team D is one save, yet Team C scores 1 full point more than Team D, the same 1-point difference as is assigned between Team F and Team H, even though the distance between the two teams is 20 saves rather than just one. Teams would then calculate points scored for each of the assigned categories (home runs, wins, etc.) and, again, the team with the most points (based on rankings) wins.

Teams play different schedules based on the sport. Football schedules often include 13 to 14 weeks of head-to-head play followed by 2 to 3 weeks of

Table 14.1 Example Distribution of Ranking Points for Fantasy Baseball League

	Total Saves	Rank	Points
	(all players, entire season)		
Team A	46	6th	5
Team B	17	10th	1
Team C	73	2nd	9
Team D	72	3rd	8
Team E	35	8th	3
Team F	48	5th	6
Team G	39	7th	4
Team H	68	4th	7
Team I	90	1st	10
Team J	22	9th	2

playoffs (the final week of the season traditionally features many high-profile players resting for the actual playoffs, so fantasy leagues usually conclude before then). Sports such as baseball and basketball involve the entire regular season, often because of the ranked-scoring format previously mentioned.

Leagues have different nuances depending on stability of owners and the spirit the group hopes to exude. For example, leagues that have existed for more than a decade may opt to become "keeper" leagues in which a select number of players on each owner's current team can be kept for the next season (thus not being available to all for the next draft). Other leagues enact rules that keep the league enjoyable for all, such as creating a Bad Example for Youth (BEFY) fine to be placed on any owner of a player who is arrested for a crime.

Interview: Jeffrey Thomas, Founder and CEO, World Fantasy Games

Q: What do you believe are the primary reasons for the rapid growth in fantasy sports over the past two decades?

A: The strength and growth of the industry can be traced back to word of mouth and passion that can only be found by drafting a fantasy team and managing it. In the late 1980s and early 1990s, media started getting involved, mainly newspapers. Then, the Internet arrived; Fantasy Sports Trade Association research shows that the industry has more than doubled in the last 10 years and specifically has grown at a rate of 20% to 25% in the past 4 years . . . peaking now at approximately 30 million consumers in the U.S. and Canada. Fantasy football is 80% of the market and has led much of the growth in the industry. Other sports are doing well, but none can claim even half the market of fantasy football.

Q: Why are people drawn to participate?

A: Private research points to three reasons: love of the sport, peer recognition/competition, and prizes. This helps explain the popularity of fantasy football versus other sports, since football is the most popular sport in the U.S. The design of the NFL also helps, with weekly rather than daily games. Peer recognition and competition come into play because of the pure time element. The structure allows for a logical flow of communication between players and gives everyone enough time to do their analysis and set their team.

(Continued)

(Continued)

Q: What impact have fantasy sports had on other aspects of sports culture?

A: When I launched my first fantasy sports company in 1993, most consumers had not heard of fantasy sports. Now, if I'm in a sports bar, I typically hear someone talking about their fantasy team or see a show on television with fantasy sports statistics streaming on the screen. Times have changed! Fantasy is now ingrained into our culture. It's also an extremely valuable marketing tool. Imagine Major League Baseball after the strike without fantasy. Fantasy baseball players were the first to really care about the players again during a time when the majority of consumers complained about million-dollar crybabies. Fantasy football has been the most valuable marketing tool of the past decade for the NFL. Think about it: Consumers from Atlanta now study the third-string wide receivers in Seattle or San Diego. The fantasy player spends 3 to 5 hours online per week specifically on fantasy; each minute they spend benefits the league and the players.

Q: Are you concerned that fantasy sports are sometimes linked to other forms of deviance in sport, such as gambling and addiction?

A: No. Ninety-five percent of the market is free or includes low fees that essentially underwrite software development and operations fees. Few companies have excellent profit margins.

Many times fantasy is a promotion or a customer-acquisition strategy to support other company or brand goals.

Q: How do you see fantasy sports evolving in the years to come?

A: Fantasy is going global. The rest of the world is way ahead of us technically and in adopting more flexible gaming laws, but their version of fantasy is 5 to 7 years behind us. Companies that expect to do well globally must have staying power . . . and a 5- to 10-year strategic plan.

MOTIVATIONS FOR PLAY

Various forms of fantasy sport communities exist, with their function largely stemming from the owners' motivation for participation in the league. Employing a uses and gratifications (see Rubin & Perse, 1987) framework endorsing the belief that people select and use media for the fulfillment of personal needs, Farquhar and Meeds (2007) identified five needs that are satisfied through participation in fantasy sports. The first two, arousal and surveillance, were determined to be the primary motivations, while entertainment, escape, and social interaction functions were uncovered as well. Spinda and Haridakis (2008) defined these types of needs as motives for play, uncovering six main factors: ownership, achievement/self-esteem, escape/pass time, socialization, bragging rights, and amusement. Thus, when combining these two lists, we can compile a list of five primary reasons for fantasy sport play.

The first factor is *autonomy*. A common thread of modern sport discussion arises from the fan who thinks he or she could run a team more effectively than the current ownership or manager/coach. Fantasy sport provides the opportunity to (at a much more simplified level) prove this axiom. Owners feel smart when they add a player who suddenly does well and even feel intellectually superior when their team becomes a winner.

The second reason for play is *enhanced enjoyment,* a combination of the arousal/entertainment/amusement functions listed above. Fantasy sport provides another reason to watch games with a much greater focus. Some owners play these games for the same reason that a person places multiple (and often conflicting) bets on the same spin of the roulette wheel: It makes the game more complex by providing more angles from which to view the game. Consider a Colorado Rockies fan watching a game between the San Diego Padres and Los Angeles Dodgers. He or she may be rooting for one team to win because it enhances the chance that the Rockies will make the playoffs, but he or she also may have an outfielder for the Dodgers and pitcher for the Padres on a fantasy team. The permutations for what the person is rooting for within that game become quite multifaceted, which tends to heighten engagement and, hence, enjoyment of the game.

A third factor is *camaraderie*—a dimension of the social aspects listed previously. Many office environments feature fantasy sports leagues because it not only gets them through the workday but also provides a subject on which to converse with colleagues. The same is true with neighbors, friends, relatives, and even old high school and college companions. The interaction keeps the relationship going while giving people a common bond.

Fourth is a reason not specifically mentioned before but that is nonetheless becoming increasingly prevalent: *addiction.* Obviously, this is a motive for continued play rather than for initially deciding to become part of the fantasy sport community, but it is a growing phenomenon. Quite a few people make a living off of fantasy sport play by offering advice for players always looking for an edge against their league counterparts. High Stakes Fantasy Football offers drafts in Las Vegas, Chicago, and Los Angeles with entry fees of $1,250. Increasingly, people are looking to fantasy sport as a form of gambling and, even when it is free, many more get a "high" from the potential for success in their fantasy league.

The final reason for play is perhaps the most obvious: *fantasy*. Ever wondered what it would be like to have Los Angeles Lakers basketball star Kobe Bryant and Boston Celtic standout Kevin Garnett on the same team? Here is your chance. Ever want to feel superior to that know-it-all friend? Sign up for a fantasy sport and let the dice roll. There is a unique culture surrounding fantasy sport that exists separately from even the regular sporting world. The graphics of a televised football game are now a clear example: Coverage of the actual game is being shown on the majority of the screen, but the statistics from other games impacting the fantasy sport world scroll below.

FANTASY SPORT COMMUNITIES

Decades ago, one could stereotype the community of fantasy sport with a modicum of accuracy. The world was dominated by "stat geeks" who were more than willing to spend hours seeking out the data needed to play the games. The ultrafan was the prototypical fantasy sport player. That, without question, has changed in the mainstreaming of fantasy sport. As a result, many different types of communities exist that were analyzed and combined for this chapter.

First, there are still the statistical enthusiasts. They love crunching numbers to determine whether a middle infielder would rebound after a down year or to uncover the degree to which having the first pick offers owners intrinsic advantages or disadvantages. However, these players differ in the games they play, as the degree of detail is quite impressive. A basic fantasy baseball league may have four or five batting and pitching components, while these communities may be assessing as many as two dozen statistical categories to determine fantasy superiority. Playing games within this type of community requires astute observation, attention to detail, and a willingness to place fantasy value over value in the "real game."

A second community is the fan-first players. They enjoy and care about fantasy sport but will not care about it so much as to disregard the fate of their favorite "real" teams. They draft players that they think are the best for their fantasy team while simultaneously realizing that if given the choice between winning their fantasy championship and their favorite team winning a real championship, their loyalties will ultimately lie with the team with which they grew up.

A third group of players exists that is casually dubbed the "homers." Not only do they care about their favorite teams more than any fantasy game, but they will also actively select players from their favorite team to essentially be rooting for the same team in the fantasy and real worlds. An example would be an Indiana Pacers fan who selects Pacers players in the first four rounds of the fantasy draft. He likely realizes his decisions will be a detriment to his fantasy performance (obviously, a Pacer player was not always the best available selection) yet only desires fantasy sport glory if it is paired with the success of his favorite regular team.

A final fantasy sport community includes those players that opt for fantasy sports merely for the social aspects. They still have a desire to win, but, most importantly, they would like to be a part of the conversation. A prime case would be an office league in which many of a person's administrative superiors play; a newcomer may wish to join just to get to know people and have something to discuss over coffee in the morning. Some of these players would not even classify themselves as sports fans, much in the same way that millions of people who do not care about football nonetheless watch the Super Bowl for fear that they would otherwise be missing something.

Obviously, other forms of fantasy sports communities exist (as hybrids of the four listed above, but also as uniquely separate organized entities). The important aspect to remember is that as the fantasy world expands, so does the breadth of fantasy sporting communities.

SOCIETAL IMPACT

The advent (and subsequent mainstreaming) of fantasy sports impacts the communication and sport landscape at many levels ranging from fandom to social attitudes and interactions to media entities and even to deviant behaviors. This section will expound on each of these four influences.

Impacts abound, but none more so than on the *role of the fan*. Fantasy sport changes fandom in the same way that gambling alters attitudes about winners and losers—it creates a game within a game. Walk into a packed sports bar in America and you will see these often conflicting paradigms at play. All are watching the same game, but for different reasons: Some are fans of the home team, others of the visiting team, others of certain players on either team as they relate to their potential fantasy sporting prowess, and still others care not as much about who wins but by how much in relation to a Las Vegas point spread. Many of these motivations for consumption converge and conflict because in fantasy sport, "allegiances to the real team and to other fans of the real team are frayed from the start," but we are drawn to it because "fantasy sports do not merely offer [a] point of transcendence through interaction; they are predicated on it and, in a way, necessitate it" (Serazio, 2008, p. 31). Perhaps Sandomir (2002) states the situation best when arguing that fantasy sport causes people to "root, root, root for no team" (para. 1).

Social attitudes and interactions are influenced by fantasy sports as well. Consumption of sports media is at an all-time high (see Raney & Bryant, 2006), meaning that a family that used to adjust its weekend schedule around when its favorite team played now may try to work around an entire sporting schedule, as each game may be of import in the fantasy sports world. It no longer matters if your favorite team is on; any game may feature a player in which you now have a rooting interest.

Fantasy sports interactions, though, inevitably occur after the games have been played, meaning that interactions surrounding sports can become a weeklong and (in extreme cases) even round-the-clock endeavor. Even with football, where games are only contested once per week, owners spend significant amounts of time determining starting lineups, brokering trades, and chatting (in person and virtually) about previous performances. The downside is that an estimated $435 million of workplace productivity is lost *each week* because of fantasy football play ("Productivity is Fantasy," 2007).

Scholars have also found that fantasy sports can reinforce traditional aspects of sports culture, including masculinity (Davis & Duncan, 2006) and hooliganism (Poulton, 2008). Not surprisingly, the majority of fantasy sports owners is male, and along with that arise the predictable patterns of dominance and exclusion. Thus, fantasy sport becomes the new form of male sports club in which it becomes tacitly permissible for "boys to be boys" because little feminine resistance (or even participation) is present in the majority of fantasy sports leagues.

Fantasy sports have also changed the way *media entities* conduct their business. Pregame shows feature analysts drafting their own teams and fantasy sports experts advising owners who to "start or sit" for a given game. National sports radio programs now routinely feature callers looking for fantasy advice. Major Internet entities such as Yahoo!, ESPN, and cbssportsline.com make fantasy sport a heavy portion of their online sports offerings, as people are much more likely to become unique, logged users for fantasy sports than merely seeking other forms of sports information.

Case Study: Fantasy Sports in a Digital Age

As this chapter would attest, fantasy sports have grown in overwhelming proportions, spawning an industry devoted to feeding the fantasy desires of fans for all types of sports. Even athletes have come to promote their fantasy potential for fans, which has not only increased popularity for the sport but has also helped to shed individual attention on athletes in team-based sports. However, as fantasy sports rely upon the use of an athlete's name and statistics, an interesting legal issue is presented about who owns the rights to this information: the players, team owners, sport organization, or the fans?

The question about intellectual property emerges when such considerable revenues are generated through the various fantasy leagues that have developed in a digital age. When little revenue potential was generated, there was limited concern by organizations or the players to control access to the information. Yet in a digital age, sport organizations are likely to have only begun to tap into the possible resources that can be gained from fantasy sports. For instance, in 2005, Major League Baseball Advanced Media (MLBAM) was granted exclusive rights to all of Major League Baseball's intellectual property, which includes player names, statistics, and likenesses that could be used in the development of any online content. MLBAM (the Internet and interactive media organization for MLB) then offered exclusive rights to only a handful of fantasy game providers.

While this has not yet transcended into other sport organizations, it raises interesting questions about the overreaching control that these organizations have over their players, and a number of fantasy outlets have contested the right to use anything that is already in the public domain. C.B.E., a small fantasy sport provider, contested the move by MLB to restrict its access to player information. The court ruled that because C.B.E. drew its content to provide an avenue for fantasy sports from the public domain, a number of legal questions related to intellectual property were not affected, including the facts that (1) ability to make a living as a baseball player was not affected (actually noting that the marketing assisted many players' financial return), (2) statistical information on the players did not constitute a "likeness," and (3) fantasy sport relied upon only "facts" rather than any type of interpretation or depiction of actual events.

Some are concerned that this rule will have a negative impact on the rights that athletes have in controlling and marketing their personae in the future. For fantasy sport enthusiasts, however, the ruling helped ensure that fantasy sport leagues will

(Continued)

(Continued)

remain affordable as sport organizations lose control of the right to charge licensing fees for the statistical data that serve as the foundation for the leagues.

1. Should information that is available in the public domain belong to any one organization or individual?

2. What types of sports are not influenced by the access of information currently found in the public domain?

3. Who should ultimately control the right to the communications on an individual athlete?

Media also are influenced by fantasy sport in larger ways, perhaps most noticeably in featuring individual accomplishments to the detriment of team achievements. A sports fan following a Mets/Phillies baseball game may be checking which pitcher got the win or who hit the home runs before noticing that the Mets actually won the game. In television, on-screen graphics have become more commonplace, partially because of the information age but also because the growing number of fantasy sports fans demand it. Perceptions of athlete worth are altered in the process. For example, a running back who leads the league in rushing may not be as valued as the person who always gets the ball at the goal line because of convoluted notions of fantasy sports worth.

Lomax (2006) notes that media outlets have not yet uncovered ways to fully realize the profits fantasy sports can provide but that the future is clearly in determining how to capitalize on this avid and growing fan base. Media outlets are hoping that fantasy sports ultimately will provide insight into not only what fans want but also perhaps even in predicting whether the collective knowledge of millions of fans can aid the prediction of future sporting successes. This has already proved successful in the film industry, as the fantasy site Hollywood Stock Exchange (hsx.com) has proven to be a very reliable indicator of how a film will perform in its first four weeks at the box office (see Smith, Sharman, & Hooper, 2006 for more information on harnessing decision-making insights).

A final impact of fantasy sport lies in the area of *deviance,* particularly in the form of addiction and gambling. Bernhard and Earle (2005) note that "if we broadly define gambling as an activity that risks something of value (substantial amounts of money) on an event whose outcome is undetermined (such as the whims of a professional baseball season), fantasy baseball clearly qualifies" (p. 29). Indeed, all forms of fantasy sport qualify under this definition, meaning there is (and will always be) an underbelly to these games as it has become a part of the "active fan" experience (Real, 2006). Internet use expedites the gambling process, and so it is with fantasy sports as well. Just as there is always a sporting event on which to place an online bet somewhere in the world, there is also a fantasy league looking for a new player and a guru offering new sage advice. Many chuckle over the concept of fantasy sport addiction and, in most cases, it is relatively harmless. However, people have lost their jobs and become estranged from their families because of fantasy play. Consider the obsessiveness of the fantasy sports players within the FX series *The League,* which debuted in the fall of 2009. Characters were depicted as placing fantasy sport success ahead of other fundamental obligations to family and career,

Gambling and Sports

once even having a character jokingly call FOX Sports broadcaster Terry Bradshaw to find out the injury status of a player on their team. The ties between fantasy sport, addiction, and gambling are perhaps weak at the current moment, yet the obsession of fantasy sport players can certainly border on deviance and can make these connections quite clear on individual bases. Scholars are also attempting to determine whether fantasy sports owners are more or less likely to gamble money on games and also whether fantasy becomes a gateway to various forms of addictive and deviant behavior.

A Matter of Ethics: What to Do with the Fantasy Fanatic?

The rapid increase of participation in fantasy sports has prompted new terms in our language, most of which are associated with player ratings and performance statistics. One term, however, is a product of the relational consequences of extreme participation: the *fantasy sports widow.* The term is typically used to describe women who feel

(Continued)

(Continued)

emotionally abandoned by their husbands and boyfriends who devote too much time and energy to sports. There is a degree of intended humor in the term, yet it also points toward the potentially real problem of fantasy sports addiction.

In response to this phenomenon, Allison Lodish founded Women Against Fantasy Sports (WAFS), largely a social media phenomenon with Facebook groups and Twitter feeds,

> as an outlet for people to ridicule, mourn and lament the loss of their partners who spend an inordinate amount of time online consuming player data, drafting and managing their teams, scouring stats, scores, and injury reports and trash-talking with friends and players in their leagues. (Women Against Fantasy Sports, 2010)

Thus, the announced purpose of WAFS is to offer a kind of support group for those whose partners may spend too much time with fantasy sports.

On the one hand, it appears WAFS serves a positive purpose. On the other hand, however, a close review of the group's website reveals that it was started as a project for an executive MBA class and that one of the cofounders, Azar McMaster, acknowledged that part of the website's purpose was to allow people to "buy cool stuff that pokes fun at our addiction." Indeed, it appears that WAFS is perhaps more about promoting fantasy sports than it is about questioning its role in our society. This doesn't necessarily mean you should condemn WAFS, but it does raise questions about the relational effects of fantasy sports.

1. Can fantasy sports participation damage interpersonal relationships?

2. Should we think of excessive participation as an addiction, as we do with alcohol or gambling?

3. Is it ethical for an organization such as WAFS to promote itself as offering a supportive community even if it appears to benefit from the very phenomenon it critiques?

4. Has participation in fantasy sports affected *you* in your relationships? Your job?

Concerns also exist regarding the expansion of fantasy sports to amateur athletics, more specifically college football and basketball. For decades, college athletes have argued that they have become marketable figures within the media and, thus, deserve financial compensation. Fantasy sports now moves that debate even farther along, as sports websites are attempting to tap into the love of college football and basketball to draw fantasy sports enthusiasts to their domains. The NCAA is currently embroiled in a debate as to whether college football athletes' names can be used to support money-making fantasy websites (Moser, 2008). Concerns about point shaving and other gambling ties already exist in college sports, and fantasy (as a burgeoning billion-dollar business) could exacerbate these issues. Many feel the Pandora's box has already been opened with March Madness, as tens of millions of brackets are completed each year, most with illegal financial components tied to the rise and fall of college basketball teams in the NCAA tournament. This fractured relationship between college sports and gambling is typified by cases such as the one of former University of Washington football coach Rick Neuheisel, who was fired from his job in the summer of 2003 for entering a neighborhood March Madness betting pool. If fantasy sport invades the collegiate ranks, many fear more of these potentially conflicting cases will occur.

THE FUTURE OF FANTASY SPORT

With so many people now participating in fantasy sports and so many variations of fantasy play now available (golf, tennis, and the Olympics now have fantasy versions), it is fair to wonder whether the popularity of the games has reached critical mass. However, the demand for virtually all forms of sport has proven to be much more elastic than most estimates, and the same is also likely true for fantasy components of the industry. Some roadblocks remain, but other heavily argued debates such as intellectual property issues (see Bolitho, 2006) have been settled predominantly in favor of fantasy sporting outlets (Van Voris & St. Onge, 2007).

In addition, fantasy sport should become prevalent in more aspects of modern life, including the world of education. For instance, scholars already are arguing that the games can be quite beneficial in the understanding of sports marketing (Gillentine & Schulz, 2001) and the teaching of information literacy (Waelchli, 2008). Fantasy sport inherently provides demographic and behavioral information about the tendencies of millions of people, and educators in fields as diverse as public relations, mathematics, and management will continue to reap the rewards of this self-generated data.

Finally, it appears that the line between the real games played by professional (and potentially, in the future, collegiate) athletes and the fantasy games played with the statistics derived from the real will continue to be blurred. The more media outlets and other gatekeepers report on fantasy sport, the more it enters the bloodstream of the modern sports athlete. Professional sports players already are asked questions about their fantasy performance and respond with a great deal of accuracy and specificity. This combination of real and fantasy sport is quite different than other forms of blurred realities presented in staged formats such as professional wrestling. It is much more akin to the types of conversations currently happening surrounding computer-mediated communication, as fantasy players often use technology to delve into a secondary world in which their uniquely constructed team wins and loses even if all of those players lost the actual game that was played. It is difficult to discern what the ultimate outcome of this collaboration of sporting worlds will be, but there is no question that fantasy sports are here to stay as a significant factor of modern sporting culture.

REFERENCES

Bernhard, B. J., & Earle, V. H. (2005). Gambling in a fantasy world: An exploratory study of rotisserie baseball games. *UNLV Gaming Research & Review Journal, 9*(1), 29–42.

Bolitho, Z. C. (2006). When fantasy meets the courtroom: An examination of the intellectual property issues surrounding the burgeoning fantasy sports industry. *The Ohio State Law Journal, 67*(4), 911–960.

Davis, N. W., & Duncan, M. C. (2006). Sports knowledge is power: Reinforcing masculine privilege through fantasy sport league participation. *Journal of Sport & Social Issues, 30,* 244–264.

Fantasy Sports Trade Association. (2010). Homepage. Retrieved on November 12, 2010, from www.fsta.org.

Farquhar, L. K., & Meeds, R. (2007). Types of fantasy sports users and their motivations. *Journal of Computer-Mediated Communication, 12*(4), article 4. http://jcmc.indiana.edu/vol12/issue4/farquhar.html.

Felps, P. (2000, September 20). Fantasy sports players getting a big assist from the Internet. [Electronic version]. *The Dallas Morning News .*Retrieved November 7, 2007, from http://www.amarillo.com/stories/092300/tec_fantasysports.shtml.

Gillentine, A., & Schulz, J. (2001). Marketing the fantasy football league: Utilization of simulation to enhance sport marketing concepts. *Journal of Marketing Education, 23*(3), 178–186.

Klaassen, A. (2006, August). That's real money—$1.5B—pouring into made-up leagues. *Advertising Age, 77*(32). Retrieved on November 12, 2010 at: http://www.highbeam.com/doc/1G1-149270692.html.

Lomax, R. G. (2006). Fantasy sports: History, game types, and research. In A. Raney & J. Bryant (Eds.), *Handbook of sports and media* (pp. 383–392). Mahwah, NJ: LEA.

Moser, K. (2008, August 15). New fantasy football league tests NCAA's rules on amateur status. *The Chronicle of Higher Education, 54*(9). Retrieved on November 12, 2010 at: http://chronicle.com/article/New-Fantasy-Football-League/21835.

Poulton, E. (2008). Toward a cultural sociology of the consumption of "fantasy football hooliganism." *Sociology of Sport Journal, 25*(3), 331–349.

Productivity is fantasy during football season. (2007, September 2). *St. Petersburg Times*, p. 1D.

Raney, A. A., & Bryant, J. (Eds.). (2006). *Handbook of sport and media.* Mahwah, NJ: LEA.

Real, M. (2006). Sports online: The newest player in mediasport. In A. Raney & J. Bryant (Eds.), *Handbook of sports and media* (pp. 171–184). Mahwah, NJ: LEA.

Rubin, A., & Perse, E. (1987). Audience activity and soap opera involvement: A uses and effects investigation. *Human Communication Research, 14*(2), 246–268.

Sandomir, R. (2002, September 13). Reality of fantasy football: Root, root, root for no Team. *The New York Times.* Retrieved October 27 2009 from http://query.nytimes.com/gst/fullpage.html?res=9F05E4DE1131F930A2575AC0A9649C8B63.

Schwartz, A. (2005). *The numbers game: Baseball's lifelong fascination with statistics.* New York: St. Martin's.

Serazio, M. (2008). Virtual sports consumption, authentic brotherhood: The reality of fantasy football. In L. W. Hugenberg, P. M. Haridakis, & A. C. Earnheardt (Eds.), *Sports mania: Essays on fandom and the media in the 21st century* (pp. 229–242). Jefferson, NC: McFarland.

Smith, B., Sharman, P., & Hooper, P. (2006). Decision making in online fantasy sports communities. *Interactive Technology and Smart Education, 3*(4), 347–360.

Spinda, J. S. W., & Haridakis, P. M. (2008). Exploring the motives of fantasy sports: A uses and gratifications approach. In L. W. Hugenberg, P. M. Haridakis, & A. C. Earnheardt (Eds.), *Sports mania: Essays on fandom and the media in the 21st century* (pp. 187–202). Jefferson, NC: McFarland.

St. Amant, M. (2005). *Committed: Confessions of a fantasy football junkie.* New York: Scribner.

Van Voris, B., & St. Onge, J. (2007, October 16). Fantasy sports win right to player names, statistics. Retrieved October 17, 2007, from http://www.bloomberg.com/apps/news?pid=newsarchive&sid=a7JHYb1l18mY.

Waelchli, P. (2008). Librarians' sport of choice: Teaching information literacy through fantasy football. *College Research Library News, 69,* 10–15.

SUGGESTED ADDITIONAL READING

Einolf, K. W., (2005). EconFantasy.com: Where fantasy becomes reality in an economics-of-sports simulation. *Journal of Sports Economics, 6,* 338–339.

Fine, G. A. (1983). *Shared fantasy: Role-playing games as social worlds.* Chicago: University of Chicago Press.

Hiltner, J. R., & Walker, J. R. (1996). Super frustration Sunday: The day *Prodigy's* fantasy baseball died: An analysis of the dynamics of electronic communication. *Journal of Popular Culture, 30,* 103–117.

Levy, D. P. (2005). Fantasy sports. In William H. McNiell (Ed.), *Berkshire encyclopedia of world sport.* Great Barrington, MA: Berkshire.

Poulton, E. (2007). "Fantasy football hooliganism" in popular culture. *Media, Culture, and Society, 29*(1), 151–164.

Walker, S. (2006). *Fantasyland: A season on baseball's lunatic fringe.* New York: Penguin.

Zimmerman, M. (2000). *The complete idiot's guide to fantasy baseball.* Indianapolis, IN: Alpha Books.

CHAPTER 15

Communication and Sport in the Future

S prinkled throughout these chapters has been the underlying notion of immense change in the ways we participate in, consume, and interact within sporting constructs. It would take a crystal ball to accurately project what sports culture will look like in the years to come, let alone to determine what the communicative impact of these changes would or could be. Still, it is evident that many changes in economic, media, and social structures are already navigating sport into new directions that may cause optimism for some and concern for others. For instance, one major facet of our discussions has been sports media, yet many highly regarded experts are arguing against even the use of the word *media*, claiming that the concept itself is too ambiguous and outdated. Consider *Wired* editor Chris Anderson's beliefs on the traditional terminology no longer applying:

> I don't use the word "journalism." I don't use the word "media." I don't use the word "news." I don't think that those words mean anything anymore. They defined publishing in the 20th century. Today, they are a barrier. They are standing in our way, like a horseless carriage . . . We're in one of those strange eras where the words of the last century don't have meaning. What does news mean to you, when the vast majority of news is created by amateurs? Is news coming from a newspaper, or a news group or a friend? . . . You don't need this access to a commercial channel to distribute (news), anyone can do it. (Hornig, 2009)

It is not just media that is undergoing dramatic change. Technology, economic models, and the advent of social networking ultimately have already been changing and will continue to change the way we interact within and about sport in the future, emphasizing the role of communication even more. Within the more traditional subdisciplines of the communication field, much evidence exists that the influence of sport is escalating. Church sports leagues are *growing,* meaning that the study of this pairing from organizational and interpersonal viewpoints must *grow* as well. The use of sport-laden language in other public arenas such as politics and public relations is *growing,* meaning the study of sports rhetoric must *grow* as well. The number of fantasy sports players is *growing,* therefore the study of the media outlets partnering with these new media players must *grow* as well. In sum, the wider the field of communication and sport becomes, the more direct the ties between the two flagpole terms become.

This chapter will outline the potential ramifications of these types of changes in the communication and sport combination by re-examining the key players within the community of sport that were outlined in Chapter 2. Specifically, we'll delve into what the future looks like for sports participants, organizations, media entities, and fans and then finish by combining them into the eclectic mix of communication phenomena that will inherently get messier and more blurry in the years to come.

THE FUTURE SPORTS PARTICIPANT

The role of the sport participant continues to change based on a number of outside influences ranging from economic to political to cultural to mediated. A person who participates in sport is now more likely to do so in a structured manner or not do it at all, opting for indoor-based video games and other forms of entertainment that supersede free-form play. Those who do participate in organized sports will continue to be pushed to specialize as the concept of the well-rounded athlete is trumped by the notion of keeping up with the others if you wish to succeed or even participate. Most athletic trainers would counter that children should not specialize in sports, mostly because year-round play of any sport such as soccer, basketball, or baseball results in the overuse of some muscles and bones to the exclusion of others. However, children now participate in leagues that travel much greater distances than ever before and push the limits of the human body in ways not expected for previous generations. Children participate in multiple games in a single day and often try to gain competitive advantages through potentially dangerous physical maneuvers, such as Little League baseball players throwing curveballs at early ages when such practices are not recommended (Whitehead & Patrick, 2006).

Athletes at all levels will also increasingly find themselves debating appropriate uses of performance-enhancing drugs (PEDs), even debating what constitutes performance enhancement. Medical advances continue to make steroids that are more effective and safer to use than ever before, and an increasing number of people use steroids for nonathletic purposes, including treating allergies and chronic ailments. Thus, the controversy surrounding the use of steroids in sports will likely continue to percolate, if not escalate, over time. If and when steroids become commonplace remedies for mainstream America (and international societies), is it fair to exclude athletes from being able to use them if they hold the potential to make their lives better outside of the sporting arena? Is it reasonable to think steroids (and other PEDs) can be regulated in any meaningful way when they continue to evolve in substance and usage?

At higher levels, athletes are finding an increased expectation for a pseudorelationship with those who consume sport, a concept relatedly known in communication circles as parasocial interaction (see Rubin, Perse, & Powell, 1985). Rubin and McHugh (1987) find that physical attraction is not as important as social interaction within parasocial relationships; this is undoubtedly true in 21st-century sport. Athletes are offering dramatically increased access to their personal and everyday lives. As of the fall of 2009, Shaquille O'Neal had 2.2 million followers on the social networking website Twitter. Athletes such as football wide receiver Terrell Owens have their own reality television shows, while other athletes like footballer Emmitt Smith and gymnast Shawn Johnson participate on *Dancing with the Stars*, offering people an opportunity to see what they are like beyond the arena in which they perform. Athlete blogs are now commonplace, with people such as basketball players Gilbert Arenas blogging during warm-ups and halftimes of games and Stephon Marbury offering 24-hour web streaming of even the most mundane aspects of his life, including sleeping and going to the restroom. The result is an increased expectation that there will be some sort of continual and personal interaction between athlete and fan. Kassing and Sanderson (2009) examined the case of Floyd Landis, a cyclist who won the 2006 Tour de France only to have the title stripped from him because of heightened testosterone ratios in a midrace drug test (Landis finally admitted to drug use in 2010). Fan postings at the now defunct floydlandis.com fell into categories of (a) empathy and sympathy, (b) confirmation, (c) testimony, (d) sharing a common enemy, and (e) offerings, all jointly indicating a shift in the types of social support and interaction offered by fans to athletes.

Cycling's Floyd Landis

This relates well to another way in which the role of the athlete changes as its highest levels—an enhanced perception of the cult of celebrity. The athletes regarded as the common everyman such as Joe DiMaggio have morphed into figures that, almost out of necessity in popular culture, become larger than life. A hybrid form of commercialism now exists in which sports become a vehicle for attaining a certain lifestyle. Sports are not always played because people even like sports, let alone just because an athlete regards it as a job. Instead, sport becomes a vehicle for selling records, attaining modeling contracts, and celebrating "bling" and other lifestyles on television programs on MTV.

Finally, one must note the dramatic degree to which sport is becoming increasingly internationalized. Sometimes the effects are positive (cultures become exposed to soccer or American football in ways that previously were ignored), yet other issues prove problematic (such as the LPGA attempt to market Asian players with similar-sounding names to a resistant public). Regardless of these largely commercialized effects, the bottom line is that athletes from different nations have ample opportunities to compete together and this will become even more commonplace in the future. (NBA commissioner David Stern foresees a European division in the somewhat near future, while NFL commissioner Roger Goodell continues to play regular-season games in London and more recently in Ontario in hopes of eventual expansion.) Integration is good, yet the result may be sports in which the preponderance of winners may not be from one's home country. Internationalizing golf, for instance, is positive, yet one must wonder if Americans will follow it at current viewership levels if the majority of Grand Slam winners are not American, with many not speaking fluent English. One only needs to witness the diminished profile and television ratings associated with internationalized tennis to know this is a real possibility.

Thus, from the ways in which kids are accustomed to playing sports to the expectations professional athletes bring to athletic competition, it is fair to surmise a major sea change that results from a hyperconnected sports culture.

THE FUTURE SPORTS ORGANIZATION

Turning to the player in the sports communication process that is the sports organization, perhaps one of the biggest influences that currently resides in sport and may only be exacerbated in the future regards access not just to sports but also to sport instruction and facilities that are necessary to become a successful (or sometimes even just a healthy) athlete. There are fundamental issues, such as the lack of inner-city swimming pools or recreational club funding. However, there are even larger issues that make access to sports cavernous between the "haves" and "have nots." Multitudes of people may play the same sport but experience it in starkly different ways. As an example, for decades foreign athletes have moved to the United States to be offered better facilities and a higher level of personal instruction. Now this is happening within the United States, with families uprooted to move to where the opportunities reside, usually accompanied by a great deal of financial hardship.

Case Study: The Right Sport Pedigree

The ability for a sport program to experience success has the likelihood to influence a coach's ability to recruit talented athletes. While this has been a basic feature of college sports for quite some time, an increasing number of high school athletes are making decisions about their high school careers as open-enrollment policies throughout the country have made it possible to relocate. The intent behind open enrollment was to allow families the right to ensure their children received an appropriate educational experience. It is no longer uncommon, though, to find sport participation as a major factor in such decisions. Football is one such sport where parental positioning

(Continued)

(Continued)

is likely to occur as key player matchups, supporting personnel, or coaching strategies can be deciding factors for landing college scholarships. Have a son who is interested in being a quarterback at a Division 1 program, then playing for a coach who prefers an offensive ground game, is unlikely to help your chances.

At the start of the 2008 high school season in California, Joe Montana (a Hall of Fame quarterback in the NFL) made a decision to transfer his son to Oak Christian Academy, which had won five championships since it was established in 2000. The tuition is more than $20,000 each year, and the school employs both academics and athletics to attract families of some of the state's most gifted athletes. For instance, despite his father's athletic pedigree, Nick Montana is considered to be one of three high-profile athletes competing on the school's football team. Wayne Gretsky's son Trevor and Will Smith's son Trey also attend and play at Oak Christian. As a result, the school is often referred to as "Celebrity High." The Montanas' decision to move not only rested upon the possibility of working with the coaching staff for the program (the current starting quarterback for Notre Dame had recently attended the school) but also on the ability to be in closer proximity to Steve Clarkson (one of the most prominent private quarterback trainers in the country). At the start of fall camp his first year, Montana's arrival brought about the departure of three other quarterback hopefuls whose families made decisions to transfer to another school. It's easy to see that with Joe Montana's experience in the NFL, it is likely that Nick would be assuming the starting position. Regardless of the starter's talent, it is unlikely that a college coach will recruit the team's backup quarterback.

1. In what way can state open enrollment policies be detrimental to the future of high school athletics? Do private schools present an unfair advantage when compared to public high schools in a state?

2. What message is communicated to children when a family is motivated to change schools based largely on the athletic program's prowess?

3. What do you think the future holds regarding the merged communication of high school, collegiate, and professional sport practices (e.g., redshirting, pay for play, etc.)?

This relates to sports organizations because they are becoming tiered in the process. Those that can afford to be Class A programs are; those who cannot experience a drop-off from people who seek better options. Even in college athletics, this is increasingly becoming the case. The University of Texas generates $72 million from its football program alone, a figure higher than all but about a dozen of the other athletic programs in the nation. A great deal of that amount gets funneled back into the program, making it even more likely to produce a consistent winner.

These disparities certainly happen with professional organizations as well. Certainly, salary caps and luxury taxes are enacted to be a necessary counterbalance for a healthy overall league, but money continually yields disparate results. For instance, the New York Yankees have always been a financial behemoth in the world of baseball; however, the advent of the Yankee Entertainment and Sports (YES) Network in 2002 made the team even wealthier in a way that very few other teams could ever conceive. For all of the discussion of parity in baseball, the 2009 season featured eight playoff teams of which seven were ranked in the top 10 in total payroll.

Thus, many sports organizations (from professional down to secondary schools and local public entities) must find their market and work within it. For professional teams, this can involve finding ways to market a team that will very likely be a consistent loser. Because of expansion, leagues such as the NFL now offer an extensive 32-team lineup. Even if a different team won a championship from the year 2010 on, it would take until 2041 before each team had a taste of winning the Super Bowl. Even assuming random odds (claiming each team was of the same relative skill level), the chances of that happening are well into billions to one. Given the large economic disparities, the odds are quite honestly astronomically thin for some teams.

The odds of producing a successful (as defined by winning championships) program at local levels are no less daunting. School systems continue to receive a major proportion of their funding through property taxes, essentially ensuring a tiered system of hegemonically entrenched power for public school attendees. To make matters even more challenging, towns change demographically to the point that teams that experienced "glory days" in the 1960s or 1970s may have little chance of ever revisiting them today. Thus, the game for organizations becomes finding a niche and redefining what success would mean for their organizations. The future will inevitably involve financial realities in the face of increasing hypercompetitive mindsets from young athletes and the people who influence them.

THE FUTURE SPORTS MEDIA ENTITY

When *TIME* magazine named its 2006 Person of the Year, one must wonder if the editors realized how prescient their choice would become. Past honorees included Nikita Khrushchev, Martin Luther King, and Queen Elizabeth II, yet the magazine opted to think outside of the box in 2006, naming "You" the recipient of the award. Their reasoning was simple and possessed no small amount of foreshadowing of the world in which we currently reside: The massive amount of contributed content from millions of people on the Internet was influencing daily lives in virtually all realms of society. This is certainly the case with the current state of sports media.

In 1964, communication theorist Marshall McLuhan proclaimed that the "medium is the message." The argument was that the media used to convey a message influenced how it was received. Lou Gehrig's "Luckiest Man on the Face of the Earth" speech is different when hearing it as opposed to reading it. However, we currently live in a world where one must query "what medium"? When *TIME* named "You" as its choice, the examples were largely based on aggregate Internet sites, venues such as Wikipedia and YouTube in which collective contributions provide a wide swath of information. In his 2004 book *The Wisdom of Crowds,* James Surowiecki (2004) articulated a thesis that "when our imperfect judgments are aggregated in the right way, our collective intelligence is often excellent" (p. xiv). These sites still thrive, but the media convergence (sports highlights on cell phones; news updates on Twitter; websites that beget their own TV shows) merges sport in a way in which the delivery of it is no longer about the medium as much as it is immediacy combined with access. ESPN once was almost exclusively a television company. Now it has secured measurable markets in traditional media such as radio and magazines as well as new media such as interactive websites and personal digital assistants, embodying what we now refer to as **Web 2.0.**

This is just the start of the complete remaking of the sports media industry, and that remaking will continue at a brisk pace in the years to come. One of the largest ancillary components is and will continually be the impact of **social networking.** Perhaps Twitter is a fad, but it is abundantly clear that social networking is not (a Twitter 2.0 is extremely likely to develop). Media entities now must find a way in which to incorporate social networking into their content without disenfranchising other key constituencies within their fan bases. One could haphazardly assume that more and bigger is better, adding Twitter feeds and Facebook groups to traditional television offerings and mainstream websites, yet there is the potential for pushback from fans who want to hear from experts instead of other avid fans. The risk is that by attempting to be everything to all fans, media entities would fail to reach any fans in the complete manner in which they desire.

The final result could be increased fragmentation of sports media offerings, even megasporting events that are currently shared experiences. ESPN has already experimented with offerings such as "360" coverage of certain major games, such as Duke/North Carolina college basketball. In such a model, multiple channels collectively render the experience: One may focus on the coaches, one may focus strictly on the game at hand, one may focus on showing "inside" production, and so forth. DirecTV satellite coverage fragments sports event coverage as well, offering, for instance, one channel just devoted to the 12th tee at Augusta's Amen Corner during Masters coverage. Fragmentation may take on new perspectives for fans who seek different things. Already websites such as nfl.com offer different tabs of coverage, ranging from chatting with like-minded fans to focuses on fantasy football implications to reading expert analysis and, yes, the unfolding of the actual game itself.

Some media are finding that new forms of media are cornering markets that make traditional offerings virtually obsolete. Local sports newscasts find they can no longer compete with Internet coverage of high school games. *Chicago Sun-Times* sports columnist Jay Mariotti resigned in 2008, opting for a job with AOL. His primary reason came from covering the 2008 Beijing Summer Olympics, where he was asked to write alternate stories (e.g. a "Phelps wins" story and a "Phelps loses" story) to make a publishing deadline, while Internet journalists were able to function without such set deadlines, resulting in more immediate and accurate reporting.

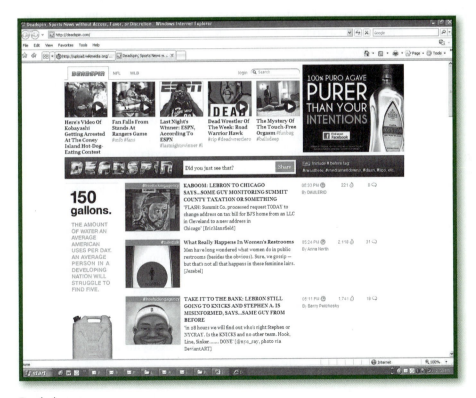

Deadspin.com

However, as journalism moves to being Internet based (many mainstream newspapers such as the *Seattle Post-Intelligencer* already have moved from print to entirely online), questions abound regarding the skills and credentials of journalists. In 2009, the *Dallas Morning News* decided to collapse editorial leadership of the sports and entertainment divisions of the newspaper, so one must ask: What is a journalist today? Is it merely someone who can "pull a number" as measured by web hits? Differentiations used to be made between traditional reporting and, for instance, blogging. However, these distinctions continue to blur. Will Leitch founded a popular website, deadspin.com, and parlayed that exposure to become a contributor to many mainstream publications, including *The Sporting News.* In this case, Leitch had the journalistic credentials (editing the school newspaper at the University of Illinois), yet ultimately reached higher levels of sports media by creating a highly successful blog more than anything else.

Media entities continue to struggle with these distinctions when deciding who should be allowed in media rooms and press conferences. Who should be let in—the blogger with half a million Twitter followers or the local newspaper journalist with a readership a tenth that size? The Southeastern Conference (SEC) attempted to adopt new media credential policies in 2009, resulting in a great deal of protest. For instance, the conference said it would only give credentials to full-time journalists, which excluded many grizzled veterans who had been placed on half-time during the economic downturn. In addition, the SEC attempted to ban more immediate forms of coverage, such as live blogging. Without question, these types of nebulous definitions are a major issue for the future of sports media as they literally affect who has access to cover major sporting events.

Moreover, the economic models for sports media offerings are becoming blurred as well. Broadcast networks (e.g., ABC, CBS, FOX, NBC) are finding that rights fees no longer justify purchasing of major sports contracts, leaving cable networks (e.g. ESPN, TNT, TBS) to become increasingly prevalent players as their funding model can include increases in subscription rates that make sports programming more viable. Channels have now been created by sports leagues themselves, ranging from the professional leagues (MLB Network, Tennis Channel, NBA TV) to collegiate conferences (Big Ten Network, SEC Network). All of these changes force new economic models to the fore, particularly as some sports rise because of a young fan base (such as BMX cycling, snowboarding, and Ultimate Fighting Championship), while others may diminish as older fan bases continue to age (such as in baseball, boxing, and tennis).

At this point, one could conclude that the future for sports media is economically bleak and operationally problematic. However, there are other sides to the media equation that could be viewed in a more positive light. One could easily argue that the Internet is the most democratic form of media ever introduced. Hegemony involves power and influence over others, which was implemented in forms of dominance of traditional media. However, when anyone can create a blog or aggregate sports website, the people who drive a story can literally be the fans. Media outlets can let fans help with the work, with websites now offering breaking news and holding the potential to highlight stories that were previously stifled when media sources were limited (by page limitations in print and by time limitations in television). What percolates to the top of the media conversation may not be the most important stories of the day and it may not be driven by the most credible journalists of our time, yet it has the opportunity to enter the sports media zeitgeist, providing insight on our society simply by underscoring what is of greatest issue to sports fans today.

Interview: Frank Deford, *Sports Illustrated* and *Real Sports with Bryant Gumbel*

Q: Has the quality of sports journalism changed in the decades you have been in the industry?

A: I believe there are more good sportswriters now than in the past. Of course, at the low end, because of nonsense talk radio and irresponsible blogs, there's more bad sports journalism. So it's better and it's worse.

Q: One could argue that the games have not changed as much as the delivery systems for consuming them. Would you concur?

A: Games change only in the most incremental way, so of course the technology that "delivers" them has been far more radical. On the other hand, the change in the cultural and economic sports universe has been exponential, every bit as dramatic as the advance in communications.

Q: Digital media has allowed the common fan to have a voice in newfound ways. What are the benefits and drawbacks of this new form of fandom?

A: Well, I guess the benefit is that the fan with an opinion can now post it online or express it on the radio instead of just telling his buddy next to him at the bar. I'm sure it feels good to be able to get your feelings off your chest and into cyberspace.

(Continued)

(Continued)

However, I haven't seen anything to suggest that this changes anything, though. So far as I can tell, the voices in sport that matter, that people listen to, are still the professionals in broadcast and print. When you give everyone a microphone, you don't necessarily get influence; rather, you only get cacophony. The way fans still can best exercise their power is by buying tickets (or watching on TV and affecting ratings). The weight of money upon sports counts for far more than free expression. Talk *is* cheap, vocally or digitally.

Q: **Sport used to be a great equalizer of social classes, but the new economics of sports (e.g., higher ticket costs, pay-per-view packages) makes this argument increasingly untrue. What are the ramifications of this stratification?**

A: There's certainly a danger in pricing the fan out of the games, yet for all the talk, attendance in most all sports continues to go up (not counting this recession, which has hurt most enterprises). I do believe sports are more vulnerable than other entertainments, though, because so much of sport is televised. You want to see the new movie, you have to go to the theatre and pay. You want to see a concert, a Broadway show, etc.—same thing. But you want to see a game, well, just turn on the TV. The flip side is that sport is so available to see, it will continue to make fans. Notwithstanding higher prices, sport appears to me to be far more popular than it was years ago, so if I had to bet, I'd say the market will adjust. I also think that there is still a huge upside to women getting interested in sport, so the potential for growing a larger percentage of the population as fans is certainly there.

THE FUTURE SPORTS FAN

As we have already learned, issues of social class used to divide athletes into stratified groups, with higher classes being amateur athletes and lower classes being professional or, if not talented enough, marginalized. Now, the economics of modern sport separate fans in even larger dimensions. As mentioned previously in Chapter 13, the New York Yankees opened a new stadium in 2009 with a wide range of attendance pricing options from $15 to $2,500. It is hard to imagine that people are getting remotely the same experience. In the NFL, some teams were able to increase prices even during an economic downturn, yet the Jacksonville Jaguars found themselves unable to sell out any of their home games in 2009, resulting in local television blackouts of all of these games.

Television screen at Cowboys Stadium

The continual influx of money creates an even more stark notion of the "haves" and "have nots." Jerry Jones's $1.2 billion new stadium for the Cowboys offers extreme luxury for some fans while others purchase "party passes" that do not even include actual admission to see the game but rather just the opportunity to be present at the stadium during the game, enjoying the festivities from a bar-like atmosphere while watching on television. Cities are increasingly told that their constituents must pay additional taxes to fund modern sports "cathedrals" (see Trumpbour, 2006). Examples of the economic divide could be offered *ad nauseum*, but the bottom line is that the current (and likely future) sports fan will often display a great deal of resentment—toward players with contracts north of $100 million and toward teams that continue to find new and innovative ways to make money off of their "product." Fans who do pony up significant amounts of dollars to attend games can feel entitled to display their fandom in any manner they feel necessary. As a consequence, athletic events are becoming coarser in their decorum, and fewer families are opting to attend games because of deviant behaviors and obscene language (see Wann, Melnick, Russell, & Peace, 2001).

Beyond the influence of dollars, the integration of new media influences fandom as well, most notably in how they receive and interpret their news. While media entities struggle in their attempts to differentiate between investigative journalism and blog entries, many fans take these forms of information as one and the same, with few distinctions being made. Rumors become fact; opinions become talking points in press conferences; blogger perceptions result in changed fan behavior, usually in a negative direction.

With the economic realities combined with more uncertain elements of fandom, it is not that surprising that an increasing number of fans are opting to avoid the entire live enactment of fandom altogether, opting to become the home-dwelling devotees outlined in Chapter 2. When tickets to the game cost thousands of dollars, the decision to invest in high-definition televisions and comfortable seating becomes the lesser (and more practical) of two economic evils. The same trend happened in the film industry a bit earlier. The more movies and movie food cost, the more people opted to rent movies instead. The more people talked and had cell phones ring during movies at the theater, the more people felt staying in their own media rooms was more of an escape than actually leaving the house. Sport fans experience a fair amount of cognitive dissonance with the cost and hassles of fandom, making simpler at-home options more appealing.

COMMUNICATION AND SPORT: ENTERING HYPERDRIVE

It is difficult not to notice that whenever we talk about the current state of sport within a communicative context, words such as *extreme* or *ultimate* come to mind. All "players" within the community of sport tend to regard it like surfers looking for the next wave, always hoping for a better ride than before. When attempting to extrapolate on the future of sports, the extreme really does seem to be where the sporting action is. Consider the X Games, hardly a new event given their introduction to the sports world in 1995. Still, the X Games continue to expand, setting new rating and downloading records (Gorman, 2009) and influencing more mainstream sporting events, such as the Olympics, which now offers several events featured in the X Games, such as snowboarding. It is no accident that the X Games are experiencing growth, particularly with younger people, because they offer a sense of adrenaline-packed hypersport.

Take another case of old versus new sport. Earlier generations were enamored with boxing. Fights of the Week were commonplace, everyone knew who held the heavyweight title, and the sport was heavily featured on *Wide World of Sports* and the Summer Olympic telecasts. Now, boxing has

Snowboarding builds an Olympic following

been superseded by Ultimate Fighting Championship (UFC), a sport origi-
nating in the 1990s and referred to by Senator John McCain as "human
cockfighting." UFC regularly draws higher pay-per-view numbers than boxing, and, in a stunning indication of the future of sports viewership, has
more male viewers in the 18 to 34 age demographic than baseball's World
Series (Meltzer, 2009). When factoring in that UFC costs money via pay-
per-view while the World Series is offered for free on a mainstream broadcast network (FOX), this trend is undeniable. Again, hypersport appears to
be the future.

This is not to say that major sports that we loved as children will disap-
pear in the near future; it simply is an argument that the expanding world
of sport tends to be gravitating toward 720-degree flips and extreme violence. This is also manifest in an area that has received relatively little
academic attention as of yet, the world of sports gaming. Leonard (2006)
discusses this paucity of focus, making a compelling case for examining it in
the future. He notes that more than 30% of all video game sales are sports
games and that "it has become commonplace in the world of sports to blur
reality with the virtual through the deployment of video games" (p. 405).
Years ago, liking sports largely meant playing them. In recent decades, this

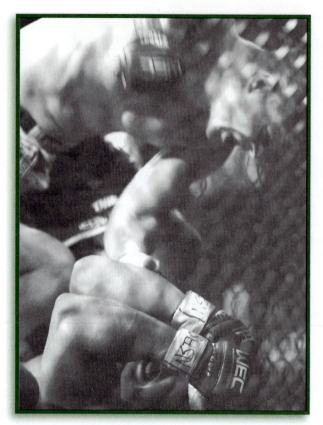

Mixed martial arts goes mainstream

included not just playing but consuming them. Now, it appears one can love sports without playing or consuming sports media, instead opting to "play" in a new, virtual domain. ESPN even features these new forms of players in programs pitting some of the best Madden NFL video game players against each other for titles and prizes.

What are the key phrases to remember regarding different levels of the sporting populace? For participants in the enactment of sport at the amateur levels, the key word is likely *specialization*. This book has outlined the new attempts to start honing athletic skills earlier and in more precise (sometimes overwhelming) ways. For those who play sport at the highest levels, the word is likely *globalization*. Leagues are constantly looking for new fans (and, hence, revenue streams). Searching for connections with other countries appears to be the next and most promising frontier for these aims. For those who consume sport, the word is likely *integration*. No matter the media format, one will undoubtedly be gaining new information and finding new ways to consume sports in ways that offer an immense amount of information with an emphasis placed on minutiae. For all of these various entities together, that word is likely *crosspollination*. No single form of sport, no "player" in the community of sport, can be discussed without the other elements. Convergence will often result in confusion but also in a sense of cultures and tastes colliding that could benefit sport in the long term.

In essence, people involved in the community of sport are continually looking for a value-added proposition. Maybe it is the professional athlete seeking other forms of celebrity as well. Maybe it is the third grader playing sports because he or she seeks the added value of a better relationship with parent or classmates. Maybe it is the fan playing fantasy sports or placing a monetary bet on the game he or she is watching. Maybe it is the sports organization seeking to commodify its product in ways both inventive and previously unimaginable. Sport in the future will very likely be about offering a new edge, an ancillary component to the act of participating or consuming itself.

Nonetheless, the basics of sport remain relatively the same. Think back to Chapter 1. The basic tenets remain in place for the foreseeable future. Sports will still be fun. They will continue to be educational. They will foster unity—and sometimes division. They will continue to be among the most vital and diverse industries in the United States. The other variables may change, but the basics will not. A first introduction to sport will likely still consist of a small child playing catch with a parent or, perhaps, batting around a balloon with a sibling. The love of that activity is innate, before any notion of sport takes hold. Those tendencies will not change; however, the communication-laden enactments, protocols, dialogues, and conceptions will be in constant flux. Winners will survive, losers will fade away. As it is with sport, so it is with trends that will shape it in the years to come.

REFERENCES

Gorman, B. (2009, Feb. 2). Winter X Games 13 sets record across platforms. *TV by the Numbers*. Retrieved June 1, 2009, from: http://tvbythenumbers.com/2009/02/02/espn-winter-x-games-13-sets-records-across-platforms/12008.

Hornig, F. (2009, July 28). Who needs newspapers when you have Twitter? Retrieved on July 30, 2009, from http://www.salon.com/news/feature/2009/07/28/wired/.

Kassing, J., & Sanderson, J. (2009). Is this a church? Such a big bunch of believers around here! Fan expressions of social support on Floydlandis.com. *Journal of Communication Studies, 2*(2) 309–330.

Leonard, D. (2006). An untapped field: Exploring the world of virtual sports gaming. In A. Raney & J. Bryant (Eds.), *Handbook of sports and media* (pp. 393–407). Mahwah, NJ: LEA.

Meltzer, D. (2009, Sept. 18). Kimbo still ratings gold. Retrieved on September 30, 2009, from http://sports.yahoo.com/mma/news?slug=dm-tufratings091809&prov=yhoo&type=lgns.

Rubin, A. M., Perse, E. M., & Powell, R. A. (1985). Loneliness, parasocial interaction and local television viewing. *Human Communication Research, 12,* 155–180.

Rubin, R. B., & McHugh, M. P. (1987). Development of parasocial interaction relationships. *Journal of Broadcasting & Electronic Media, 31*(3), 279–292.

Surowiecki, J. (2004). *The wisdom of crowds.* New York: Random House.

Trumpbour, R. C. (2006). *The new cathedrals: Politics and media in the history of stadium construction.* Syracuse, NY: Syracuse University Press.

Wann, D., Melnick, M. J., Russell, G. W., & Peace, D. G. (2001). *Sports fans: The psychology and social impact of spectators.* New York: Routledge.

Whitehead, J., & Patrick, D. (2006, Aug. 18). How much is too much for young arms? *USA Today.* Retrieved on November, 12, 2010, from http://www.usatoday.com/sports/baseball/llws/2006-08-17-injuries_x.htm.

SUGGESTED ADDITIONAL READING

Eitzen, S. (2009). *Sport in contemporary society: An anthology* (8th ed.). Boulder, CO: Paradigm.

Fort, R. D. (2006). *Sports economics.* Upper Saddle River, NJ: Prentice Hall.

Gerdy, J. R. (2000). *Sports in school: The future of an institution.* New York: Teachers College Press.

Mahan, J. E. (2006). The new online arena: Sport, marketing, and media converge in cyberspace. In A. Raney & J. Bryant (Eds.), *Handbook of sports and media* (pp. 409–431). Mahwah, NJ: LEA.

Paolantonio, S. (2008). *How football explains America.* Chicago: Triumph.

Smith, A., & Westerbeek, S. (2004). *The sports business future.* New York: Palgrave Macmillan.

Photo Credits

Chapter 1

Photo 1.1: Photograph by Ed Edahl.
Photo 1.2: © Can Stock Photo Inc./shariffc
Photo 1.3: Photograph by Bobak Ha'Eri.
Photo 1.4: © Library of Congress/George Grantham Bain Collection.
Photo 1.5: Photograph by Pete Souza.

Chapter 2

Photo 2.1: Photograph by TwoWings.
Photo 2.2: Photograph by Wasted Time R/ Wikimedia.
Photo 2.3: Photograph by Sebastian Danon.
Photo 2.4: © iStockphoto.com/fstop123.
Photo 2.5: Photograph by Darlenela5.

Chapter 3

Photo 3.1: U.S. Navy photo by Photographer's Mate 3rd Class Clarck Desire.
Photo 3.2: Photograph by Glenn Simmons.
Photo 3.3: Photograph by Mike Russell.
Photo 3.4: © BrokenSphere / Wikimedia Commons.
Photo 3.5: Photograph by Marcin Wichary.
Photo 3.6: Photograph by Kipp Jones.
Photo 3.7: Photograph by DaveZ28.

Chapter 4

Photo 4.1: Photograph by Ewen Roberts.
Photo 4.2: Photograph by Matt Boulton.
Photo 4.3: U.S. Navy photo by Musician 1st Class Tina M. Catalanotto.
Photo 4.4: Photograph by Bryan Allison.
Photo 4.5: Photograph by Stevan Sheets.

Chapter 5

Photo 5.1: Photograph by dbking.
Photo 5.2: Photograph by dbking.
Photo 5.3: Photograph by Torrey Wiley.
Photo 5.4: Photography by Bobak Ha'Eri.
Photo 5.5: Photograph by Manningmbd.

Chapter 6

Photo 6.1: © Library of Congress.
Photo 6.2: Photography by SJSU Public Affairs.
Photo 6.3: Photograph by Mark Mcgee.
Photo 6.4: Photograph by Chris Ptacek/ Wikimedia.
Photo 6.5: Photograph by Tim Hipps, Special to American Forces Press Service, U.S. Army.
Photo 6.6: Photograph by Christopher Holder.

Chapter 7

Photo 7.1: Abbie Rowe, National Park Service, Courtesy Harry S. Truman Library.
Photo 7.2: Photograph by Chuck Kennedy.
Photo 7.3: Photograph by Tim Hipps, U.S. Army.
Photo 7.4: © iStockphoto.com/3dbrained.
Photo 7.5: © iStockphoto.com/SorenP.

Chapter 8

Photo 8.1: Photograph by Keith Allison.
Photo 8.2: Photograph by Arttoones.
Photo 8.3: Photograph by Brandon O'Connor.
Photo 8.4: Photograph by Mb.matt.

Chapter 9

Photo 9.1: © iStockphoto.com/ bigdaddyrockstar.
Photo 9.2: Photograph by Derek Jensen.
Photo 9.3: Photograph by Tksteven.
Photo 9.4: Photograph by K. Kassens.
Photo 9.5: © iStockphoto.com/Purdue9394.
Photo 9.6: © iStockphoto.com/PhotoInc.

Chapter 10

Photo 10.1: Photograph by Aaron Vazquez.
Photo 10.2: Photograph by Fuzzy510.
Photo 10.3: Photograph by Keith Allison.
Photo 10.4: © iStockphoto.com /asiseeit.
Photo 10.5: Photograph by Airman 1st Class Jonathan Steffen.

Chapter 11

Photo 11.1: © iStockphoto.com/bonniej.
Photo 11.2: © iStockphoto.com/ActionPics.

Photo 11.3: Photograph by de:Benutzer:Hase.
Photo 11.4: Photograph by Bobak Ha'Eri.
Photo 11.5: Photograph by EJ Fox.

Chapter 12

Photo 12.1: © iStockphoto.com/sshepard.
Photo 12.2: Photograph by Kjunstorm.
Photo 12.3: Photograph by David Ruddell.
Photo 12.4: Photograph by David Ruddell.
Photo 12.5: Photograph by Ed Yourdon.

Chapter 13

Photo 13.1: © iStockphoto.com/J-Elgaard.
Photo 13.2: Photograph by Mahanga.
Photo 13.3: Photograph by Brendan Haywood.
Photo 13.4: Photograph by lasvegasvegas .com.
Photo 13.5: Photograph by Madmaxmarchhare.

Chapter 14

Photo 14.1: © iStockphoto.com/Double_ Vision.
Photo 14.2: ©iStockphoto.com/spxChrome.
Photo 14.3: © iStockphoto.com/Pgiam.

Chapter 15

Photo 15.1: Photograph by colinedwards99.
Photo 15.2: N/A.
Photo 15.3: Photograph by Mahanga.
Photo 15.4: Photograph by Rama.
Photo 15.5: Photograph by Staff Sgt. Leo A. Salinas.

Index

SAGE Research Methods Online
The essential tool for researchers

**Sign up now at
www.sagepub.com/srmo
for more information.**

An expert research tool

- An **expertly designed taxonomy** with more than 1,400 unique terms for social and behavioral science research methods
- **Visual and hierarchical search tools** to help you discover material and link to related methods

- Easy-to-use navigation tools
- Content organized by complexity
- Tools for citing, printing, and downloading content with ease
- Regularly updated content and features

A wealth of essential content

- The most comprehensive picture of quantitative, qualitative, and mixed methods available today
- More than **100,000 pages of SAGE book and reference material** on research methods as well as editorially selected material from SAGE journals
- More than **600 books** available in their entirety online

Launching 2011!

$SAGE research methods online